Entertaining In Dallas!

a guide to sources and facilities

1994
Edition

by
Carol Fraser Hall

PANACHE PRESS

Dallas, Texas

Printed in the United States of America

ISBN 0-9635174-1-4

Library Of Congress Cataloging-In-Publication data

PANACHE PRESS, Dallas, Texas

Design by Suzanna L. Brown of O! Suzanna Design
Illustrations by Mary Tomás of Alma Graphics
Printing by Great Impressions Printing & Graphics, Dallas

*T*o my spouse for indulging me with still another year of sampling and exploring the entertaining possibilities of Dallas; to my children whom I hope have benefited from the many celebrations of life's happy occasions; to my many friends, who shared their expert opinions and guarded sources; and to Charron Denker, my partner in the first edition of ENTERTAINING IN DALLAS! whose imprint is still apparent in this subsequent publication.

Entertaining In Dallas

CONTENTS

Foreword 7

How To Use This Book 9

I Getting Started 11
a few thoughts on entertaining

II Confidence Builders 15
what & where to learn

III Entertaining at Home 27
kitchenware, table accessories & linens

IV The First Step 41
the art of inviting

V Basic Ingredients 57
markets, wine, bakeries, & take-out

VI Let The Pros Do It 91
caterers & party planners

VII The Right Place 117
hotels, clubs, restaurants & special sites

VIII Decor and Theme 157
flowers, party supplies & more

IX Entertainment 169
the right beat & other acts

X Finishing Touches 185
rentals, lighting, sound & such

Advertisers 203

Directory Of Sources 223

Telephone Directory 247

Index 259

About The Author 271

Entertaining In Dallas

Foreward

E ntertaining should be fun, an extension of one's own creativity and a gesture of appreciation for others. Because everyone needs to start somewhere, we can make it easier with finger-tip access to the area's most reliable and unique sources that will add panache to your efforts. There is something in this directory for everyone — from the bride who will take her first cooking lesson to the veteran charity chairman in search of a facility, an invitation designer, an entertainer or a party planner for a major fund-raiser. In between, there are a lot of us who are trying to keep up with the latest resources in Dallas and the surrounding area. In fact, knowing about a new sources, whether for a cake or a caterer,may be the incentive to invite a few good friends for dinner or to plan a major family celebration or business event.

There are other publications in Dallas covering specific aspects of entertaining; namely, weddings and corporate and convention events. It is not our intention to duplicate those efforts. Ours is directed to the hostess and would-be hostess, and perhaps also to the charity and corporate planner, who would be utilizing many of the same talents and venues. We have omitted the themes, ideas and facilities that are primarily geared for children's parties. Those sources are so potentially expansive that an entire book could be devoted to that subject alone.

This is our second edition. We have become all the wiser in the interim. Changes and the emergence of new talent are constant. As we mentioned last year, no matter how thoroughly researched, we know there are wonderful suppliers in the Dallas area that we have not touched upon. It is not our intention to slight those who are as well-qualified as those included in our book. For the sake our readers, however, we have attempted to be selective in our coverage. As always, we look forward to your suggestions and comments for future editions.

We hope you will read "How to use this book" on the next page. We have in the format of this edition with regard to the Directories following the text. We have also included a select "Advertising Section." Our advertisers are very important to our success. We hope you will support them as they have supported us.

Enjoy!

How To Use This Book

ENTERTAINING IN DALLAS! progresses, by chapter, through all the steps of entertaining. The chapters are divided logically and can be easily accessed by referring to the "Table of Contents" at the beginning of the book or to the comprehensive listing of subjects in the "Index" at the end of the book.

As you read through the book, you will note that the individual write-ups do not have addresses and phone numbers adjacent to them, largely because of the vast number of entries and the space required. Instead, there are two directories for easy referral towards the end of the book. There is a "Directory of Sources," in which sources are listed *alphabetically*, along with addresses and phone numbers. Because of present day use of the computer, each entry is listed as it is alphabetized in the book. Russell Glenn Floral Design will be listed under "R." Those businesses starting with "The" are the only exception. The dani group, one of Dallas' premier catering companies, for example, is listed "dani group, the."

All references are also listed, *by chapter and by subject*, in a convenient and compact "Telephone Directory," following the "Directory of Sources." As an example, invitation sources, calligraphers and invitation designers will be listed, by subject, under Chapter IV of the "Telephone Directory."

As you know, our Advertisers are special to us. Their ads are in a separate "Advertising Section," that begins on page 203.

I

Getting Started

a few thoughts on entertaining

*B*uilt on either truth or myth of the past, Dallas excels at the art of entertaining. Dallas conjures up images of lavish balls, charity and corporate extravaganzas, fabulous at-home soirees, and Hollywood-inspired hoedowns. Perhaps the myth — exaggerated by the excesses of the 80's — has inhibited the novice and the modest. Anyone can entertain with flair and grace. It is an acquired art and we hope our book can, at least, direct the hostess and would-be hostess in the right direction for the area's best resources.

The reality of the 90's has curtailed the lavishness and, perhaps, restored realism to entertainment and to the joys of simpler celebrations and sharing occasions with good friends. This does not mean that our expectations and our taste are lessened. We have already honed our expertise and experiences. We have learned to expect excellent food, service and creativity. We think these distinctive features will always be achievable, whether for a picnic, a simple family birthday cake celebration or cocktails honoring a visitor.

Fortunately, people are gregarious. As a result, we have always had an interest in socializing with one another. Social entertainment is a large part of our lives, or at least should be. The interaction provides an opportunity to share pleasures and special moments — birthdays, graduations, holidays, weddings, as well as personal and business triumphs — with our family and friends. Often, it is the celebrated moment that provides our memories and strengthens the fabric of friendship with others. It is also an opportunity to be creative and individualistic.

Dallas has always been a sociable city. We've frequently said that Dallasites share more time with one another than do residents of other large cities. Perhaps, this is homage to a Southern past and a remembrance of by-gone, small-town days.

On reflection, this may be why Dallas has such extensive talent and resources devoted to the fine art of entertaining. Could there be such talent in other similarly sized cities? And, because there are so many resources, we thought that a source book would be a boon to the frequent host and hostess as well as an incentive to the infrequent host.

Entertaining for the 90's is already taking on a new feel and new scene. Caterers, florists and party planners all report the change in available dollars for entertaining and in attitudes toward entertaining. Certainly, with reduced budgets, entertainment is one of the first items to suffer from financial shrinkage. This does not mean that hospitality should or will cease. It is part of our social, business and charity structure. Likely, we will approach it with greater sensibility and more intelligent use of our resources. In terms of personal involvement, the trends of the recent past will continue. The pressured schedules of busy lives will dictate how we entertain, with a dependence on smaller festivities, dinners based on or supplemented by take-out, or events given over to professionals if the budget will allow.

As we launch our updated updated tour of sources and creative talents, we offer you a few ideas about entertainment in the 90's that should enable you to continue to entertain with style. It could be, through serious examination of the elements of entertaining, you may actually concentrate more on style and quality. For example, you may devote greater attention to the menu and to the wine, or become more creative with the details of a theme or holiday setting.

a few thoughts on economy

This is not a guide book for bargain sources. But, in order to reduce costs and maintain style, we have a few suggestions.There are those who would forgo the *foie gras* for the flowers and vice versa. A list of alternative choices could fill an entire book, but a few representative ideas may help you determine the elements that are most important to you.

▲ *start with a budget*. It will give you an overview of your expenses and define the perimeters in terms of cost. This may make it easier to judge what you can afford or intend to spend.

◆ *make the party simple*. But, at the same time, be creative with what you have.

▼ *limit the size*. A beautifully executed party for a few will be more rewarding than a large party done poorly.

● *experiment with varying formats*. Consider coffees, teas, dessert parties, picnics, ice cream socials, or cocktails and hors d'oeuvres rather than dinner. Experiment with ethnic menus and less expensive foods, or launch the summer season with a pool party with pizzas and subs for a few families. Consider the Tex-Mex fiesta instead of classic cuisine with fine wines.

■ *give a party with friends*. Sharing the expenses, the work and the fun can be a happy solution for all.

▲ *segment party costs and economize on those elements that are less important to you and that will not affect the overall impression.* Skip the printed invitation or scrimp on decor, using outdoor plants or the centerpiece of a single, perfect rose. A trip to the Farmer's Market can yield the best produce of the season for a meal that is frugal but fabulous.

◆ *do all the work by yourself.* Self-help can substantially reduce, or eliminate, the expenses of caterers and outside help.

▼ *use tax deductible entertaining!* Take a table at a charity event, such as luncheon for a good cause. The money will go to a worthy organization and you will have entertained with all the benefits of the charity and its hard-working committee.

● *make the occasion special.* Your guests will be honored to share an engagement announcement or the christening of a new baby.

■ *enjoy the bounty of your garden,* be it food or flowers. Your guests will be impressed with the flowers or food of the season. This is an opportunity to show off, with the help of nature.

▲ *concentrate on the guest list.* After all, your guests should be your primary consideration.

We hope that there will always be the time and the place for the extravagant celebration, relative to one's means. On the larger scale, when giving the grand or great party, rely on the advice of professionals — party planners, caterers, hotels, florists. Their talents and experiences can add the pizzazz needed. These professionals know the sources and have the inventory to assist you — frequently with cost-cutting ideas, shortcuts and ready-existing inventory.

a few thoughts on planning

One element that should not suffer from economy is planning. Thinking through the occasion will mean a more relaxed host or hostess, one who is fully prepared when the first guest appears at the front door. We are believers in making and following lists, which may be the greatest prudence of all in avoiding the pitfalls of mistakes and redoubling of effort.

We are a filofax society. The planning for a party, no matter how small or how large, will be easier with forward planning and organization. Our source book will have the phone members to get the party underway, the food and flowers ordered, the caterers and entertainment engaged, the hotel or other site reserved. For the hostess who does her own cooking, a daily schedule of duties prior to an event will distribute the work load and ensure that nothing is forgotten. Personally, we are great believers in doing what can be done in advance, like setting the table and arranging the seating. We prefer to find that there is one napkin or fork missing the day or two before the party than an hour before the guests arrive.

With major parties, an organized event sheet is definitely in order. A schedule and checklist are indispensable. We know of some parties where help did not show and others when full orchestras did not arrive. The checklist needs to provide for confirmation of every major facet a few days in advance.

On the other hand, everyone needs to be flexible for emergencies, which are better handled when you are prepared in all other aspects. A lady and a gentleman show their mettle by handling a mishap with the aplomb of Miss Manners in making the best of an awkward situation.

The perfect party begins and ends with keeping your guests happy. This should be the primary focus of your efforts — whether the effort is for your friends, for business or for a charity undertaking.

Our aim is to make you wiser to the scene and to the entertainment opportunities that exist in our savvy, well-seasoned and well-stocked city.

great occassions for entertaining

birthdays	*harvests of the season*
anniversaries	*Labor Day*
graduations	*Fourth of July*
Thanksgiving	*major sports events*
Christmas	*New Year's*
bar mitzvahs	*Super Bowl*
betrothals	*new baby*
weddings	*new business*
Mother's Day	*new neighbors*
Father's Day	*Olympics*
christenings	*St. Patrick's Day*
Halloween	*school's in*
Easter	*school's out*
Oscar night	*Texas Independence Day*
Bastille Day	*Valentine's Day*

II

Confidence Builders

what and where to learn

*C*onfidence and time seem to be the major stumbling blocks to recurrent and easy entertaining. Yet, most of us entertain without consciously labeling the activity as "entertaining." Asking a friend to join you for lunch at a restaurant, or asking a new neighbor to come for a drink, is part of everyday social activity — or at least should be. Sharing time with friends in a relaxed environment is part of the richness of our lives and important to all of us for our well being.

Developing a flair for the everyday event is just one step toward building the confidence to undertake more involved parties and varied forms of entertainment. If the intention is to invite a friend for lunch to observe her birthday, or to celebrate a new promotion, the process of researching a restaurant takes little more than awareness of the Metroplex dining scene by regular perusal of local newspaper restaurant reviews. The author meets for lunch monthly with a group of friends, a pleasant custom observed now for almost twenty-five years. The "sport" of the luncheon sharing is to discover the newest and best potential on the restaurant scene. We feel like reviewers ourselves, being among the first to impress our friends with word about the newest restaurant. There are many occasions when one's favorite restaurant provides an element of comfort and the confidence in knowing what to expect. But, be adventuresome and expand your horizons to the diversity in our city.

Many of us have gotten away from, or perhaps never even began, the simplest form of entertaining — just asking someone to come by for a drink or a cup of tea. Having a reason — to meet an out-of-town friend or a new neighbor — makes the engagement special. Introducing our friends enriches their visit with insight into our lives.

When the author had young children, one mother always asked a few neighbors over for post-car pool coffee to celebrate the first day of the school year. How flattering it is in this hectic day and age to visit on a one-to-one basis and, per chance, to discover a potential new friend or a mutual interest. How easy is the sharing of freshly brewed coffee and warm-from-the-oven muffins to start the day on a friendly note. Likewise, for the cocktail hour, a nice bottle of wine and a modest hors d'oeuvre — home-made or store-bought — is all that it takes to set the scene for a pleasant occasion.

So many of us have lovely belongings that are not used often enough. The wedding-gift wine glasses, or grandmother's charming coffee cups, along with the appropriate napkins arranged on a tray or table, provide the center-piece of a lovely and inviting vignette.

As a further enrichment of our everyday lives, it is not difficult to master the small occasions and then extend the format to grander or larger events, all with ease and panache. The author endeavors to encourage the combination of elegance with ease to enrich our social lives.

To master the style and extend the range of entertaining, the author has numerous confidence builders to suggest. The recommendations come in many forms — taking a few cooking lessons or wine appreciation classes, subscribing to food and wine publications or even being on the look-out for the city's many food and wine events. Any of these will help stimulate both the novice and the expert with new ideas for entertaining. With a little practice, aided by our recommendations and sources, the novice will be ready to enter-tain the most intimidating guests.

the Cooking Scene

Schools & Classes

Perhaps most basic to confidence building is to learn one's way around the kitchen. For even the most confirmed user of catering companies, classes with chefs may extend the horizon of ideas to incorporate into one's entertain-ing scheme and to personalize menus and occasions.

Cooking lessons may be the first step for the novice. These need not be formal lessons if funds or scheduled time are short. In fact, the city housewares shops are a treasure of demonstration courses both by cookbook authors and celebrated chefs. During almost any given week, cooking demonstrations on anything from appetizers to desserts can be found at **Williams-Sonoma, Plate and Platter, Panhandlers** or **Macy's**, among our favorite local cookware shops. Often these are free to the onlooker, or available for modest charge. We recommend checking regularly with the weekly "Food Section" of THE DALLAS MORNING NEWS, or directly with the cookware shops for upcoming visitors and events. What a feast of inspiration for the observer with an hour or two to spare! Some of the shops give evening and Saturday demonstrations and lessons, which may be more convenient for those with limited time.

Fortunately, outstanding cooking instruction is readily available in Dallas and the surrounding areas. Twice annually, in September and in January, THE DALLAS MORNING NEWS publishes an extensive list of "cooking schools" and their schedule of courses. The list is almost overwhelming, but it does contain options for every palate and purse. We suggest that you examine the section, carefully narrow down the options, and check with friends about their personal experiences.

By all means, if you are a novice, start with a course in basics. Several area schools offer excellent starter courses. And, incidentally, cooking lessons make excellent gifts to wife, husband or friend for a birthday, to a new bride, or for a group of friends celebrating an event together.

The addresses and phone numbers for the schools and teachers listed below can be found in the "Directory of Sources," which starts on page 223, and in the "Telephone Directory," which starts on page 247.

▲ **Cake Carousel**. There are other cake decorating classes, such as at Brigner's Cake Supply in Garland and the Wilton Method classes at J.C. Penney, but Carol Beshears of Cake Carousel seems to be the favorite teacher for instructions on cake decorating. Classes cover Basics and More Basics, Wedding Cakes and classes on the various and glorious edible flowers we see on celebration and wedding cakes. Classes are held at the Cake Carousel's Richardson location.

◆ **Christine Carbone**, ex-protege of Jean LaFont and Universal Restaurants, specializes in giving private cooking lessons at your home. Six hours of classes, however divided, is $275. and yields a lot of confidence and proficiency. Christine also likes to do cooking class parties, using the dinner party as an extension of her class. She shops with the hostess and then teaches the participants prior to their enjoying the meal. Christine also caters for a small group of regular clients, and is sought after for both food styling and sculpting, her last effort being a Arcimboldo centerpiece! (Giuseppe Arcimboldo, if you recall, was the Sixteenth century Italian artist famous for fruit and flower paintings depicting human forms.)

▼ **Cooking Lessons with Cammie**. Cammie Vitale has been on the Dallas scene for 13 years, and has fortes in Italian and Chinese cuisine — both popular at the moment. She has lived in Italy and studied in Hawaii. Classes include tips from menus to fine points of table decor. Hands-on classes are limited to eight a year and are $35. She will also arrange private lessons.

● **Cuisine Concepts** in Fort Worth is popular with Metroplex "foodies." Congenial director Renie Steves gives private lessons, as well as two-day courses in such subjects as Sauce-making and Holiday Meals, from September through April. But, the school is best known for its ambitious schedule of "star" guest chefs, which we find the biggest lure. Previous years, for example, have included food celebrities Jacques Pepin, Anne Rosensweig, Joyce Goldstein and dessert chef Nick Malgieri from New York Cooking School. Particularly popular are Dallas' own "stars." Stephan Pyles, Michel Platz and Lori and David Holbein were on the sell-out schedule last year. Classes are

$200. for two sessions with the all-star casts. Groups are small and comfortable in Renie's custom-made home kitchen. Renie published a successful cookbook, *DALLAS IS COOKING*, in the Fall of '92. Her second book, *FORT WORTH IS COOKING*, is now available in the stores.

■ **Deborah Orrill.** When not in Dallas, Deborah dons a toque for the famed La Varenne Cooking School, as Director of their International Professional Program, a twice-yearly, five week program in Burgundy. Locally, Deborah teaches private lessons in homes for two to six students with a minimum charge of $100. for two hours, including all ingredients. Deborah has a few regulars for whom she does this in a dinner party format. If you want information on the La Varenne Program at any level, Deborah is the person to ask. Deborah may also have some major plans on the horizon, so keep your eyes on the local food news for the latest information.

▲ **Fun Ed's Eunice Ritchey's School of Cooking** sponsors the complete range of cooking basics — from baking bread to Thai, Chinese, or Sushi classes by the popular Anita Frank. Classes are fast-paced and low-cost, usually about $21., plus the ingredients. Fun-Ed's very popular class in dining etiquette, the most basic course in "getting started," is geared to the novice in giving parties and to the young executive on the corporate ladder. What a great gift-giving idea to give to newly-weds as a confidence booster! The three hour class is $25.

◆ **Gourmet Cookery School**, in Irving, is a well-established school, with Dolores Snyder behind the stove. She teaches both basics and courses on entertaining, such as her "high tea class." Classes are frequently in the evening at a cost of $35. per three-hour class. Dolores will also do cooking class parties at your home, as she did for one of our friends. The honored bride-to-be and several of her friends learned and prepared. The beaux came later for dinner and all was a huge success!

▼ **Mange-Tout Cooking School.** Susan Johnson, graduate of the Cordon Bleu and a veteran of twelve years of teaching, stages classes from her Highland Park home. Day-time classes from 9:30 to 1:00, on subjects which include pastries or Chinese food, for example, cost $35 and include lunch. Evening classes, such as "Grilling for Couples," include dinner and wine. Susan also has a small newsletter, which contains comments on local restaurants and food sources and, also, some recipes. Susan is a co-venturer, with Jean Crow, in the Humble Pie Baking Co., which is listed in Chapter V under "Desserts."

● **Messina's Culinary Centre** is the sibling to Jennivine's Restaurant, with classes being taught by Billy Webb and Jennivine chefs as well. Messina's conducts mostly Wednesday evening classes with emphasis on regional and ethnic foods from around the world, plus occasional classes on herbs, Cajun food and seafood, to give recent examples. Classes are priced at $30. and include a buffet dinner with wine following the class. Messina's is also available for special group classes and for the rental of their 50-person space.

■ **Out of a Flower.** One of the area's best schools is Out of a Flower's Cooking School for Young Chefs and Adults, a fairly new venture for Michel Bernard Platz and his partner, Jose Sanabria. Platz, one of the city's best chefs and teachers, is the former Executive Chef of the five-star L'Entrecote Restaurant at the Loews Anatole Hotel. Theirs is a hands-on experience, rather than the usual demonstration approach. Platz and Sanabria run their highly regarded cooking school out of a well-equipped kitchen on the second floor of The Brewery in the West End. Platz and Sanabria's ice cream business is booming — and their reputation as teachers so stellar — that classes are now "on demand" rather than the schedule previously published. Put together a group of at least five and, *voila*, Platz will suggest a choice of menus and the classes, usually on Saturdays, will be packed with information and experience. Afterwards, you will enjoy your meal with your cook-mates. The classes run $52. a person.

Platz enjoys giving classes for children and teenagers, so if the object is developing *savoir faire* at an early age, we recommend looking into his "School for Young Chefs," which he started while still at The Anatole. A week-long summer class for young chefs, either French cuisine or pastry, costs $130. for the five, half-day classes. He also has a Christmas holiday cooking class which fills up rapidly.

If you are curious about the name, Out of a Flower, Platz and Sanabria sell a line of ice creams, sorbets and specialty desserts, all flavored by edible fresh flowers and herbs. These items can be found at their kitchen in the Brewery and at Dallas specialty food shops, such as Marty's and The Whole Foods Market. We were so impressed to see the distinctive Out of a Flower containers in New York's City's famed Dean & DeLuca emporium, whose selection is tantamount to being labeled "the best." See also the listing of Out of a Flower under "Desserts" in Chapter V.
*Please see the advertisement for **Out of a Flower** on page 212.*

▲ **Plate and Platter** on Lovers Lane, mentioned above, has a more serious demonstration kitchen than most of the cooking supply shops. Plate and Platter issues a full Spring and Fall schedule of courses, which can be obtained by calling or stopping by their shop and asking to be put on the mailing list. The classes are conducted by Dallas' best chefs and, occasionally, by authors who are eager to acquaint you with their publications. In a recent week, for example, Robin Novak of Cafe Pacific, Scott Davenport of Sfuzzi Addison, William Guthrie of Hotel St. Germain and Kent Rathbun of the Melrose each gave demonstration lessons. Two two-hour presentations are $15., great values for what you get. The classes, which are limited to 30, fill up rapidly.

◆ **Sushi Sensei**. Anita Frank, Dallas sushi expert and the Director of Fun-Ed's Eunice Ritchey Cooking School, teaches advanced classes in Japanese cooking at her Oak Lawn area home. She also offers a service suitable for parties, where she brings the class to your home. A three-hour class costs $40. Her sushi classes for beginners are staples at Fun-Ed's Cooking School.

▼ **Tina Wasserman** is one of the city's better-known names for cooking lessons. She specializes both in pastries and in foods for Passover and other Jewish holidays. Look for her popular classes on Christmas desserts, including croquenbouche, in the Fall and Winter issue of THE DALLAS MORNING NEWS "Guide to Cooking Classes."

● There are several other "schools" such as **Brookhaven, Mountain View** and **North Lake Colleges'** extension classes, which give inexpensive demonstration cooking classes among the full roster of adult education classes. **Plano Parks and Recreation Department** also sponsors classes. Most are listed, almost weekly, in the Food Section of THE DALLAS MORNING NEWS. Costs are very reasonable.

Just a reminder– the listing for the above cooking schools can be found in the "Directory of Sources," which begins on page 223.

Classes with Chefs in Their Kitchens

The cooking class scene is a plentiful one, particularly after one has mastered the rudiments. We often wish that we could pursue, on a full time basis, the full cornucopia of classes available to the curious public. Some of the really outstanding classes to consider are those by the area's best chefs and by visiting, nationally-known chefs. Most will have ideas and menus to teach and to inspire. Besides, in most instances, the classes are fun and a great camaraderie exists among the participants. Most will have at least one strong common trait — an interest in food and entertaining.

■ **Baby Routh**'s gregarious chef, Kevin Rathbun, has been active with lessons, both for the AIWF and in his own kitchen. During the summer of 1993, for example, Chef Rathbun gave a series of sell-out Saturday lessons that included: recreating the Baby Routh favorites at home; a pastry class (the route to our hearts!); and, lastly, a class on food and wine pairing. Each $45. class included lunch.

▲ **Christian Gerber**, co-owner and chef of Juniper Restaurant hosts classes in his kitchen. Last year, along with 18 other students, we reaped the benefits of the demonstration class, enjoying the meal afterwards and the camaraderie as well. The Provençale class menu included bouillabaisse, a well-herbed rack of lamb and a lemon souffle with raspberry coulis, perfectly suitable to duplicate for a dinner party for friends. Classes are usually $45. Per person, including dinner, and make a nice gift or party for a newly wed couple.

◆ **Cuisine International**. Some of our local citizens attend the famous European cooking schools of Lorenza da Medici in Tuscany, La Varenne at Chateau du Fey in the Burgundy countryside and Le Petit Blanc at Le Manoir aux Quat' Saisons near Oxford in England. We want you to know that the exclusive world-wide representative for these schools and several others is here in Dallas, making the choice and the arrangement all the easier. Judy Terrell Ebrey is the representative, who will be happy to help narrow the choice. Prices for the schools range from $2000. to $4500. a week.

▼ **The Mansion on Turtle Creek**'s celebrated chef, Dean Fearing, can be counted on to give rapid-paced, informative classes, sparked with the popular chef's up-beat charm. Dean is particularly popular among cooking class followers. Recently, Dean gave a series of $80. classes, each geared to the single course of a meal. For example, one class was devoted to learning three different entrees and their variations. The subsequent week, the subject was desserts. Happily, the classes sample the delicious outcome following the two-hour sessions in The Mansion's well-equipped kitchen. The Mansion, from time to time, offers entire gastronomic weekends, tied to lessons with Dean. Few hotels, in fact, are as ambitious as The Mansion in staging food-oriented events.

Not to be overlooked was the week-long class this past summer at Rosewood Corporation's La Samana property in St. Martin. This must have been heaven for the "foodies" to spend a week at La Samana, with four award-winning chefs, preparing your meals and sharing their culinary secrets. Chefs included Dean Fearing, The Crescent's Jim Mills, Paul Gayler from The Lanesborough in London and Marc Ehler, chef of La Samana.

● **Sfuzzi**, in Dallas, Addison and Plano hosts cooking classes. Executive chefs Kevin Ascolese, Scott Davenport and Dan Dreyer, respectively in each location, have Saturday morning classes. Last year, their two hour classes, on subjects such as hors d'oeuvres and sweets, cost $20. and were great successes! Sfuzzi Public Relations Director Mary Edwards reports that the Sfuzzi in Plano also plans classes for children.

Cookbooks by area chefs

Patrick Esquerré	*a long-awaited La Madeleine cookbook, due in early '94*
Andree Falls	*THE PARIGI COOKBOOK*
Dean Fearing	*THE MANSION COOKBOOK & SOUTHWESTERN CUISINE, New recipes from The Mansion on Turtle Creek*
Kevin Garvin	*SEASONED IN TEXAS: The Adolphus Cookbook*

Renie Steves	*DALLAS IS COOKING*
	FORT WORTH IS COOKING
Stephan Pyles	*THE NEW TEXAS CUISINE*
Victor Gielisse	*CUISINE ACTUELLE*

Charity and the Cooking Class Circuit

◆ The local chapter of the **American Institute of Wine and Food** has been the workhorse of the food scene, and among its many and varied programs are chefs who demonstrate or discuss food trends, such as current changes in nutritional thinking. During 1993, local chefs, including Baby Routh's Kevin Rathbun, Chena Civello of Civello's Raviolismo and Mai Phma of Mai's Oriental Cuisine, gave a series of Saturday classes focusing on ethnic foods utilizing unique products available in the Dallas market. A Fall cooking series for the AIWF, organized by Dakota's executive chef Jim Severson, was a series of classes at the Farmers Market. Jim lined up his chef-friends, the "who's who" of the city's chefs, for eight Saturdays, to share their expertise and their enthusiasm for our local produce at the Farmers Market. Also on the Fall '93 list was a class by Paris food writer and cookbook author, Patricia Wells, at the Veranda Club's fabulous demonstration kitchen. For anyone who is interested in learning more about food and wine, as part of becoming a more confident hostess, we can wholeheartedly encourage joining the Institute. Its many and varied events are usually mentioned in the newspaper, but the only sure way of keeping up with the Institute's activities, some open only to members, is to be a member.

Other annual food events to look into

■ **FOCAS' "April in Paris" Benefit** and **SOS' "Taste of the Nation,"** are only two of the established Dallas charities that sponsor food events as their annual fund-raisers. The former, supporting the Foster Child Advocate Services, has an annual tasting of the best of the area's restaurants and chefs: It attracts sell-out crowds for the $75. per person event. The latter event, spear-headed by *chef extraordinaire* Stephan Pyles, is a dinner to raise money for the North Texas Food Bank and international food relief efforts. In addition to helping a very needy cause, the guests at the $150. per person dinner are treated to a team of Dallas' best chefs, including Pyles, The Mansion's Dean Fearing, The Riviera's Lori Finkelman Holbein, David Holben, now at Mediterraneo, and Victor Gielisse of the much-missed Actuelle Restaurant. This fund-raising format also includes, on a subsequent evening, a $40. broader sampling of foods prepared by restaurant and food-industry professionals. In 1993, the Taste of the Nation Chef sampler was held at the Crescent Court Hotel. The 38 noted area chefs attracted a capacity crowd.

▼ **"Raiser Grazer,"** sponsored by **Les Dames d'Escoffier,** is held each year in February. Members of the prestigious organization, limited to women food and wine world professionals, prepare tastings from hors d'oeuvres through dessert. The 1993 event, held at the Tower Club, featured a "Route 66" theme and cuisine along the famous highway from California through New Mexico and Texas and on. The finale was great: a child sized car made by cake-maker Becky Sikes of Ida Mae's Cakes' fame, and car cookies by Sherry Carlson of Dessert Dreams. Mark your calendars for the 1994 Raiser Grazer on February 24.

● **The VNA "Walkabout,"** held each May, is now in its fourth year as a fund-raiser for the Visiting Nurses Association with the cooperation of the American Institute of Food and Wine. In 1993, ten restaurants in the Quadrangle area offered a sampling menu to the participants, who afterwards gathered in the Quadrangle Courtyard to enjoy champagne and dessert — the latter a contribution of the Loews Anatole Hotel. The unique aspect of this food-oriented event is the opportunity to visit the participating restaurants for a very modest investment and, at the same time, help a worthy cause.

▲ For those who want to go further afield, the **Texas Hill Country Wine and Food Festival** is held each April in Austin. Not only do the partici-pants enjoy the best of the state's food and wine bounty, coupled with seminars on topics of related interest, but the evening events include samplings of Austin's and San Antonio's best restaurant and music scene. The 1993 Festival included a bonus day of lessons from instructors from Peter Kump's New York Cooking School, including Kump himself and pastry instructor Nick Malgieri. The Sunday event always includes a wine and food fair at nearby Fall Creek Vineyards in Tow, Texas. Dallas chefs and purveyors are a significant part of the festive scene.

Because of the popularity of the charity/food format, other organiza-tions are getting on the bandwagon. For the most part, food and wine events have become an enjoyable way to support the various charities and, at the same time, become acquainted with the culinary talents of the involved chefs and restaurants.

And why attend these events? In addition to support for their causes, they stimulate an interest in food and its presentation and cultivate an aware-ness of our local culinary talent.

Please refer to the "Directory of Sources," beginning on page 223, for the phone numbers of the various sponsoring organizations.

Classes

While most hosts and hostesses can increase their entertainment confidence by boning up on cooking skills, they should also look into the available and recommended wine appreciation courses to complement the scenario. New Texas wine laws will make informative wine tastings in the wine shops more available. There should be an accelerated pace in these tastings.

◆ **La Cave Warehouse** on Munger in the West End offers occasional wine tastings of new releases. The Warehouse is just that, a temperature-controlled facility, and an exciting bonanza of wines, mostly from owner Francois Chandou's home Bordeaux area. Call to find out about his informative classes. Chandou also puts out an informative newsletter for his customers.

▼ **Marty's** has become increasingly active in wine tastings and the new Texas laws mentioned above will allow the wine and epicure shop to accelerate the pace. Stop by to check on the schedule, or be certain to be on the mailing list in order not to miss out. Last year, off-site tastings featured fine Burgundies, Champagnes selected on a recent buying trip, and a Port tasting, each with a distinguished speaker. The $20. cost of each was credited against purchase of the evening.
*Please see the advertisement for **Marty's** on page 218.*

● **Tony's Wine Warehouse & Bistro** on Oak Lawn has on-going tastings and samplings for $15. Their calendar is one of the busiest in town. Tony's bistro also allows for easy tasting and discoveries with every meal.

■ **The Wine Emporium Etc.** has the best schedule of wine appreciation classes, taught by the enthusiastic and informed proprietor Bill Rich. Rich teaches a $65. basic survey course of four classes, covering wine's major characteristics and the major wine producing areas of the world. He also has on-going, one-night classes on specific wines, such as Red Burgundies and California Cabernets, for $25. and $20. respectively. His classes are small and sell-out rapidly, so book early. The set-up for classes at the rear of his Lovers Lane store is well arranged.

Like food events, local wine events are proliferating. Dallas hosts a number of wine-focused events that can provide crash courses in wine appreciation. Once again, we recommend watching the Food Section of THE DALLAS MORNING NEWS for the frequent notices of tastings and "wine dinners" at area restaurants. Each September and October, the popular Quadrangle Grille for example, features a **"Celebrate Texas Wine"** festival, with a series of tastings, parties, dinners, and even a Texas winery tour to the Hill Country. Another popular wine festival is the **"Annual Texas Wine & Food Festival"** benefitting the Creative Learning Center. Hotels and restaurants, such as Baby Routh, The Mansion and the Hotel St. Germain, have frequent special dinners, usually featuring the wine of a specific vineyard.

▲ **THE DALLAS MORNING NEWS** hosts a prestigious national wine competition each February or March with as many as 1500 entries from 16 states. The usual format for the event, now in its tenth year, is a three-day tasting and judging event, later followed by a gala awards' dinner and other public events.

◆ **The Dallas Opera**, in taking a nod from the very successful Houston and Chicago opera-benefitting wine auctions, initiated an international wine auction in 1993 in conjunction with THE DALLAS MORNING NEWS awards' weekend. The success of the first annual auction, Vintage Dallas, held at the Fairmont Hotel in early March, attracted collectors and novices alike. For the collectors, there was the opportunity to find wines no longer available on the retail market. For the novice, it was an opportunity to begin a cellar and learn about wine pricing. Several pre-auction events helped raise the consciousness about wine and collecting. In any case, the benefits accrue to a deserving charity. The second Dallas Opera auction will be held on March 25, 1994.

▼ **The American Heart Association** also sponsors a major wine auction, *Côte du Coeur*, each February. This alliance of heart and wine gives credibility to "the French Paradox," the term given to the results of a study demonstrating the correlation of French eating habits accompanied by moderate wine drinking and a decreased evidence of heart disease.

● **The New Vintage Festival**, held appropriately in Grapevine, made its debut in April of 1993 with aspirations of becoming an annual event. The multi-faceted event emphasized educating the palate with Texas wine tastings, an afternoon food and wine tasting, and finally a gourmet dinner, featuring the best of Texas and guest speaker and wine connoisseur Sarah Jane English.

Vintner Dinners

Vintner dinners have been an increasingly popular form of entertainment and education. A number of the hotels and restaurants have become very active in this area and, at the same time, provide excellent meals to showcase the wines. Among the most active are:

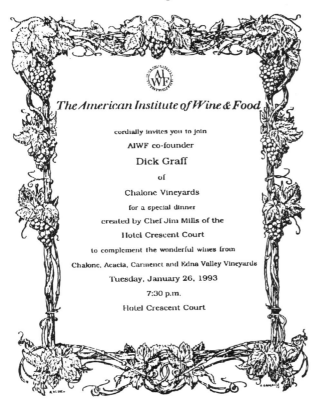

The American Institute of Wine & Food

cordially invites you to join

AIWF co-founder

Dick Graff

of

Chalone Vineyards

for a special dinner

created by Chef Jim Mills of the

Hotel Crescent Court

to complement the wonderful wines from

Chalone, Acacia, Carmenet and Edna Valley Vineyards

Tuesday, January 26, 1993

7:30 p.m.

Hotel Crescent Court

Baby Routh
Quadrangle Grille
The Mansion on
Turtle Creek
Hotel St. Germain
Four Seasons Resort
& Club

We recommend these events in an attempt to educate the aspiring wine connoisseur. The host and hostess may soon find that the pursuit of food and wine is full-time entertainment of itself!

Good Advice

▲ Last but not least on the subject of wine enlightenment, inexperienced buyers should consult the merchants at the better wine shops. Particularly knowledgeable sales assistance is available at **Grailey's, Marty's, Po-Go's,** the **Wine Emporium Etc.** and the **Sigel's** on Greenville Avenue. We recommend that you refer to our section on wine shops in Chapter V for additional information.

Now, prepared like chef and sommelier, the level of your entertaining should be both confident and extraordinary.

A reminder — *all the addresses and phone numbers for the above-mentioned sources are listed in the "Directory of Sources," which begins on page 223.*

III

Entertaining At Home

kitchenware, table accessories & linens

*O*pening one's home to friends to share occasions, both large and small, is the logical next step to gracious entertaining. While entertaining at home may occasionally entail sprucing up the living areas for the occasion, or decorating the home thematically for holidays, the kitchen and the dining areas are our focus in this chapter.

For the most part, we assume that the average hostess-to-be has already been given, bought or inherited the basics for wining and dining at home. From time to time, replacements or the updating of tableware and linens are a necessity and a pleasure. Many veteran party-givers are constantly on the look-out for new accessories to expand their entertaining inventories, whether these be the purchase of new dessert plates to give a fresh look to inherited china or a set of glasses to create a new mood for outdoor dining. When entertaining with any frequency at home, a variety of looks is important to the entire scenario and the pleasure of one's guests. Few of us want our friends or family to see the same scene repeated with every at-home entertaining experience. To always set the same scene is much like serving the same menu on each occasion. In other words, approach your at-home entertaining with the variety needed to give your guests the anticipation of something a little different on each occasion.

Fortunately, Dallas has a wealth of choices to start or refresh the components of successful home entertaining. The city has many resources, many more than we can possibly list and describe. We are mentioning our favorites, some of which enjoy a high profile in the community, and others which we hope are not on everyone's usual shopping itinerary. All of them have wonderful items and ideas to offer to the hostess, whether she be a novice or a veteran, and in varied price ranges and styles.

The addresses and phone numbers of the shops listed in this section can be found in the "Directory of Sources," beginning on page 223.

▲ **Barneys New York** in NorthPark is known for its contemporary but classic accessory items. Barneys carries lines not usually seen elsewhere, such as the wonderful British pottery lines by Maryse Boxer, as well as Italian and French faience made just for them. Their glassware selection is marvelous and includes some very special Venetian glassware and selections from London Glass Works. Their vases and centerpieces would be handsome additions to any entertainment scene. We only wish that the store would expand its attractive gift and home accessories' department close to the scale of its New York parent operation.

◆ **Cathy's Antiques** in the Crescent and **The China Cupboard** in Lakewood have some wonderful china and crystal gleaned from estate liquidations. The browsing at both places is fun and the discoveries frequent. We should note that The China Cupboard, run by the knowledgeable Mr. and Mrs. Bell, specializes in Meisen and Dresden, most of it of serious interest to the collector. There are rooms filled to overflowing. It's quite a cache.

▼ **The China Teacup** in Irving should be kept in mind for hostesses who have missing pieces of fine china patterns. The shop carries pieces of 2000 obsolete patterns and will happily search for your needs if not available in the current inventory.

▲**Classic China** now has a new name and has consolidated its two locations to its Arapaho address in Richardson . The shop, as the name indicates, specializes in fine china and has extensive selections of Lennox, Spode, Royal Daulton and Wedgwood, all discounted about twenty percent.

■ **The Copper Lamp,** tucked away in Old Town on Greenville Avenue, is *the* place in Dallas for estate silver. Stacked high on tables are silver pieces of all makes, quality and styles — bowls, trays, coffee and tea services. Should you want to buy slightly-used forks to supply your buffet table, the selection is plentiful. Lost a piece of your flatware? If the friendly owners don't have the needed piece filed away, they will scour their network of sources to locate your pattern, even if it has been off the market for a considerable time. The Copper Lamp is quite a unique operation and local treasure.

▲**Crate and Barrel** is every young person's dream of first possessions for the home. The contemporary lines are getting softer with age as more pine and color have been added to the extensive collection of kitchen and dining ware. Baskets, trays, copper, glasses and plates of every description fill the two Dallas stores. You can be sure that when the look is "in," it will be found at the NorthPark and Galleria locations of the Chicago-based company. The author frequently searches the well-organized shelves for extra bowls, sets of glasses or whatever is needed to round out the permanent party supplies. Recently, in looking for the new look in colored goblets, Crate and Barrel had attractive ones in several colors at inexpensive prices. It is not difficult to understand the store's popularity and success.

◆ The budget-conscious should occasionally explore the **Crate and Barrel Outlet Center** in Inwood Plaza. Their inventory varies, with anything from outdoor plastic tableware to hurricane lamps and discontinued table settings. It's a bargain-hunter's dream. Incidentally, another bargain (but quality) outlet is the **Chantal Cookware Factory** on Denton Drive that opens for seasonal sales of it quality merchandise. Call first for the schedule of sales.

▼ **East & Orient Company** on North Henderson is Dallas' antique shop that comes closest to a decorative museum. Owner Betty Gertz has an eye for the most elegant and refined antiques for the serious collector. Carefully arranged among the larger pieces are extraordinary porcelains from various heritages, which would be the focal point of any entertainment scenario. Fine silver is one of Betty's many specialties, as is decorative porcelain. A visit to East & Orient is a feast for the eye and the imagination.

● While in the neighborhood, explore the street's other shops, **William Farrell**, Russell O'Neil's **In Good Company, Les Antiques**, all of which have treasures for the table. Just on the other side on North Central Expressway, on Knox Street, there is a trio of good shops with antique accessories, many of them suitable for the table and entertaining scene. **Peregrinator's**, the **Highland Park Antique Shop** and **Drrew Ltd.** should all be on the list for those who ferret out good accessory finds. For contrast, **Vertu**, around the corner on Travis Street, is the destination of those who love the contemporary look. A visit to the Travis Walk shop will spark inspiration from the assembled vignettes and table settings.

■ We miss **Gump's** but, fortunately, their unexcelled collections of tableware and small antiques are available from their frequent catalogue collections. They are as close as their "800" number, listed in our "Directory of Sources." Gump's still maintains its mail-order warehouse in Dallas. There are occasional newspaper notices on inventory sales, so watch the newspapers. You know the stock will be great and the finds rewarding.

▲ Speaking of catalogues, the **Horchow Collection Catalogue** is a major source for miscellaneous home entertaining accessories. Watch the catalogue for china, pottery, cutlery and linens, culled from sources around the world. Some of it ends up at great savings at the outlet centers, **Horchow Finale**, on Inwood near LBJ and on Spring Valley in Richardson.

◆ We could do an entire book on mail-order for entertaining basics and food. We'd like to put in a good word for **Gardners Eden** which is obviously geared to those who like to entertain out-of-doors. Any issue, each better than the last, will contain never-seen-before items to enhance the patio and home scene. A recent summer issue had bamboo garden torches, inexpensive Chinese blue and white porcelain, tablelinens, hurricane lamps, antique hyacinth glasses, baskets, outdoor furniture and more. If you use your out-of-doors for entertaining, you can easily be hooked! **Smith & Hawken** has a similar catalogue, likewise filled with flower pots and vases, bistro and Parisian park furniture, alfresco earthenware and summer linens, all to embellish the outdoor setting. Both have the author always anxious for the next catalogue, and their ideas and accents for dining and entertaining.

▼ If the garden will be the entertaining space, check out **Llewellyn and Lee** in Preston Center East and **The Garden Secret,** a fairly new shop on Routh Street east of McKinney, for garden antiques, unusual lights and more. The stock is ever-changing and expanding.

● **International Wine Accessories.** We'd like to put in a good word for IWA, Inc., the Dallas-based supplier of supplies for wine connoisseurs. "Accessories" covers everything from glassware, uncorking machines, budget wine racks to serious wine cellar storage and all the frills. Their frequent catalogue will keep you up-to-speed on books and videos, all devoted to learning more about the fruit of the vine. Lucky for us, the ten year old company is here in Dallas, on Audelia near LBJ.

■ **The Ivy House** is a delight for the fine china collector. Located in Greenville Avenue's Old Town, the Ivy Shop should be on everyone's list to look for Wedgwood and Spode, as well as better-edited selections of Cerelene. The well-organized shop is run by knowledgeable personnel. In fact, owner Earl Buchman is an expert on antique Wedgwood and always has a collector's reserve on hand. Understandably, they do a big wedding gift business. And, watch for their sales when adding to your own home inventory.

▲ **La Mariposa**, across from the Quadrangle in an old house, is the destination for all those South of the Border accessories. The shop is chock full of folk art, tin art, clay candelabra, serapes for use as tablecloths, woven runners and napkins, pinatas and all the ingredients for an authentic Mexican look. We particularly like the tin lanterns with cactus cut-outs and the oversize margarita glasses, straight from Old Mexico.

◆ **Lady Primrose** at the Crescent has a revolving display of everything imaginable to set the table and accent the entertaining scene — old English china and silver, antique decanters and candlesticks. Browse frequently to keep up with the shipments from abroad purchased by owners Caroline Rose Hunt and Vivian Young. Their finds bring charm and the patina of the Old World to the traditional scene.

▼ **Lovers Lane Antique Market,** just west of Inwood Road, is a sibling operation to the well-established McKinney Avenue Antique Market mentioned below. In fact, many of the same merchants are represented in each location. Several of the individual dealers, such as Melanie McNutt and Charlene Marsh, are known for their excellent taste and their ability to search out interesting "finds." Certainly, the lover of English platters, majolica and one-of-a-kind table accents will have an ever-changing inventory to consider. And, don't forget the bride-to-be when shopping here. This may be a pleasurable way to introduce her to the joys of incorporating older treasures with her new possessions.

▲ **Macy's** has a world-wide reputation for housewares. Stocking an entire kitchen — from knives to pasta machines —from their Galleria emporium would be easy. On the same third floor, there is Wedgwood, Lennox, Nataska and Waterford for the dining room as well. Macy's has frequent specials, particularly on sets of cookware and kitchen machines. Prices are competitive indeed.

● **The Market**, with its multiple Dallas locations, is primarily a home decorating establishment, and the dining room is certainly important in the overall scheme. Their dining room vignettes are fun to look at for ideas and for purchases. The looks are dramatic — brass chargers, candelabra and lots of crystal. They also have a selection of fashionable chinaware and less expensive flatware.

■ **McKinney Avenue Antique Market** is an ensemble of 35 individual antique shops where one never knows what will be found among the charming vignettes. One dealer is a particularly good source for antique platters, those lovely nineteenth century Spode and Mason's works of art that can be the focal point of a display or buffet table. Candlesticks, fancy linens, and silver serving pieces are other good finds among the primarily British and American antiques.

▲ Nearby on State Street is **Mary Cates & Co.** which often has table accessories and small items related to cooking and entertaining, such as a recent collection of old, decorative molds for use and for fun. Mary is always on the watch for collections of the unusual.

◆ **Marguerite Green At Home**. Maggie Green's name brings instant recognition on the Dallas decorating scene, and we are happy her retail shop is back! After a year tucked away on Bowser in Oak Lawn, At Home is now more visibly located on Lovers Lane — fortunately for both shop keeper and purchaser. At Home is sheer ecstasy for the collector of beautiful entertaining accessories. A designer of note for more than 30 years, Maggie Green regularly travels to Europe to bring home the well-edited inventory. We admit to coveting the antique porcelain cake stands, Wedgwood silver luster and majolica galore. We love the Eighteenth Century French dessert plates, tureens, platters of varying heritages, charming candlesticks and virtually everything to make a table distinctive. But, this is not a shop for solely the antique. The old is supplemented by contemporary accessories, such as pottery by Lynn Evans and colorful, hand-blown crystal by Smyers, which all seems to blend so well with the surrounding treasury of small antiques and incidental furniture. Shops such as this exist in London, Paris and New York, but this is an original for Dallas. The stock changes frequently with new acquisitions incorporated into the ever-changing tableaux. This is a corner of paradise for lovers of exquisite table appointments. The distinctive dinner party may start right here.

● **The Mews**, in the Decorative District and selling both wholesale and retail, is an exciting new assemblage of wares from some of Dallas best collectors and designers. Among those participating, for example, are antique collectors Claire Martin, whose fine English porcelains will be the focal point for any table, francophile Ann Schooler, and talented artisans Mary Kehoe, Malee Rauscher and Mary Jane Ryburn. Front and center in the shop is local designer Gary Young. Many of the one-of-a kind items found there will make any dining and entertaining scenario distinctive.

■ **Neiman Marcus** has the city's largest selection of imported and exclusive brands in fine china, stemware and silver, not to mention small antiques, crystal and everyday ware to complement any gracious scene for entertaining. The extraordinary selections at Neiman's — sterling by Buccellati, flatware and accessories by Christofle, fine china by Herend, Cerelene and Puiforcat, crystal by Bacarrat, Waterford and Steuben and pottery by MacKenzie Childs are tomorrow's fine antiques. Neiman Marcus, Dallasites' favorite and most reliable purveyor of quality merchandise, also has linens and small bibelots that will add to any hostess' treasured inventory. Some kitchenware is available in the gourmet shops at NorthPark and Prestonwood.

▲ **Nuvo** on Cedar Springs is a gift-cum-card shop, which we discussed last year under invitations. Now, Nuvo is coming to the forefront as an accessory shop reflecting excellent taste. and ever-changing discoveries. Among furnishings by Phillippe Starke and Michael Graves can be found well-edited collections of china, linens and inspirational table settings. The look is contemporary but classical at the same time. We could easily add some of their small indulgences — glassware, china and vases — to our personal collections for entertaining at home. Nuvo's split personality allows for card and invitation stock, primarily Crane and Caspari, much of it pre-packaged or fill-ins.

◆ **The Panhandlers** has moved a bit further north to Preston Forest and continues to carry kitchen items, but with a new twist — that of meeting all discounted prices on appliances and equipment. They also sell some china tableware. A second Panhandlers shop is now located in Plano, facing Preston Road in the Preston Park Village. The merchandise is much the same, but there is more activity in the way of cooking demonstrations.

▼ **Pappas Design**. Sisters Mersina Pappas and Pam Pappas Mattingly have opened a Mediterranean-inspired interiors and accessories shop adjacent to the family-owned Pappadeaux Seafood Kitchen on Oak Lawn. It's a great place for provincial earthenware for the table, along with placemats, napkins and a nice line of glassware. Scattered among colorful table settings are candelabra and bibelots to enhance warm climate environments. The Pappas sisters have brought a touch of their heritage to the entertaining and home atmosphere.

● **The Perfect Setting**, a favorite and once lesser known haunt for pretty table accessories, moved from its Snider Plaza location in early 1993 to the former Loretta Blum space on Oak Lawn close to Empire Bakery. The shop's long-time specialty has been Herend china. It could be that fans of the exquisite, hand-painted Hungarian china had wanted to keep the shop their secret, but the new location will certainly heighten its visibility. The shop also carries Mottahedeh and other choice lines. Any fancier of the beautifully-set table will be happy with the inventory here. Understandably, it is important for bridal selections.

■ **Pier One Imports**. A visit to Pier One will convince the shopper that there is no excuse for not having at least one set of whimsical dinnerware, mats and napkins. When stocking up or filling in, notice the candlestick vases. Pier 1 shops are all around town in convenient location.

▲ **Plate and Platter** is paradise for the bargain hunter and for the person who needs to equip an entire kitchen — from coffee machines, to Henkel knives to Calphalon pots and pans — all at discount prices. The shop has quite an array of china patterns of such well-regarded names as Wedgwood, Dansk and Villeroy and Boch. The glassware is a bargain too. The author has a toss-up whether to head first to Plate and Platter or to Crate and Barrel for party-type fill-ins; i.e., less expensive dinner and glassware for buffet parties when we don't want our finest wares balanced on knees or taken to the patio. Many about-to-marry couples register with Plate and Platter for their kitchen choices. Plate and Platter is also discussed under "Cooking Classes" in Chapter II.

▼ **Polly Dupont** in Richardson has an extensive selection of china patterns, many of the usual, plus Ginori and others. The owners are very knowledgeable about their business and are value conscious. The sales on various lines are frequent.

◆ **The Polo Shop/Ralph Lauren** in Highland Park Village is a great place to purchase for the home as well as the wardrobe. The second floor has complete displays of Ralph Lauren's china line, with accompanying linens and fabrics to decorate a kitchen and dining room a la Lauren.

● **Room Service**. While this is another shop geared toward the home furnishings market, Room Service always has charming pottery, glassware, casual placemats and accessories to grace table tops. Owner Ann Fox has a big following among the young set for her decorating flair, which is evident in the shop. She can probably come up with some solid suggestions about creating a cozy dining and entertaining milieu.

▲ **The Sample House and Candle Shop** has been a Dallas institution for as long as we can personally remember. The collection is eclectic and charming, and among the always-packed inventory are the ingredients for many a theme party and accents for entertaining. Glassware, spongeware pottery, colorful Quimper dinnerware, papergoods, baskets and, of course, candles and holders can always be found. The inventory changes, particularly with seasons and fashions. Surely, there couldn't be a household in Dallas without wares from the Sample House.

▼ **The Silver Leopard** on Oak Lawn is a treasure-trove of new and old silver, including fine European flatware such as Buccellati. The antique wine coolers, candelabra, samovars and trays would enhance any entertaining setting. The Silver Leopard also carries fine china lines, such as Puiforcat and Cerelene, and has recently expanded into crystal to complete table components.

● **The Silver Vault**. The name is perfect. Imitated from the great London silver vaults where some of Britain's best antique silver dealers have their shops, the Lovers Lane shop brims with huge silver trays, antique silver baskets and wine accessories for the opulent look in fine dining and entertaining. While the shop, which features both antique and new pieces, does not carry flatware, it has a large selection of serving pieces, both antique and reproduction. As direct importers, their prices are fair for their excellent quality merchandise. For those who live further North, The Silver Vault has fortunately added a Plano location at Preston Park Village.

■ **Smink**. Check out the smart and contemporary shop next to Ruccus near SMU on Mockingbird. Sisters Jennifer and Autumn Smink offer unique decorations and accessories, as well as their own line of custom accessories including candlesticks, vases and glassware. These are whimsical wire and glass constructions. If you like Calder and Miro, you'll love their line of small accents.

▲ **Edward Stalcup, Inc.**, has settled in comfortably in Preston Center East, after almost 20 years in another location, making it even more convenient for faithful followers. The inventory shows Ed's enduring good taste – a

blend of placesettings, silver, crystal bowls, lamps, cachepots, sprinkled with a few small antiques. There is always something to be found for a gift and for one's own home entertaining and table accents. Collections can be begun and added to – candelabra of pottery, brass, crystal and silver; Motteheda plates; Stratfordshire figures; and napkin rings, to name just a few. The shop's settings provide ideas for the best use of one's favored possessions, such as the demi-tasse service arranged on an antique gallery tray, or a side table accented with crystal Val St. Lambert or porcelain Herend animals. Speaking of Herend, the shop is one of Dallas' better sources for the fine, hand-painted china, and the charming Herend Village pottery can also be found there. The latter is affordable for replacing or adding to one's casual dining inventory. Regular shoppers and collectors are on the look-out for one-of-a-kind *trompe l'oeil*, sculpted plates by Sarah Coke King and the hand-made pottery by a group of talented Dallas artists. Understandably, and coupled with the very personal service on the part of the owners and long-time employees, the shop does a significant bride's business. *Please see the advertisement for **Edward Stalcup, Inc.** on page 212.*

■ The **Saint Michael's Woman's Exchange** in Highland Park Village has a wealth of accents for the table and thematic decorations for the season, be it Christmas, Easter or a summer picnic. During the summer, the red and white checkered picnic items were reason enough to have a party. Because we love their invitation services and gift wrapping services, we stop by frequently and can always find appropriate items for our own entertaining needs and gifts for the many brides on our list. Recently, we admired all the crystal rose bowls, perfect for the dining table's centerpiece, and the variety of faience for casual parties. To qualify as a "woman's exchange," a certain percentage of their stock must be hand-made, another reason to shop there for the one-of-a-kind treasures. If the party occasion calls for a gift, the store can wrap and deliver, a service for which it has long been known. We hope you will refer to the write-up of Saint Michael's Woman's Exchange under "Invitations" in Chapter IV.
*Please see the advertisement for **St. Michael's Woman's Exchange** on page 210.*

◆**Stanley Korshak** at The Crescent is another favorite for selecting new dinnerware and accessories for the table. The shop's mode is contemporary, and few Dallas stores have such fashionable looks in china and flatware selection. The linen and place mat choices featured in their "At Home" department are always the "look of the moment." And, for the Southwestern style, there is a large selection of pottery by Luna Garcia and Mexican silver pieces by Las Castillos from Taxco. All in all, we love Korshak's tasteful choices. The author has picked up many accessories there during the years to update her more traditional setting. Korshak's has added an instantly popular bridal shop, so we suspect that the brides who are flocking there will become equally enamored of the "At Home" Shop. Last but not least, the sales help is wonderful and creative.

■ **Tiffany & Co.** is the author's favorite establishment for wish-list acquisitions. Oh, to be a bride again and receive all one's first permanent belongings from Tiffany's exclusive sterling silver and tableware collections! If one is in the market for a silver service, or for extraordinary crystal candlesticks and vases, this is the place. Frequently, there are excellent values, that come with the Tiffany reputation for quality and incomparable service. Be sure to notice their new and affordable line of wine glasses and their expanding line of both fine china and pottery. Tiffany has always been known for its displays of dining accessories, particularly the imaginative table settings. The Galleria store has table vignettes at all times. Do stop by and admire the stylish ensembles. There are always ideas to be gleaned. And, speaking of ideas, the full range of Tiffany's books on entertaining should be part of every hostess' library — *TABLE SETTINGS BY TIFFANY, TIFFANY PARTIES* and the newly published *THE TIFFANY GOURMET COOKBOOK.* Tiffany also publishes a book on weddings, which is filled with exquisite ideas for the elegant wedding.

▲ **Translations**, an accessories shop owned by Mary Bloom and Debbie Tompkins, opened in Preston Center East last year and has a steady stream of customers looking for unique ideas in gifts and table accents. Good taste gurus Mary and Debbie can be counted on to have an exquisite hand-blown plate or glass, a unique candelabra and even outstanding gift foods to add taste to the entertaining scenario. One thing is predictable about the shop — it is a changing tableau to suit the season and the latest discoveries on the gift market.

◆ **Williams-Sonoma** has everything conceivable for the kitchen at their Highland Park and Galleria locations. Serious chefs can find the ideal gadget and cooking supplies, not to mention heavy French copper cooking ware, knives, butcherblocks, baskets and more. Williams-Sonoma always has the latest and best in kitchen machines, be it for pasta or for bread. If the dedicated cook is particularly happy here, so is the collector of casual glassware, pottery, platters for the Thanksgiving turkey, and every size of souffle and au gratin dish. We are fans, and be sure to get on their mailing lists in case shopping from home is your forte. The frequent catalog is a great inspiration for gift-giving to the friend or spouse who likes to cook and to entertain.

▼ As a reminder, the thriving Lovers Lane area has several other shops where entertaining accoutrements can be found. One is the charming **Tulip Tree, II** which has pretty accessories for the table and the patio, and **The Wicker Basket,** just around the corner from Lovers Lane on Eastern, where the hostess can find any possible basket for flowers and serving needs. **Brenda Schoenfeld**, while primarily a jeweler specializing in Mexican silver, has wonderful table accent pieces from her family's home city of Taxco, especially the flamboyant Los Castillos serving pieces and flatware.

● As a special hint, don't overlook the restaurant supply houses when equipping a kitchen or adding to your entertaining inventory. Though ostensibly "to the trade," few will question your purchase if you follow the rules on minimums. We have many friends who shop these places regularly for their cooking equipment and for the pottery and glassware used by restaurants. **Ace Mart Restaurant Supply** on Northwest Highway near Bachman Lake is one of the area's largest. **Watson Food Service Industries** is another of the major suppliers in the city, whose warehouse brims with everything from expresso machines to everyday pots, pans, strainers, wooden spoons and even cutlery and china.

Linens

Because we have numerous requests about linens — an important part of table dressing, we decided to segment the linen component of our listing, so that our readers could focus on them together. Certainly, several Dallas stores, not specializing solely in linens, have wonderful selections. **Neiman Marcus** always has some of the most luxe of linens to accompany the choices of china and silver made by brides. **Stanley Korshak at The Crescent** has one of the best selection of napkins, placemats and unusual linens to add special flair for the properly-groomed and fashionable table setting. In addition, there are several shops, such as **Ed Stalcup, Inc.**, where good choices are always available.

■ **Designs Behind the Scenes.** At least one source, a tip from a well-versed party planner, makes affordable tablecloths, either from their extensive fabric stock or yours. Table tops (square coverings) are their usual way to dress up a space or coordinate the "look" with their floral and plant business. Their tops start at $15. and go up to $45. depending on the fabric. They will make round cloths as well, with a charge of $25. to $35. with your fabric.

▲ **Ginette Albert** took over a 35 year family business about three years ago, selling custom linens to Dallasites in their homes. She represents numerous fine lines, all custom, and mostly from Europe. This is an opportunity to select linens in your home to coordinate with your setting and china. Ginette takes orders from samples, such as appliquÈed mats and napkins from Madeira, embroidered or monogrammed cocktail napkins and hand towels, and fabulous lace-edged buffet napkins from England. Whether ordering for yourself, or for the bride-to-be, the linens represented are only the best, to become family treasures that never go out of style.

◆ **The Linen Gallery**, at Preston Road and Lovers Lane, has filled a need as a source for fine linens. While the stock is geared more toward the bedroom and the bathroom, there is a growing selection and display of fine linen placemats and napkins. Ask to see the hard-to-find linen tablecloths that are carefully folded away in drawers. Like several local stores, they have the "in vogue" lines of Liz Wain. These hand-painted linens, mostly placemats and cocktail and dinner napkins, are the look of the moment. And don't forget, gracious entertaining requires a consideration for the guest bath. Here, the bathroom incidentals will be among the prettiest. There is also an extensive collection of bride's books and related bridal keepsakes.

▼ **Linen 'n Things**, a chain of discounted linens and miscellany for the home, has opened a large shop in Preston Royal near Borders Books and Music. Their inventory of table linens leans toward the casual and utilitarian. We are mentioning them because many a hostess has found linen sheets to utilize as to-the-floor table cloths — either by trimming the king-size sheets into 108 inch rounds or by knotting the corners, a trick we learned from flower and party maestro Rusty Glenn.

● **The Linen Sisters,** Sharon Galer and Judy Tiemann, have launched a now year-old custom linen enterprise. For the ultimate touch of coordinated and complementary linens, Sharon and Judy are designing runners, placemats and napkins in cottons, brocades and even silks to dress up the focal point of the party and to tie together your wonderful table accessories. Runners start at $150. and napkins start at $15. The duo, who do "trunk shows" at their homes, also have taken space at the McKinney Avenue Antique Market where their very attractive linens can also be seen and ordered.

■ **Fishburn's Dry Cleaning and Laundry** is appropriate for mention at this point. Don't put off using your heirloom linens for fear of guests who

spill. Two generations of Slaters are presently involved in this family-run business which has catered to the carriage trade since 1907. The eighteen store operation is the city's premier caretaker of fine linen appointments for the table, whether by hand laundering or dry cleaning methods. The carefully hand-finished items will be ready for the next special event. The drop-off points are conveniently located throughout Dallas and the suburbs — but, don't forget, for today's busy hostesses, Fishburn's picks up and delivers.

Many of those now assembling a fine linen trousseau are the brides who will be enjoying those linens for years to come — thanks to the fine care they will receive at Fishburn's. This may be the right moment to suggest that those same brides should remember to preserve and store their wedding gowns for future generations. Fishburn's has been caring for wedding gowns for almost 50 years now and has been the reason that many Dallas brides are able to enjoy wearing the gowns their mothers and grandmothers wore on their own wedding days.

*Please see the advertisement for **Fishburn's Cleaning and Laundry** on page 211.*

▲ **Tablecloths Unlimited** is a small and specialized rental company, which we have listed in Chapter X under "Rentals." We are mentioning them here because owner Dawn Cartwright sells her slightly-used linen cloths and, occasionally, napkins, at the end of each season. Prices range from $25. for a square table top to $95. and up to fit 48 and 60 inch round tables to the floor. Fabrics are always superb and the workmanship excellent. Give the company a call and ask to be put on the list for their periodic sales.

◆ **Westminster Lace**. We are aware that it is increasingly difficult to find formal linens, which certainly could be a reflection of a more casual dining and entertaining style. North Park's Westminster Lace, as the name suggests, has lacy lines from which to choose, if the look you want is elegant or fancy.

▼ There are numerous fabric shops throughout the city that will fabricate tablecloths for parties, a great way to coordinate the entire look. We can recommend **Calico Corners**, with several locations throughout Dallas, and **Rutherford's** on Lovers Lane. **Quiltcraft Industries** is a to-the-trade source that specializes in making tablecloths, among its other fabric specialties. A hemmed and unlined cloth for either a 48 or 60 inch round is $45. with your fabric.

● Under **Miscellaneous** is some very good advice from friendly readers. The major rentals companies at all times have bins of slightly used cloths which they sell inexpensively, from approximately $3. to $10. These may not be acceptable as cloths by themselves because of slight top stains, but they make quite adequate undercloths for those who have or rent decorative linen table tops.

A reminder — *the addresses and phone numbers are listed in the "Directory of Sources" beginning on page 223.*

The Dallas Symphony Orchestra League
invites you to a
New Members Coffee and League Presentation
Thursday, the second of September

UNE FÊTE ARTISTIQUE

Please join us for a glass of wine
to celebrate the publication of the 1993 edition

ENTERTAINING IN DALLAS!
a guide to sources & facilities

by Carol Hall with Charron Denker
design by Suzanna Brown

ARCODORO
2520 Cedar Springs
Thursday, December the third
five to seven

please reply by December 1

IV

The First Step

the art of inviting

*I*n hosting many parties through the years, we've learned that Dallas abounds in shops specializing in invitations, and in designers and specialists who will add a novel dimension to the art of inviting. During that time, the emphasis on invitations has changed considerably, partly as an effort to compete for our attention and as a result of increased sophistication in the design world. Not too long ago, we used our engraved or monogrammed stationery, or plain note cards, to invite friends for cocktails and dinner. Many still do, and it is a charming alternative to the printed party invitation. That practice makes considerable sense when the printing of a few invitations frequently costs the same as printing one hundred.

We also used fill-in's for birthday parties, showers and the like. This, too, has become a lesser alternative, partly because the options have become so varied. Telephone calls are the easiest route, if the party is small or impromptu.

The engraved invitation, plain and in impeccable taste, is still the standard for formal events, and we can happily report that social etiquette is alive and well, particularly for weddings. This does not mean that alternatives are not plentiful. Certainly, gracious options are available for second or very intimate marriages, and the use of calligraphy and thermography — faux-engraving — is frequently seen for black-tie celebrations. A few of the Dallas stationers, such as **Campbell Stationers**, and the social secretarial services, namely **R.S.V.P.** and **Party Service**, are expert in assisting with the selection of proper invitations for formal occasions.

But, no wonder that the art of the invitation has reached new heights. The invitation creates an instant impression to the prospective guest. With few words, but with visual impact, it announces the theme, the facts of who, where and when. It conveys the elegance or informality, the celebration of a marriage or the intimacy of a dinner party at home. It creates a mood of excitement and anticipation. *In short, it is the first impression of what is to come, and you will want to make it favorable.*

We have listed our favorite and most reliable shops where invitations can be purchased, usually in blank form, to be hand-written or printed in a usual format — or with witty sayings — that include the message and establish the tone. This is not to suggest that all invitations come in conventional form! There are many, more shops than are listed here, but we think that you will enjoy the selections available at these, our favorite suppliers.

The addresses and phone numbers for the shops and designers listed in this chapter can be found in the "Directory of Sources," which begins on page 223.

▲ **Campbell Stationers** is THE place for top-of-the-line engraved invitations and social stationery. Not only does the Preston Center emporium carry a full line of quality Crane products and engraving, Campbell's is the retail arm of the Southwest's finest engravers. Consequently, their engraving styles and expertise far exceed their competitors. The more serious look of their stock also reflects their extensive corporate business. Their other valuable asset is Sue Parker, the local expert on invitation etiquette, especially for weddings and formal occasions.

◆ **Carté** is an attractive, fairly new invitation and card shop on Oak Lawn. Their invitation stock is particularly well selected, with lots of large square invitations, the look of the moment. The posted samples will give you an idea of their good taste in the finished product. Carté has been adding several custom-designed lines. Carté has its own calligraphy machine, which makes truly elegant invitations more affordable. A calligraphy set-up/type-set is $25. and includes the first ten invitations. Each additional invitation is $1. Carté also uses the machine for calligraphy envelope addressing, also at $1. per envelope. Meanwhile, business has been expanding to small gifts, photo albums and brides' books to complement their growing wedding invitation business.

▼ **Geppetto Designs.** Stationery consultant Merrie Ann King represents some of the best of engraved papers for weddings, parties and social stationery. Merrie Ann brings with her the experience as several times mother-of-the-bride and a reputation among her peers for flair and taste. When ordering for a wedding, consider the total package of paper needs, of personal stationery and party and rehearsal dinner invitations. There is little to compare with the instant recognition and timeless elegance of fine engraving. For financial savings and for less formal occasions, thermography — the faux engraving — is also available from the represented lines, all at very competitive prices.

● **Inkcorporated Stationery and Invitations** is an outstanding two-year enterprise by Suzanne Droese who oversees a Preston Center business that offers creative designs for invitations, personal stationery needs, and corporate and promotional materials. A departure from the usual makes the enterprise special. Included are many lines new to Dallas as well as several custom designed lines. We particularly liked the whimsical Kangaroo & Joey line with coordinated envelopes and the Beaux-Arts-looking and appropriately-named Ars Antiqua line. Of course, laser printing and calligraphy machine processes are available. More significantly, Suzanne will oversee any special design and printing to make your invitations truly distinctive, and her scope is not limited to stock invitations, with an increasing number of designers and printers among her sources. The Inkcorporated name has been associated with a number of major charity invitations, including the Weekend to Wipe Out Cancer, the Kidney Foundation, the Crystal Charity Ball and the Dallas Garden Society. During the past year, we have been aware of the origin of some of the most effective invitations, one a simple and colorful mixture of geometric shapes, festively tied together and each bearing another part of the message, in this case for a store announcement. It was inexpensive and effective. Another was the holiday greeting, which came gift-boxed. Inside was a miniature carton of Cheer with accompanying greeting from the staff of Inkcorporated. We know their ideas are endless! By appointment only.

*Please see the advertisement for **Incorporated Stationery and Invitations** on page 215.*

■ **It's a Wrap**, primarily a gift wrapping service, tucked away in newly expanded space near Patrizzio's in Highland Park Village, also has a limited, but very select, stock of invitations to go along with their tasteful collection of merchandise. If it is pool party time, you can be assured that they will have one or two of the best. We're always fascinated with their small-scaled gifts, favors and toys, something for everyone.

▲ **Ken Knight**, in the Quadrangle, has what we think is the city's best card shop. Fortunately, among his growing inventory of miscellaneous accessories, are occasional boxes of blank cards and post cards which would make great invitations. Ken, former owner of Arresta and a former Horchow Catalogue buyer, has extraordinary taste. He can easily come up with some clever ideas for invitations.

◆ **Marj's Stationry** in Inwood Village, specializing in party needs and invitations, has been on the scene for a number of years. Theirs is a shop carrying the best lines of ready-boxed invitations and a very complete line of Crane's papers. The party paper selection is always choice.

▼ **Needle in A Haystack**, despite its name and split personality as a needlepoint shop, is one of the Park Cities and North Dallas' favorite shops for invitations. Their stock is extensive — with everything from Crane, as well as from Regency and Cambridge, for engraved invitations and social stationery to Paper by the Pound. Originally owned by the wife of the Glad Tidings paper line, the shop still carries the most complete selection of that popular and clever line. Whether the party is baby shower or ice cream social, there will be an invitation of interest. Owner and avid needlepointer Bhavna Parimar points out that the convenient Preston Road shop does its own printing and can personalize wedding and photo albums and many of the accessories that are part of the entertaining scene.

● **Papyrus**, with both NorthPark and Galleria locations, is a fairly new entry on the Dallas paper products scene, carrying cards, wrapping papers and a growing supply of invitations. Like Carté, Papyrus has one of the new calligraphy machines, which can be a price boon to those who are printing fewer than 50 or 100 invitations. We love to browse among their paper gift items as well.

■ **Party Art**, with a second floor Preston Center East location, is run by artistic Ruth Ann Caudle, who specializes in customized, hand-created party invitations. We are always awed by the whimsical and hand-painted art, frequently incorporating photographs, ribbons, bows and lace. With such attention to detail, her invitations are always treasured mementos for a bride-to-be or birthday honorée. We were happy to see that the attractive, music-sheet-collage invitation for the '93 Dallas Symphony League Fashion Show was a Party Art creation! Her prices start at $50. for very unique works of art. We will also note that her very individualized cards and invitations have picked up a national following. Applause!! Please, by appointment, and take heed — that despite a Preston Road address, the studio is actually on the street behind.

▲ **Party Bazaar** is covered below for their contributions on the party supply scene. The shop has been a Dallas staple for multiple generations and many of us are like homing pigeons when we think of parties. Their invitation selection, both blank cards and the fill-in variety for children's and casual occasions, has grown considerably. They carry all the usual, including Caspari and David M, plus others as well. Printing prices are somewhat less than their competitors, with $30. covering both typesetting and printing of the first 100. Color adds another $30.

◆ **Party Cat** from Austin has opened a Dallas office! We were so impressed with their quality and cost savings when we only had to call, mail or FAX an invitation copy to Austin and the order would be sent out in two days. Now, the same service is available in their Preston Center location (in the Lobello Building). There is always stock on hand for a two-day turn-around in printing. Pricing for printing is simple: Party Cat does not charge for a set-up fee, by the line, or for color. Pricing is based on quantity, $20. for 50 invitations, as an example, and $25, for 100. There are 15 or so type styles to choose from, as well as nine or ten colors. There is the opportunity, also, to order from the complete selection of numerous well-known lines, if you order the minimum and if you plan ahead for the two week delivery. There are also books to order from — these too at 10% to 20% discount depending on the vender and volume. Meanwhile, if you want to continue ordering by Fax or phone, the 800 number will reach ex-lawyer and owner Claire Saunders in Austin.

▲ **Party Place**, in both Preston Center and at Park Place in Plano, lures a good number of party givers, particularly for their extensive collection of party paper products. The Party Place has a varied selection of off-the-shelf invitations, mostly geared to the informality associated with paper goods and party favors. Recently, they've added space in their Preston Center location. Likely, all the same stock was there before, but now it's spread out for ease of selection. Their in-house laser printing is reasonable, under $40. for 100 invitations including color. Their selection of fill-in invitations is better than the norm. They also have the largest selection of attractive (and money-saving) post-card-type invitations. Party Place is also listed in Chapter VIII under "Party Supplies."

▲ **Party Service** should not be overlooked when considering invitations for a major event. While the company provides event planning and social secretary services, they also handle lines of invitations and have access to many graphic artists who will custom-design a unique invitation. For the special anniversary or birthday celebration or important corporate party, the impact of a distinct invitation will be significant. Besides, there will be the opportunity to discuss other aspects of the party to add to its pizzazz. Party Service is also listed under "Party Planning and Secretarial Service" in Chapter VI.

▲ **Print Shoppe** on Lover's Lane is an understandable favorite among those who enjoy taking care of their own printing, or who have more exacting printing requirements. Type-setting capabilities are outstanding, and their expertise comes through with more than just the standard invitation form. For one-stop shopping to go with printing expertise, The Print Shoppe is the place to visit. The popular spot has a nice selection of packaged invitations, including our favorite Greeting Graphics, Caspari, David M and Odd Balls. In fact, the selection of invitation stock is more varied and appealing than ever.

Join
Holly and John
at their
Rehearsal Dinner
Friday, April 16
8:00 p.m.
Mariano's Restaurant
Old Town

Casual
R.S.V.P.

Laser typesetting for the typical invitation runs about $12.50 and printing 100 invitations costs $28. Color adds $15. The Print Shoppe also carries complete lines of fine engraving and thermography, including the top-of-the-line Crane. And thinking of engraving, The Print Shoppe can handle the full range of wedding needs, such as place cards and wedding programs, and social stationery as well. Naturally, we've also listed The Print Shoppe under "Printing." See below for listing.

Please see the advertisement for **The Print Shoppe** *on page 221.*

▲ **R.S.V.P.**, as part of its social secretarial services, is active in selecting engraving and custom-designed invitations for their many clients in the social swim. Owner Barbara Paschall has access to fine sources of invitation designers to provide not-to-be-duplicated invitations. You can always count on a distinctive look from and invitation bearing the R.S.V.P. imprint and return address.

◆ Another invitation source in Highland Park Village is **Randall Morgan-Village Stationers**, which has a nice selection of Crane fine papers and well-chosen, traditional party invitation lines, along with gifts and accessories for the table. Of course, they can handle the engraving and the printing too.

▼ **Royale Party +** in Preston Forest has become a popular source for cost-cutting invitations, particularly for children's parties and all those get-togethers for teenagers and charities. Royale Party + seems to have the city's largest selection of the popular Paper by the Pound (one pound, about 120 invitations, for $7. with envelopes at $.30 each) and its related designer line with borders and motifs. The stock, in fact, has expanded significantly, and printing is inexpensive. (We do want to mention that the samples displayed are from the companies represented and not samples of the laser work done on premises.) There is also a corner in the rear of the store for budget wedding invitations.

● **Ruccus**, on Mockingbird near SMU enjoys its reputation as one of Dallas' best greeting card shops. In the rear of the store is a nice selection of prepackaged invitations from the major makers and some fill-ins as well. Of course, they will take care of all your printing needs.

■ The **St. Michael's Woman's Exchange**, in Highland Park Village, has continued to enjoy its new look after a renovation two years ago. St. Michael's enjoys a special niche in the community and their many supporters

go to great lengths to ensure the best community sources for the shop. Additional emphasis has been put on a growing selection of party invitations, many of them for children's parties and for casual occasions which can even be bought by the piece and printed through one of their inexpensive sources. (We paid about $25. to typeset and print 25 invitations.) We love the Odd Balls line with wonderful thematic art for garden parties and kitchen and wine showers. Likewise, the William Arthur collection, tucked away in a book, offers the nicest thermography we have seen on fine papers with lined envelopes and charming borders. While ordering invitations for the party, don't forget embossed or monogrammed cocktail napkins and other paper goods — among the shop's other specialties. You will find the devoted, volunteer staff particularly helpful, which in itself is a good reason for shopping here. See also to the listing of St. Michael's Woman's Exchange under "Kitchenware and Table Accessories" in Chapter III.

Please see the advertisement for St. Michael's Woman's Exchange on page 210.

▲ **Suzanne Roberts Gifts** has been in Snider Plaza near SMU since 1975 and has a dedicated clientele. While technically a gift shop, among the Spode, Royal Worcester and MacKenzie Childs is one of the city's largest selection of Crane's note cards and writing paper, plus books of engraving samples for weddings and social stationery. Likewise, the charming Caspari Collection of invitation cards is one of the best, especially the precious baby motifs perfect for showers and announcements.

◆ **Tiffany & Co.** While we have written up Tiffany elsewhere, we want to mention that Tiffany has long been among the most respected names in engraving and fine invitations, a complement to their business in weddings and in accessories for elegant entertaining. Receiving an invitation with a Tiffany embossed envelope flap is not overlooked by the cognoscenti. See our listing under "Kitchenware and Table Accessories" in Chapter III.

● **William Ernest Brown,** located now only in NorthPark, is the city's elegant place to shop for an invitation. The well-appointed shop and comfortable chairs make stationery shopping a pleasure. For a really special event, and for a large choice of engraving, do not miss their well-edited options. Their invitation choices represent a few different lines and their displayed samples are an inspiration of what can be done. There is also a good selection of cards with motifs for baby announcements and for children's parties.

▼ **Write Selection.** Everyone loves Write Selection in Preston Royal and their knowledgeable, attentive staff. Their suggestions are always creative and appropriate, whether it be for a baby shower, bar mitzvah, teenage party or bridal luncheon. The shop's shelf selections are usually more diverse than many of the competitors, as are the vast number of lines available for special order. Owners Betsy Swango and Ynette Hogue have quite a following among the party set, and no wonder!! Expect to pay $25. for an invitation set-up and $30. per 100 for in-house printing in black. Color is extra.

■ The major specialty stores, such as **Neiman Marcus** and **Stanley Korshak**, also carry invitations and will order Crane's engraving. For many years Neiman Marcus was the best-known Dallas source for fine wedding engraving and still does a tremendous amount of wedding and social stationery. Now that Stanley Korshak has a fine bridal salon, we can anticipate that the brides will find it also convenient to coordinate their wedding invitation purchases in the same location. Both stores also have a selection of packaged invitations and boxed note cards as well.

Studio Specialists

◆ There are a few new "finds" in this area, one of which is **Invitations and Party Innovations,** owned by Lisa Smiley. Lisa works from her home (in the Far North Dallas-Plano area) and uses principally laser printing for invitations, envelope addressing, napkins and whatever can be printed for a party. For one event, she even printed commemorative labels for the champagne bottles! With minimal overhead and astute shopping in the invitation market, Lisa can offer imprinted invitations at about the same price as the invitation stock offered elsewhere. In addition, she has sought out a number of designs not often seen in area shops, such as the watercolor-like Garden Flowers of Hannah Hill and Faux Designs, while still providing all the well-known favorites. Service has been a key to her success. Free delivery is offered in her immediate area and can be arranged for most other areas as well. Another at-home invitation supplier is **LazerTations**, whose work is what the name indicates, invitations done on the computer. Owner Eric Oleson has a large wedding invitation business in the Plano area.

▼ Another is **Making Statements**, a new company by Stephanie Westfall, who is now coordinating invitations for individuals and party planners, after several years of experience planning social events for a major Dallas law firm. Her stock is the full range of most invitation manufacturers at very competitive prices. And, not only does she oversee all the printing details, she comes to you for added convenience. Invitation set-ups are $15. and print-ing of 100 invitations, for example, will cost $27.50. Custom PMS colors add $10. When we talked to Stephanie during the midst of a hot July, she was custom-printing fans for a client, just an example of the additional projects that she handles.

▲ **The Write Choice** is a flourishing, seven-year old, studio business with a large clientele for party invitations, birth announcements and the like. Owner Jennie Gilchrist represents some 80 lines, including most of the better-known names. In addition, she has a number of local artists who will custom design invitations starting at about $30. Savings occur mostly by way of reduced costs for printing, hot-pressing, or calligraphy machine, which are in the $35. range for 50 invitations. Along with the selection (Jennie carefully buys for her market), there is personalized service that accompanies the savings.

▼ There are a number of other invitation "specialists" who work from their homes, providing custom design and service for invitations. These include **Invite Your Guests** and **Card Art**. Card Art owner Kristina Wood will hand-craft an invitation, announcement or greeting card to the customer's specifications. Simpler designs start at about $6. per card. All have loyal followings. **Ann Manning** also does design work at home. Her fees start at $40.

Just a reminder — *the names and addresses for the invitation specialists listed in this chapter can be found in the "Directory of Sources," starting on page 223.*

Printing and Other Resources

Most of the shops mentioned above can provide printing services for invitations. Certainly, one-stop shopping for both invitation and printing is easier and time-efficient. But, many of us will find an invitation we like at one place and still have a favorite or more economical printing sources elsewhere. Often, we pick up invitations on sale and "stock pile" them for a future, appropriate time. Also, there are the creative opportunities for having an invitation or menu set-up for printing by a calligrapher. Knowing a few good printing sources should be on everyone's list!

● **The Print Shoppe**, mentioned above, is everyone's favorite and first destination for quality printing and services beyond the norm. If an invitation is custom-made, likely the designer will choose The Print Shoppe for the exacting work. They have the capacity to die stamp and cut, screen, and do the more demanding print work. Likewise, custom color printing will be more precise. Their many samples will give an idea of the work they have done for area designers. For the discriminating individual, there will be the expansive choice of style and color for printing perfection. The recommendations of the staff are made with years of experience in the printing business. Not to be overlooked, George, Shirley and Liz have made friends through the years with charities and schools, whose printing work and yearbooks they have overseen If one counted, we are sure that The Print Shoppe has printed more

On the occasion of the visit to Dallas, Texas
of
Her Majesty Queen Elizabeth II
and
His Royal Highness
The Prince Philip, Duke of Edinburgh

The Mayor of the City of Dallas
and
Jubilee Dallas 150
request the pleasure of your company
at dinner
on Tuesday, the twenty-first of May
at six o'clock

Hall of State   Fair Park

invitations for charity events than any Dallas printer. And all who have used the shop know the dependability of the people and the product. See also the listing of The Print Shop above under "Invitations."
Please see advertisement for **The Print Shoppe** *on page 221.*

■ Do-it-yourselfers, like ourselves, should also look into quick-print options, available at the area **Kwik-Kopys, Kinkos** and **PIP Printers**, which will vary from store to store. The typesetting is usually about $15. and the printing of 100 invitations will be about $20. Custom color adds another $30. Their selections of type styles and colors will be broad. **Moreno Printing Service** on Greenville Avenue does excepional work at reasonable prices and fast turn-around. Another find may be **Dave the Printer** on Irving Boulevard where almost everyday is a "free" color day, and the colors are unique, such as "grey 420" on Mondays and "burgundy 208" on Wednesdays. Dave has 135 fonts, or typestyles, and will print 100 invitations for $29., his stock or yours, with typesetting another $15. Work must be brought in before three o'clock the previous day. **PIP Printing** on Forest across from Medical City also rotates free color days. Call to check on color and schedule.

▲ And don't forget to check out **OK PAPER** at Harry Hines and Pearl, or one of the other locations, if you want to save on paper stock. For unique and handmade papers, try **Paper Routes** in Deep Ellum.

◆ We're also fascinated with the rubber stamp approach to making invitations, which is clever way to involve children in their own invitation process — and certainly not limited to children!! We love the **Private Collection Rubber Stamp Company**, owned by collector-turned-entrepreneur Cheryl Darrow. There is virtually nothing that cannot be "stamped" on to cards and envelopes from the 20,000 decorative stamp inventory for a party motif. As some of you may know, the Preston Center shop also offers birthday parties for children, teaching them to personalize and decorate with ink stamps.

calligraphy

Calligraphy affords alternatives to both handwriting and printing. And while calligraphy machines have become commonplace, there is nothing so elegant as the work of an artistic calligrapher.

In lieu of typesetting for a formal invitation, you might ask a calligrapher to make a master copy, which can be run off on fine stock at a small print shop. We had a personal experience of a calligrapher doing the invitations for a small formal wedding. The number needed was fewer than considered appropriate for engraving. The result was beautiful. Each invitation was a work of art to herald a momentous event. We've used calligraphic invitations for many events and we've always been pleased with the delighted reactions of our invitees.

For formal parties and, especially, weddings, some hostesses have the invitations addressed by a calligrapher. And, don't forget place cards done in calligraphy for a special touch at an important dinner.

There are several excellent calligraphers in Dallas with very full calendars because their work is in such demand. Prices vary, but generally an invitation master or set-up will run about $35. and invitation addressing is usually between .50 cents and .75 a line. Rates may be negotiable depending on the size of the party or wedding.

The names and phone numbers of the calligraphers in this chapter can be found in the "Directory of Sources" on page 223.

▼ **Donna Bonds** is another highly recommended calligrapher, who zis a veteran of 20 years. Donna specializes in script writing for social and wedding invitations. She is very gracious about providing on-site service for a formal seated dinner or wedding when there may be last minute changes in the place cards. She did this recently for a flawlessly executed wedding dinner at the Hall of State. It certainly eased problems for the mother of the bride. Her prices vary, are reasonable and are priced on volume.

● **Donna Sabolovic Calligraphy and Design** utilizes multiple talents in her invitation work. With a background as an illustrator, she brings more than the art of fine writing to her calligraphic work on invitation set-ups and addressing for wedding invitations. Invitations can be embellished with artistic borders, for example, or calligraphy can be incorporated into the custom design for an invitation. These provide unique touches when the occasion is very special, such as a rehearsal dinner or a very personalized wedding invitation. Donna can provide that special touch that will set the invitation apart. In addition, Donna is in demand for the calligraphy of poems, sayings, menus and more, all of which she can likewise embellish with borders or appropriate artwork. We suggest that you look ahead to the write-up of Donna Sabolovic under "Custom Designed Invitations."
*Please see advertisement for **Donna Sabolovic Calligraphy and Design** on page 212.*

■ Susie-Melissa Cherry of **Calligraphic Arts, Inc.** is always mentioned as dean of the city's calligraphers. A visit to her cheery, plant-filled Herschel Avenue studio will excite any admirer of fine workmanship and papers. Calligraphic Arts can take care of all your gracious needs for placecards, invitations, envelope addressing, menus and much, much more. Susie-Melissa set-up charges are $10. a line for Italic and $15. a line for Script; addressing is $1. and $1.50 a line, respectively. This is a place where the Book of Belles Lettres could be reproduced!

▲ Several designers use calligraphy as their art form, and we can applaud the talents of Janet Travis, who once penned a wine society's proclamation for us. With capital letters worthy of a medieval book of letters, the proclamation was far beyond our more limited imagination. Janet could design a fabulous invitation, or coordinate the collateral materials for any project. Her company is **Calligraphy by Janet Travis**.

◆ **Quill Productions** is another source for invitations and serious design using "beautiful writing," the meaning of calligraphy, as owner Paul Siegel points out. Siegel is more of a designer who happens to use calligraphy arts for logos, illustrations, monograms, menus and the like. His workmanship is impressive. Paul is also a printing broker so he can handle a turn-key job for invitation design needs.

▼ One of Campbell Stationer's recommended calligraphers is **Sue Bohlin**, who charges $7. a line for artwork as part of an invitation, $.50 a line for envelope addressing and $1.50 for each place card. Although she can provide any calligraphic source from ornate certificates to placecards, her specialty seems to be addressing envelopes in copperplate script. She reports having addressed 10,000 envelopes in 1992 !!! Sue says she "really, really loves helping clients make a tremendous first impression for their event — which is what happens when their names are written in a memorable style."

● We particularly like **Teel Gray**, who is booked long in advance for invitation set-ups and wedding addressing, and no wonder! It is so flattering to receive an invitation with her distinctive art work. And incidentally, it was she who can be credited with our own aforementioned wedding invitations. Her invitations for a Ninetieth birthday party also made quite an impression. The lovely invitations set the tone for the very special event. Many of the guests, thanks to their venerable ages, could remember when the most correct invitations always arrived with a perfect script. Her latest news is the use of her calligraphy to make an engraving plate so that the invitation and the hand-lettered envelope match!

■ We would be remiss in not mentioning other recommended calligraphers. **Betty Barna** gets high accolades from her peers, as does **Karen Kaufman** who has a company, K2 Design, always in demand for calligraphy work. Karen can do a variety of calligraphy styles. **Nancy Himes** is a Park Cities area calligrapher whose work is frequently seen on place cards and menus at SMU events.

custom designed invitations

So the readers will not think that we are solely conventional, we would like to comment on alternate forms of invitations when the occasion warrants. Receiving something in the mail that comes in an attention-getting form is certainly to be opened before anything else. We have received posters, rolled up in tubes, with the artful invitation serving as a lasting favor of the upcoming party. We have received small boxes with mementos inside, and an invitation attached to the symbolic gift. One of our favorites this year was the miniature Christmas Nutcracker, which arrived in a very small box, to be hung on the tree as a momento of the party. The tag inside announced a friend's annual Christmas luncheon, which includes an ornament exchange among the guests. We have also received puzzles, to be pieced together with all the necessary information. A printed T-shirt-invitation served as an invitation to the announcement party of Julie Esping and LeonardSteinberg's new Julie & Leonard fashion enterprise. There is virtually no limit, particularly if your budget is generous and the intention is to let your guests know that they are in for an unusual treat. We always anticipate that the party will measure up to the standards set by the invitation.

Invitation Designers

For the invitation beyond the ordinary, for a very special private celebration, for a major charity event or for a large corporate-sponsored party, we have a few suggestions for designers. In many years of doing events, we have been fortunate in locating a number of good designers who delight in creating invitations that make a statement. Most have been done for major social and charitable functions.

▲ Melinda Cato of **The Cato Company** loves invitations that have unique twists and involve cut-outs, assembling, unique folds and pop-ups. Her invitations have been issued for everything from a birthday party for a one-year-old to a Big Apple-themed deb ball to large charity events, such as the '90 Heart Ball and the '92 Art Reach Heirloom Tea. Melinda has started doing "blanks" that are available though some local retailers. Otherwise, you can contact her for custom designs that start at $50.

◆ **Donna Sabolovic Calligraphy and Design.** Donna has an impressive background in commercial art — honed with an education in art and later as an artist with Neiman-Marcus-like Joseph Horne & Co. in Pittsburgh — and excels at layout, design and illustration. In the 10 years she has been in Dallas, she has contributed to the professional art scene with book cover design for Taylor Publishing, where she has specialized in artistic lettering which led, in turn, to her work in calligraphy and doing memorable invitations for friends who knew her talent. Now, she has launched into invitation design with a wide variety of styles, drawing on her extensive background. If you want an invitation that is sketched with the likeness of the honorèe or a familiar scene, Donna will be the source. We've loved her invitations for a seventh birthday soccer party, a Sock-Hop for teenagers and another for a Casino Night, all enhanced by her

calligraphic lettering. Designs for invitations start at $50. and average about $150. for a total design package.

*Please see the advertisement for **Donna Sabolovic Calligraphy & Design** on page 212.*

▼ **Inkcorporated Invitations and Stationery**. See listing above under "Invitations." Increasingly, owner Suzanne Droese is into special design of invitations and collaborated printed materials for charity and corporate events.

*Please see advertisement for **Inkcorporated Invitations & Stationery** on page 215.*

● **Lynn Townsend Dealey** has orchestrated some of the finest recent charity invitations and we are impressed with her range of styles. The State Fair Gala invitation, so precise with its Texas symbols, and the smashingly attractive, art nouveau 1992 Opera Ball invitation are both her creations — and impressive. The litany of graphics and invitations for major events is long and includes the Children's Medical Center, the Flora Awards and the Grand Heritage Ball! Her work for the Marianne Scruggs Garden Club is notable. Many of us know Lynn by way of her appealing and clever "Adopt an Animal" newspaper ads for the Dallas Zoo.

■ Suzanna L. Brown of **O! Suzanna Design** is an artist of many styles and perfection. When not doing logos, corporate brochures, letterheads, and magazine ads, Suzanna has executed many event invitations, including for the Dallas Museum of Art and, more recently, for the Catherine the Great at Fair Park. Frankly, we like Suzanna Brown's work so much that we asked her to design this book, the greatest accolade of all! By appointment.

*Please see advertisement for **O! Suzanna Design** on page 206.*

▲ Young and talented Alison Pickens Farrow of **Pickens Design** has been gaining notice for her "painterly" art work which she translates into logo designs and other graphic work. Alison recently oversaw the design and invitation for the '92 Shakespeare Festival. We were impressed! More currently, she has overseen the invitation, brochure, T-shirts, ads and all the collateral materials for the "Weekend to Wipe Out Cancer," a major, multi-faceted and multi-day Dallas charity event. Obviously, the word about her talents is getting out and we suspect that her name will appear more frequently on the charity and major invitation circuit.

Like the other designers mentioned here, Alison designs invitations for private parties as well as for larger charity and corporate events, but the numbers should be significant enough to warrant the art work and custom-color printing. For a major event, a ball, a milestone birthday or large corporate function, the distinction of the invitation will be worth it!

A reminder -- *The invitation shops and specialists highlighted in this chapter are all listed in the "Directory of Sources," which begins on page 223.*

V

Basic Ingredients

speciality markets, desserts, wine & take-out

Selections of food and wine are among the most important aspects of entertaining. In fact, deciding on the menu can be as challenging as the format of the party and the guest list. Certainly, the "foodies" among us might even consider this the primary focus of any shared event with friends.

What to serve is, of course, dictated partially by the type of event — luncheon, tea, cocktail or dinner party — and the overall theme — Easter or luau, Valentine or Academy Awards-watching. The poolside luncheon will obviously necessitate one menu; the cocktail party another. Once having established the format and theme, the hostess also needs to think through a variety of elements, including the season, the number and ages of guests and the budget. Dallas provides a rich array of fresh food products, available for creative use and enjoyment. We also have dedicated food professionals who are enriching the food scene with superbly prepared baked goods and take-out, a great boon to every hostess.

markets

Dallas is more of a supermarket city than most. And, regretfully, while we do not have a great selection of specialty food markets, we do have a number worthy of our attention and patronage. Perhaps as a compensation, and thanks to our climate, we have access to fresh and exceptional locally grown produce that can make shopping a joy. Our summer fruit selections alone are reason for a celebration.

The addresses and phone numbers are listed in the "Directory of Sources," which begins on page 223.

▲ **Dallas Farmers Market**, a 50 year old municipally-owned institution in downtown Dallas, is one of the city's greatest food resources in terms of availability, quality and price. It is also our link to the farmers who are up before daybreak to bring to town the freshest possible local produce.

Unabashedly, we love shopping there and ferreting out the best of the growing season. It's fun, friendly and informative too. Don't let the myth of having to buy in bulk keep you away. Both farmers and dealers, whose status is designated by the sign over each stall, sell in small amounts. Weekends are, of course, the best time to shop, but go early. During 1993, the Farmer's Market has been undergoing a major facelift and expansion. Debuting in the Spring was a new shed, all-weather in structure. As part of a restructuring of the entire Southeastern entryway to downtown, the Farmers Market re-do will ultimately benefit also from new floral vending, kiosk areas and festival spaces — in addition to the new shed, which is already beginning to house vendors for meat, fish, cheese and other produce. Among them are Primo, a prime beef vender, and Marcello Comitre who has a mini-market selling produce from the city's best sources, including bread, cheese and sausages.A visit to his stall will eliminate the need for a stop at the supermarket.

◆ In addition to the major, all-year round Dallas municipal market, there are **seasonal farmers' markets** in several suburban areas, including Addison, Plano and Garland. A covered year-round market also opened this year near Big Town Mall, visible from Interstate 80.

▼ **Danals**, a six-store chain of Mexican supermarkets, is one of Dallas' better food values and sources. Danals is more chaotic mercado than traditional supermarket. Tanks of live catfish, crates of live Louisiana crabs and crayfish, squid and octopus share space with varieties of produce and non-food items. Shopping here is a multi-cultural experience.

● **Fiesta Mart** has opened its first Dallas market on West Jefferson in Oak Cliff, with more markets to come in the next few months. For the moment, this is the place to head for Latin specialties. There are raves for the bakery which has the best tortillas and empanadas in the city.

■ **Phil's Natural Foods.** The founder of Whole Foods Markets is opening a market in the former Highland Stores' space at Inwood and Lovers Lane. Look for a Spring'94 opening.

▲ **Ralph's Fine Foods**, in Snider Plaza, has been a Dallas institution for 17 years. More than a supermarket, it excels in its meat and fish market (with frequent specials to lure us!) and has a large selection of deli/take-out and baked goods. The hostess who cooks her own meals will love the availability of unusual gourmet items and the attention to special requests, particularly at the meat market. For the hostess who is "mixing and matching"home-prepared and take-out, Ralph's has a number of featured items prepared by an in-house chef that will make entertaining-in-a-hurry an easier task. If you will be entertaining a crowd at home or guests at the ranch, there are casseroles of lasagna, chicken and broccoli and a delicious potato casserole to accompany selections from the meat department.

◆ **Simon David** is the area's premier supermarket, providing top-quality produce, meats, seafood and as many gourmet items as can be packed into their sizable store at the corner of University and Inwood. For the one-stop shopper, Simon David has everything, including an excellent wine selection, take-out department, bakery and florist. Often, we see local caterers shopping there for the hard-to-find selections and the benefit of the custom meat department. Simon David is an experience as well as a social outing for the regulars in the Park Cities and near North Dallas. Because Simon David is such a stand-out in so many categories, we recommend that you also see listings under "Take-out" and "Wines."

▼ **Whole Foods Market** is the Dean & DeLuca of the organic food world. In addition to the availability of additive and chemically-free foods, Whole Foods, with locations on Greenville in East Dallas and at Belt Line in Richardson, has excellent bakery, fish and meat markets. The cheese and wine selections are extensive, as are the brands of beer. Absolutely no market in town has the comparable choices of flour, beans, rices, spices, etc., sold from bulk containers.

● A number of the **Oriental markets** of Dallas area offer a full range of products, including fish, meat and fresh produce. While there are steadily more markets to be found throughout the Metroplex, the larger ones are located where Dallas, Garland and Richardson converge (in and near Walnut Street, north of LBJ Freeway), an area where there is a rich ethnic mix. The shops provide an interesting excursion and are rapidly being discovered by local "foodies" and professional chefs in search of exotic and cost-saving ingredients. Many chefs head to **Shin Chon**, a Korean store on Walnut Street for the sheets of dried seaweed and other exotics. **Hiep Phong Supermarket and BBQ**, also on Walnut Street, has mouth-watering displays of mahogany-colored, roasted duck, chicken and pork, plus varieties of fish, such as anchovies, turtle (!) and tanks of lobster, clams and crabs, all at very reasonable prices. There are aisles of dried fish, bean and plum sauces, sacks of rice, noodles, unfamiliar canned goods, plus a melange of duck eggs, dried mushrooms, Oriental vegetables and even bamboo. **Hiep Thai** may have the best selection, viewed through the eyes of the more traditional purchaser. There is an excellent fish market — with ice chests filled with fresh snapper, striped bass, crawfish, and blue crabs — and an excellent meat market (although be prepared to see unusual cuts and parts). **Truong Nguyen**, across the street and adjacent to the popular Arc-en-Ciel Vietnamese Restaurant, is more conventional in organization, with freezers of fish and a large produce department with exotics, like lime leaves, penny wort, baby mustard greens, lemon grass and the popular bok choy. The tea selection is particularly extensive. English is definitely a foreign language at these spots and others like them.

■ **Golden Pacific Supermarket,** immediately north in Richardson is the Safeway of the Oriental food markets. The display is fascinating, perhaps more organized than the above-mentioned shops. It is definitely worth the visit for the fresh vegetables (like bok choy and lemon grass), fish (tanks of lobster and carp, as well as fresh eels, grouper, oysters and crabs) and the cultural mix of shoppers. This shop also carries a good supply of non-food items, such as vegetable steamers and Oriental china.

▲ **Kazy's Food Market** on Forest Lane, between the Texas Instruments entrance and Greenville Avenue, is an extraordinary experience. Few food shops can compare with the stocked variety: an array of exotic fish, both fresh and frozen — octopus, sushi quality tuna and salmon, crabs, clams, pompano and snapper; Japanese specialties — sushi-to-go, dumplings, tempura, noodles and large bags of rice; and fresh vegetables usually not seen in Dallas — greens, roots, daikon radishes, shiitake mushrooms. The shop is fascinating and would excite the most blasé gourmet. We have to admit, however, that we cannot identify much of the inventory. Charmingly interspersed are oriental knickknacks, videos and magazines.

◆ **Taiwan Supermarket** in Richardson, just East of Central Expressway on Polk Avenue, is the Simon David of the Oriental-owned markets. Housed in a movie-set pagoda, the market displays beautiful Oriental vegetables, pristine meats and tanks of fish that will delight a gourmet's senses. It pays to be savvy about identifying foods. All names are in Chinese. Prices, in English, are gentle.

▼ A few other Oriental markets to explore include the **Thai Oriental Food Store** in the Fitzhugh area and **Inchon Oriental Food** on Belt Line in Irving.

● **Sam's Wholesale Club** deserves mention. After initial resistance on the part of the author, but with realization of considerable savings, we have to admit that entertaining for a crowd often warrants cost-cutting measures, possible through these mega-stores. At a recent committee gathering, the hostess served an enjoyable buffet of chicken enchiladas, which came from Sam's! Dressed up with accompanying fresh salads and desserts, plus attractive accoutrements, the luncheon was a good example in gracious entertaining on a budget.

speciality

Meats

■ **Fresh 'n Tender** is a small Pakistani-owned market at Floyd Road along the North Central service Road in Richardson. The house specialties are lamb and cabrito, in addition to the frozen fish, exotic rices and beans, spices and sweets, mostly from India and Bangladesh.

▲ **Glazed Honey Hams** and **Baked Honey Hams** provide the quick answer to serving meat to a crowd, either dressed up for a holiday buffet or for a casual open house. Our favorite, to be frank, is to call ahead and order a freshly baked ham that is not already pre-cut. It seems more like a home-cooked ham. Expect to pay under $4.50 a pound for half or whole hams. Glazed Honey Hams has expanded its operations to include barbecued spareribs, smoked turkey breasts (at $5.95 a pound), and deli meats and cheeses.

◆ **Gorman's** in Mesquite is an old-fashioned butcher shop, specializing in "hanging beef." Along with beef, Gorman's handles pork, "hot links" and sausages. There are Gorman's markets also in Pleasant Grove and at Cedar Creek Lake.

▼ **Guadalupe Pit Smoked Meats** ships turkeys, hams, briskets and tenders to your door by UPS from New Braunfels. Their popular smoked turkey breasts, averaging about seven pounds a piece, sell for $41.50 including shipping. Call their 800 number for a catalogue.

● **Hans Mueller Sausage Co.** has long dispensed its sausages, deli meats and salads at its Southwell Road restaurant, adjacent to its meat facility in the shadow of Stemmons Freeway north of Walnut Hill Lane. The bad news is that the restaurant burned this year, The good news is the plant will sell retail while the restaurant and deli undergo rebuilding.

■ **Kuby's Sausage House.** Dallas does not have New York's Jefferson Market or Lobel and Sons, but fortunately, we have Kuby's, a German meat market to pamper us with the best available meats and knowledgeable butchers, who can accommodate the specifications of our recipes. And, Kuby's has more than just fine meats (at competitive prices, we might add), with deli, take-out, house-made sausages and more. It has the charm of being the gathering place for Dallas' European population, who enjoy the friendly German-style restaurant, as well as the carefully selected and prepared food items.

▲ **Preferred Meats** is the wholesaler to the best restaurants. Their meat is Dallas' best, particularly veal and game. Like other wholesalers, if you are purchasing in large quantities and can meet their minimum purchase requirements, you can purchase directly from them — if you can find them at their "Trinity bottoms" location near the Sportatorium.

◆ **Rudolph's Market and Sausage Factory**, an institution since 1895, has had generations of Dallasites trekking to its Deep Ellum shop for custom-cut meats and all varieties of sausages. Everyone should make an occasional pilgrimage to our oldest butcher shop.

▼ **Texas Wild Game Cooperative.** Owner Mike Hughes has been a success story in producing wild game in the Hill Country and supplying exotic meats to five-star restaurants. Retail customers have access to venison — filets, roast, cubed for stews, ground meat for chili and sausage — as well as wild boar, wild lamb and antelope. Texas Wild Game ships fresh meat overnight using frozen gel packs and guarantees fresh delivery.

A Reminder — The names and addresses for the specialty food stores are listed in the "Directory of Sources," which starts on page 223.

Seafood

Fresh fish seems now to be the domain of the supermarket, with excellent fish departments found at Simon David and Whole Foods, not to mention the superbly-stocked Oriental markets. The ranks of fish specialty shops are dwindling, with two major losses that we know of — Hampton's and Pescados — during the last year. Fortunately, there are still a few excellent fish markets, including those listed below.

● **Fabian Seafood Co.** Normally, buying shellfish from the back of a truck does not appeal. Fabian, however, is different and makes the trek from the Gulf to Dallas on regular runs, supplying its many, faithful customers with last-night's well-iced catch. Watch for their Dallas Morning News ads and the tell-tale lines, now at Mockingbird and Airline one block West of Central (after years of queues at Lovers Lane and the Tollroad). Once a buyer, you'll receive a postcard about the next shipment. The quality is tops, the prices below market, and be ready to shop early before the shrimp run out.

■ **Fishmonger's Seafood Market & Cafe.** Plano has a quality fish market at North Central and Park Boulevard in conjunction with an excellent fish restaurant. On our last visit, the cases were filled with fresh scrod, swordfish, tuna, snapper, and all the shell fish as well. Lobsters are usually available, and anything can be ordered to satisfy your recipe requirements.

▲ **TJ's Seafood**, located in Preston Forest, is one of the few remaining neighborhood seafood shops in Dallas. We were pleased to find that owner Tom Haden was recently bringing in lobsters with a one day advance notice. Along with the usual selection, there are some prepared foods and seafood salads, enough to put together the basics of an exceptional meal — including the Out of a Flower ice creams and sorbets that are carried in the freezer.

◆ **FishFinders, Mr. Fish Crabs 'N More**, and **Pullen Seafood** are basically wholesalers in the Fair Park/Commerce Avenue area. If you are having a large party and need a sizable order — and we stress a sizable order — these merchants may possibly accommodate you, particularly if you know exactly what you want to order. Recently, the author ordered two whole salmons for a large party. The freshness was obvious and the prices worth the effort. Pullen Seafood has recently received DALLAS OBSERVER publicity, so we can expect their off-the-street sales to accelerate. **Landlock Seafood Co**. in Carrollton is a major area supplier where large quantity purchases are also possible.

success stories

Applause to the food entrepreneurs who are putting Dallas on the national culinary map and shipping their products nationwide:

Kozy Kitchen — *tea cakes and cookies*
L'Epicurean -- *superb pâtés*
La Crème Coffee and Tea — *premium coffees and teas from around the world*
Morgen Chocolate — *truffles and handmade chocolates in the European fashion*
Mozzarella Company — *cheeses in the Italian tradition*
Out of a Flower — *ice cream and sorbets at their best*
Taste Teasers — *jalapeno-based condiments and confections*

Gourmet

▼ **Al's Import Foods**, at the corner of Greenville and Park Lane, has been a Dallas institution for over forty years. Specializing in Greek, Italian and Middle Eastern foods, Al's brims with exotic foods. If the recipe calls for prosciutto, Genoa sausage, chick peas or Greek olives, go direct to Al's. The shop has more sizes and brands of olive oil than we've ever seen, and vats of unusual coffees and spices. The meat market and prepared foods are excellent, as is the selection of Italian, Greek and unusual wines. You will be pleasantly pleased with the prices as well.

● **American Food Service** is the small retail arm of the American Produce & Vegetable Co. restaurant wholesaler located on Simonton, just west of The Galleria. If you are cooking for a crowd and find it worth your while to purchase in multi-gallon sizes, all the ingredients are here, including dairy products and bags of shredded cheeses. On the day we shopped there, the fresh produce was limited but we loved buying a flat of fresh raspberries at the wholesale price.

■ **British Emporium** and **British Trading Post.** See page 68.

▲ **Civello's Raviolismo.** This little known source for hand made designer ravioli, used by local caterers and chefs, has been around for about ten years. Now that brother and sister Philip and Chena Civello have a store-front small factory on Bryan near Peak, the casual drop-in customer can buy the day's leftovers. Our selection was duck, spinach, feta with black olives or goat cheese with cilantro and green onion, from $3. to $4. per dozen. Sauces and sausage are also available. If you are having a party and want to be sure of the availability, the Civellos will be happy to fill your advance order.

▲ **The Coffee Company** in Preston Center has a good choice of coffees and teas. The distinction here is the chocolate selection, with an excellent stock of Godiva Chocolates.

◆ **European Market and Deli.** Newcomers George Kowalczyk and Jerzy Drozen have brought their Polish food backgrounds to Dallas. Their year-old shop is stocked with unusual packages and canned goods mostly from Hungary and Poland, and from Belgium and Holland as well. We were happy to purchase poppy seeds in bulk at a considerable savings over super-market small-size containers. The ingredient makes its appearance in their tasty poppy seed cakes. And don't overlook the other European specialties, such as stuffed cabbages and sausages. For the moment, the deli case holds many of the usual meats and cheese. With their friendly enthusiasm, the own-ers should do well and we hope customers have found them in the shopping center on Forest across from Medical City.

▼ **Fresh Pasta Delights** on Parker Road near Central Expressway in Plano, is a favorite source for caterers and chefs. This is the place to go for custom-ordered pasta, especially for ravioli filled with lobster, shrimp, cheese, smoked chicken or sausage. Salads and tortellini are always on hand. Owner Jack Rayome is particularly proud of his striped pasta, which makes a dramatic as well as a tasty statement and is used by a number of caterers and hotels. Business has been great and the shop will be taking over some adjacent space to better serve the retail customers who drop by for fresh flavored pastas and sauces, such as bolognese at $5. a pint and pesto at $9. a pint.

● **Fresh Start Market and Deli** is a new venture on Oak Lawn by three transplanted San Franciscans (the name may be prophetic!). They are into "the food of the 90's" — low-fat and healthy. All the owners have back-grounds in merchandising for Nordstrom's so we can anticipate constant new finds and fresh ideas. For the time being, this is the place to seek out health-conscious foods, including the new Fit-Kit Cuisine by dani foods. ·

■ **Golden Circle Herb Farm**, in Rice, Texas, supplies a number of restaurants with unusual lettuces, such as arugula and lamb's ear, and herbs. If you will call owner Tom Spicer with an order, you can pick it up at Simon David with the assurance of getting what you want and having the freshest available.

▲ **Goodies from Goodman.** The Goodman family name has been synonymous with good food in Dallas for 76 years. We do miss their more extensive retail operations of the past, but the Preston Forest store still main-tains a good selection of gourmet foods and candies, including Morgen's irresistible truffles, as well as frozen entrees and salad and sandwich take-out. They also prepare trays for meetings, picnics, lunches and the like. The long-time familiar faces in the shop add to the comfort level! Gift baskets are a specialty. And, don't forget their catering. In a recent NORTHSIDE and PARK CITIES PEOPLE poll, Goodman came out second in the favorite caterers' category of favorite caterers.

◆ **Gourmet Food Warehouse Outlet,** now with two locations in Dallas — in Preston Forest and Hillside Village, is a two year old enterprise by the former gourmet department manager of Neiman Marcus' gourmet shop. Owners Ron Solovitz and Glen Gordon provide new brands for Dallas, all at discounted prices. And while the smoked salmon and caviar, at below retail costs, may be just what you need for a special party, we'd recommend that you become acquainted with their stock of unusual pastas, freshly ground coffees, package goods and condiments. This is a welcome addition to the Dallas food scene and a destination for an impromptu cocktail or dinner party.

● **Gourmet Unlimited.** Sandwiched among the liquor stores on Inwood Road just south of Belt Line is an oasis of party foods that include meats, a good selection of cheeses, desserts and coffee. The shop has party trays to go and David K's ice cream cakes, which must be ordered in advance.

■ **India Imports** in Irving and **Impofoods** in Richardson's Promenade Shopping Center both stock a fascinating array of Indian foods, balsamic rices, curries, aromatic spices as well as English teas, chutneys and the like. There are also homemade dessert specialties such as a Persian baklava. The shops have the feel of another and distant world. **Taj Mahal**, also in Richardson, reflects the growing internationalization of the Dallas area and meets every-one's expectations of exotic ethnic foods.

▲ **La Cave Warehouse,** the wine shop of note in the West End, imports superb cheeses from Androuet, one of Paris' best-known cheese shops. Available are Camembert, Saint Marcellin, Crottin de Chevignol and other cheeses of quality and variety hard to find in Dallas. This is a major addition to the Dallas cheese scene.

◆ **La Crème Coffee and Tea** is Dallas' premier coffee emporium and the retail establishment that handles the same full line of specialty coffees and teas served at most of Dallas' fine restaurants. If your favorite coffee is at Dream Cafe and your favorite iced tea at the Hotel Crescent Court, be assured that you can enjoy the same beverages at home. The Lovers Lane shop is paradise for the lover of coffee and teas. In addition to 140 blends of coffee and 70 different teas, La Crème, the store, offers little-known treasures — shortbread, biscotti, jams and sweeteners — most of which are perfect accompaniments to the specialty beverages. All the preferred equipment to make the perfect brew are also on hand, plus mugs and accessories galore. Wouldn't it be wonderful if La Crème's *gelatos* and *frutta granitas* (Italian sorbets), made for the top restaurants in the traditional Italian method, would be available here. Among the extensive list of flavors, all are outstanding — including raspberry, pistachio, white chocolate and lemon If you have the opportunity, try the chocolate hazelnut. It will transport you to a cafe in Florence! Most popular of the new La Crème products is the refreshing and positively addictive (at least to the author) Caffesorbetto, a blend of select coffees, cocoas and other flavors, served semi-frozen.

New owners of the La Crème wholesale line are B.B. and Judy Tuley, who have bought the company from original owners Bonnie and Jerry Itzig and will continue the same excellent standards in buying, roasting and blending the coffee and tea products. In addition to being served at most fine area restaurants, La Crème products are available locally at specialty stores, such as Marty's, Simon David, Goodies from Goodman and Ralph's. The Caffesorbetto machines and beverages have also become a staple of the Dallas refreshment scene and are conveniently found in many cafe and take-out establishments. *Please see the advertisement for **La Crème Coffee and Tea** on page 214.*

▼ **LaRosa's Italian Specialty Desserts,** one might think, should be listed in our dessert section. In reality, the shop stocks everything for the Italian kitchen, much of it made by New York transplant and owner Charles LaRosa and his wife. There are pizzas, subs and calzone, fresh grilled red peppers, Italian sausages and cheeses, fresh pizza dough imported from Brooklyn as well as the Italian desserts, such as cannoli, ricotta cheesecakes, spumoni and tortone. The shop is in the same West Parker Road strip center near Central Expressway as another food gem, Fresh Pasta Delights, which is mentioned above.

● **Macy's** has a "food hall" in the tradition of many department stores. Packaged goods are similar to those at other cookware shops, more directed toward the gift-giver than the direct consumer. Macy's does, however, have an extensive bakery, a branch of Plano-based Cafe Partier, and an excellent chocolate shop. The food counters are well-stocked with cheeses and salads to-go. Perhaps the best food "finds" at Macy's are the smoked salmon and caviar, offered at competitive New York prices. Around the holidays, Macy's is a great place to find these delicacies.

■ **Magnifico Fine Foods.** It's been a while since Las Colinas has had a serious fine food establishment (we hope some of you will remember the Valley Ranch emporium). Now, serious Irving "foodies" only have to go to MacArthur Boulevard and Walnut Hill to find all the best that the area has to offer — Empire Baking Company products, Mozzarella Company cheeses, fine meats, fish and produce, Out of a Flower's ice creams and sorbets, plus Italian specialties that are the favorite of owner and caterer Toni Magnifico. Take-out is available plus a few seats for those who can't wait to sample the offerings, such as bruschetta, classic white and tuna salad, gnocchi, osso buco and chicken saltimbocca. Toni already enjoys a fine catering reputation. We think that this new visibility will expand her popularity. *Truly magnifico!!*

▲ **Marty's** on Oak Lawn is one of Dallas' premier food establishments, where the word "gourmet" aptly applies. Marty's carries lines of epicure foods, from fresh produce to the city's best selection of cheese, caviar and more. Speaking of caviar, new Food Director Karen Joyce points out the increase in caviar sales, perhaps a good barometer of our recovering economy — following a decline of several years. Marty's carries only the best — the respected Petrossian and a new Swiss purveyor, Caviar House, whose hand-selected caviar eggs are world-famous. Marty's typically handles a number of specialty items not found elsewhere in the Dallas market, such as Italian buffalo mozzarella and Balik smoked salmon. The frozen food cases are filled with hors d'oeuvres, such as stuffed puff pastries. Marty's business is multi-faceted and covers the entire gamut of entertaining essentials — gourmet food, wine, take-out and catering. See also our listings for Marty's under "Wine," "Take-Out" and "Catering."
Please see the advertisement for Marty's on page 218.

◆ **Momo's Italian Groceries** on Forest Lane near Greenville is a recent addition to the original Momo's restaurant. In addition to some prepared pastas and sauces, the shop is selling its own pastas as well as imported sausages and prosciutto.

▼ **Mozzarella Company** is one of Dallas' success stories. After living in Italy, owner and cheesemaker Paula Lambert set out on a mission to duplicate that country's fine cheeses. Paula now has some of the best mozzarella, ricotta and marscarpone outside Italy, as well as *crème fraiche* and other delicacies. (And our statement is given credibility by a trio of recent National Cheesemaker Awards.) The cheeses are widely available in Dallas area stores, but it is still more fun to buy at the Deep Ellum "factory" where the freshest and widest variety will be found. Try the Marscarpone Torte with basil pesto and the Mozzarella Roll with sun-dried tomatoes — our favorites!

● **Neiman Marcus** has long been gift-oriented in its gourmet depart-ment, as it should be. Among its varied stock are some of the finest specialties to be incorporated into entertaining — everything from its popular Red River brand of chili to the caviar, salmon and *foie gras* available at the Petrossian Boutique. If the occasion calls for a celebration, Neiman Marcus can certainly supply the needs. See also the Neiman Marcus listing under "Tableware," "Wines," and "Desserts."

■ **Pasta Plus** in Preston Royal and on Preston Road near Campbell, has fresh pasta products, prepared in several flavors such as tomato, whole wheat and spinach, tasty sauces to top the pasta and many other ingredients for fine Italian dining. The shops stock olive oils, Dean & DeLuca herbs and other packaged products not widely found in Dallas. See also our listing for Pasta Plus under "Take-Out."

▲ **Pendery's.** Welcome to the world of chilies and spices! Pendery's, now in Inwood Village and the Galleria, has a 123 year history in selling regional Texas seasonings. Their original chili powder is the forerunner of 24 ground chilies, seven blends, eight whole chili pods, 77 herbs and spices, and seven herbal teas. Pendery's is an education as well as a destination for dried herbs and spices, jars of salsas, sauces and moles, all geared toward the food culture of the Southwest. As to be expected, the shop is also a treasury of accessories tied to regional cooking.

◆ **Tommaso's** on Spring Valley is the retail arm of a successful whole-sale operation. A variety of pastas and sauces is available in addition to their ready-prepared pasta dishes which are discussed under "Take-Out."

▼ **Williams-Sonoma**, like other of the cookware shops, has a nice selection of specialty food items, more gift-oriented than not. There are, however, wonderful pancake and muffins mixes, real maple syrups and the, like that would provide a treat for your guests and be great for the weekend trip to the farm.

● **Worldwide Foods** on Lower Greenville Avenue carries the aromatic staples of Middle Eastern and Greek cooking. The unacquainted shopper will be awed with the extensive selection of olives, bulgars, spices and beans in large vats, not to mention the dark roasted Turkish coffees. Be sure to take home some pita bread or freshly made baklava.

■ **World Service UK.** Kelli Barclay, wife of five-star chef and British-born Nick Barclay of the dani group, has opened a Greenville Avenue store specializing in British food stuffs, We admired the bangers, sausage, pork pie and pasties, all nostalgia food to Brits. The shop also carries cheese, devon cream, jams and biscuits and lots of chocolates, which Kelli says are the biggest sellers. Even if you are not from the U.K., you'll not be able to resist – and the major British newspapers are also available. While we are on the theme, consider **The British Trading Post,** run by Irish-born Louise Blackburn and her sister Myra Ballantyne. It's been at its Ferguson Road location for almost eight years. In addition to British foods, they have begun cooking lesson as well. A third shop is **The British Emporium**, which opened last November in Grapevine. Owner Sheila Kaddam owned a gourmet and catering company in England and favors foods from India as part of her continuing interest in the foods of the British Empire.

▲ Among the not-to-be-missed category are **Hines Nut and Produce Co.**, especially for nuts in quantity, and **Taxco Produce** for chilies. **Green**

Produce on Parker Street is the green grocer of choice, other than the Farmer's Market, for savvy chefs. It's wholesale, but if you cannot find squash blossoms for your favorite recipe, Mr. Green will be accommodating, providing that your quantity warrants the sale. **French Direct**, another wholesaler on Commerce Street in the Fair Park area, imports French produce direct from France. The *haricots verts*, white asparagus, wild mushrooms, and *fraises des bois* are all within our reach during their seasons and at prices and freshness that will impress any gourmet, so long as purchases are by the case. In additional to fresh produce, there are cheeses, French oils, vinegars and more. Still another produce wholesaler, **Coussemans Dallas, Inc.** located just east of the Farmer's Market will accommodate orders by the case for 24 varieties of lettuce and by the pound for an extensive selection of herbs. The vegetable selection is literally "a" to "z" — from Asian pears to baby zucchini. *Please note that Coussemans Produce will be open to the public on Saturday mornings as soon as the construction near the Farmers Market is complete. Purchases must be by the case!*

A Reminder — the addresses and phone numbers for the shops listed can be found in the "Directory of Sources," which begins on page 223.

gift basket specialists

 The gift of food is often the excuse to entertain, or the encouragement to experiment with new specialty items. Dallas has numerous shops and businesses that put together specialty baskets from their inventories, and a few that will customize the gift with the recipient in mind.

Some of the best include:

Bodacious Baskets
City Cafe to Go
Empire Baking Co.
Eureka!
Goodies fromGoodman
Gourmet Food Warehouse
La Crème Coffee and Tea
Kozy Kitchen
Marty's
Morgen Chocolate
Mother-Daughter Originals
Mozzarella Company
Neiman Marcus
Party in a Box
Spirited Cakes
Translations
Williams Sonoma

wine shops

▲ **Al's Import Foods,** mentioned above as a gourmet grocery, should not be overlooked when purchasing wines from Italy, Greece and Hungary, to accompany those special ethnic meals and recipes.

◆ **Grailey's** in Lakewood Village offers some of the city's wine rarities at the best values. Owner Lee Jaynes rates high on the knowledgeable scale. It's worth the price of a purchase to have his advice.

▼ **La Cave Warehouse,** an unmarked warehouse in the West End, is the best source in town for Bordeaux wines, which owner Francois Chandou imports direct from France, some from his family's own vineyard. Without a doubt, La Cave is the definitive resource for older Bordeaux vintages in the Metroplex, which the reader needs to keep in mind for that special celebration. When asking for advice or a quote, we loved Francois' attitude: "If for no other reason than to appear optimistic, you should always have a bottle of champagne in the fridge." La Cave offers climatized wine stage as well.

● **Marty's** on Oak Lawn tops the list for everyone's favorite wine shop and is, unquestionably, the best single wine source in town — backed up by 50 years of the Shapiro family's wine expertise. Marty's stocks somewhere in the vicinity of 1200 different labels, all of which are carefully chosen by

wine buyers with years of experience in selecting from the world's best growths. The hand-picked selections come with person-alized service and knowledgeable advice, whether for first-time buyer or the connoisseur. Manager and wine buyer Brian Schmidt points out that Marty'sophisticated clientele is also willing to experiment and knows that the wine-educated staff will meet the demands of finding new varieties Marty's reputation is associated with finer wines. Fortunately for their faithful customers, a label to label and store to store comparison will show Marty's to be the fairer in price, and the budget-minded will find real value and enjoyment in a wine to share with friends — thanks to long time associations in the wine world and intelligent buying.

Incidentally, the DALLAS OBSERVER's *"Best of Dallas 1993"* voted Marty's the *"best value on lesser known wines and Burgundies"* — which we knew all along! And, a word to the wise, keep up with Marty's wine sales. The serious buyers flock to those sales, which seem to be more frequent than in the old days. The store maintains a mailing list, so get your name on it.

One of the bonuses for buying wine at Marty's is that you can do one-stop shopping — whether for an entire dinner, picnic or cocktails with friends. Your wine can be complemented by the best take-out in the city, and the best selection of cheeses and pates, for impromptu and gracious entertaining. See also the listings for Marty's under "Wine Classes," "Take-Out," and "Catering," *Please see the advertisement for Marty's on page 218.*

■ **Mr. G's Beverage Center** on Coit and Fifteenth Street in East Plano easily has the best wine selection in the Northern suburban area. The first-time visitor will be impressed by the depth of inventory.

▲ The **Neiman Marcus Wine Department** has some well-selected, up-market wines and champagnes in their epicure department. Watch for their frequent sales, particularly on champagnes — to go with the caviar in the adjacent Petrossian boutique.

◆ **Po-Go's**. Owner Harris Polakoff has become one of Dallas' premier Wine & Spirits retailers since beginning the business in 1987. The Lovers Lane shop has a reputation for seeking out the best trendy wines at very competitive prices. The staff is at all times helpful. It's hard not to miss the information from the wine publications that are posted with each wine selection. A second Po-Go's at Walnut Hill and Central Expressway is now under different ownership but, likewise, carries a broad selection.

▼ The Greenville Avenue **Red Coleman's Liquors** has great prices on both wines and liquor. The varieties are so numerous, in fact, that wine buying takes some consideration. You might follow the suggestions of a local wine letter by Rick Avery, who ferrets out the best buys at all the local wine and liquor shops.

● **Sigel's Liquor Stores** at their shops on Greenville Avenue, in Addison and in Buckingham near Richardson, offers the best wines of all the liquor chain stores and stocks breadth and depth at competitive prices. The sales staff is knowledgeable and eager to share its expertise. The sales reductions here are also frequent, but it may help to have a basic knowledge of wines before tackling the sales bin, unless hit-or-miss sampling is your goal.

■ **Simon David** provides the most convenient wine shopping experience. As one respected oenophile said, where else can you buy Roederrer champagne, caviar, dishwasher soap and PEOPLE MAGAZINE at the same one-stop location.

▲ **Tony's Wine Warehouse and Bistro** stocks lesser known wines by the case (1400 varieties at last count!) in his labyrinth-like shop on Oak Lawn and, now, has added a bistro to complete his setting. Tony's also runs wine classes on a frequent basis. This is a place to have the tasting experience of wines by the glass without the trip to France.

◆ **Whole Foods Market,** at its Greenville Avenue location, also has a wine department with some interesting choices. After a visit to Hungary, we enjoyed finding some little-known Hungarian wines at Whole Foods, which seems to make a point of importing wines not usually carried elsewhere and which appeal to its well-versed clientele.

▼ **Wine Emporium Etc.** At the corner of Lovers Lane and Lomo Alto, east of the Tollroad, the Wine Emporium stocks diverse and well-selected quality wines spanning all price ranges. Owner Bill Rich calls upon an extensive knowledge of lesser-known wines to the customer's benefit. Always on hand are cheese, smoked salmon and L'Epicurean pates to accent the enjoyment of your purchases, See also the reference to Wine Emporium under "Wine Classes."

A reminder — *the names, addresses and phone numbers of the shops listed above can be found in the "Directory of Sources," beginning on page 223.*

desserts and more

While specialty shops, such as green grocers and custom butcher shops are rarer commodities in Dallas, the list of bakeries may be indicative of our favorite foods. Many of the bakeries are multidimensional, ranging from the increasingly scarce traditional baker with bread and cakes, such as **Stein's,** to the bakery with take-out and meals, such as **La Madeleine** and **Celebrity,** to the wedding cake specialists, such as **Ida Mae's Cakes** and **le gâteau cakery.** None-the-less, it is evident that dessert is a major item on any menu, and one of the items most likely to be purchased outside the supermarket.

● **Angel in My Kitchen.** Robin Kohler Stieber's company is aptly named. Her beautifully decorated cakes — from the cheerfully-decorated children's cakes, many with rainbows and sculpted figures, to more formal cakes for milestone events — add a note of happiness to any celebration scene. We've recently enjoyed one of Robin's exquisite cakes at a small wedding reception. Not only was the white chocolate-pistachio cake with buttercream icing delicious, it was a conversation piece, tastefully and uniquely decorated with French ribbons and fresh flowers.

■ **ArtCakes by Oggetti**, a fairly new cakery company by partners Julie Richey and Laura Larsen, is one of our more unique dessert sources. Utilizing art major backgrounds, Julie and Laura do "art cakes," creating edible scale reproductions of famous works of art — Matisse, Van Gogh, Lichtenstein have all been commemorated in icing. The popularity of the cakes is catching on and their publicity has been nation-wide. Abstract expressionism and impressionism have been their forte, but the duo has undertaken a medieval Belles Lettres style for a wedding cake. Their favorite, so far, was a stained glass success for a groom's cake. Their *pièces de resistance* start at $150. to serve 24. You can have your own Van Gogh sunflower masterpiece for $250. or Munch's "The Scream," perfect for a 40th birthday, at $200. Whatever the occasion, ArtCakes leaves a lasting impression!

▲ **Aston's English Bakery**, undoubtedly, has baked more birthday cakes for the children of Dallas than other bakery in town. It is just as popular with the set of parents whose own childhood cakes came from the Preston Center bakery. Aston's makes it easy to pick up the needed paper plates, napkins, etc. at the same time. A decorated cake serving 24 to 36 costs between $29. and $35.

◆ **The Bagel Chain** on Lovers Lane is a magnet for bagel enthusiasts who live s south of LBJ. The varieties are many – garlic, onion, rye, and even pumpkin during Halloween season. Seemingly as numerous are the flavored cream cheeses – chive, lox bits, cinnamon, walnut-raisin, to name only a few. There are deli meats for those who use bagels for sandwiches.

▼ **Bagelstein's Deli and Bakery** is the epicenter of the local bagel world. The quality is outstanding and the varieties will satisfy every taste. But, Bagelstein's is also a full wholesale bakery, supplying bread to many of the area deli's, along with their pastries, cheesecakes and special order cakes. Next door is the deli/take-out and restaurant. To complete the picture, Bagelstein's does catering and has a separate room for private functions.

● **Black Forest Bakery**, behind the old Sterling Jewelry property on Northwest Highway, is now part of Henk's European Deli. The bakery has always done an extensive wedding cake business, which is still their mainstay. Of course, there is a full range of baked goods and celebration cakes for order.

■ **Cafe Partier** is Plano's most popular bakery, with additional outlets at Prestonwood Mall and at Macy's in the Galleria.

▲ **The Cakery**, formerly in Turtle Creek Village and now in Casa Linda Plaza, is a wedding cake specialist, but all that artistry is put to good use in the celebration cakes that can also be ordered. Stop by to see the sample photos of cakes. You will be impressed. (On a geographical note, there has been an amusing musical chairs in locations. Zen Floral Studio has moved to The Cakery's former place in Turtle Creek Village, and The Cakery has moved to Casa Linda Bakery's place, which in turn has moved to a new location on Garland Rd.)

◆ **Casa Linda Bakery** has a relatively new Garland Road location and keeps the Lakewood crowd happy with their full service baked goods, from sweet rolls, breads and the evening's dessert.

▼ **Celebrity Cafe and Bakery**, also covered under "Take-Out," is one of the very popular drop-in spots in Highland Park Village for homestyle muffins, sweet rolls and their sumptuous pies and cakes. Celebrity has been spreading its wings to new locations, on the Northern fringe of downtown, to Preston Royal and a future Plano location.

● **Dallas Affaires** is a *incredible* source for both celebration and wedding cakes. Owner Travis ("Sibby") Barrett has gone from floral designer to caterer and, now, cake-maker with style and sizable following for her specialty party cakes. Sibby describes her cakes as gourmet cakes, each decorated with the obvious talents of her floral past. The look is extraordinary — wedding cakes tastefully decorated with flowers, such as roses, gardenias or casablanca lilies. There are stacked cakes, decorated as wrapped gift boxes; heart-shaped caked, with "lids" ajar and flowers tumbling out; and a favorite cake in disguise as a potted cactus. These are works of edible art!! Cakes come in 17 flavors with a choice of 23 fillings. As an example, a 12 inch cake with buttercream icing costs $47. and an Italian cream runs $57.

■ **David J's** has been a wholesaler of excellent ice cream cakes and sorbets. Their distinctive desserts have been available through selected gourmet food shops and served to us at restaurants. The good news is that there is now a retail outlet at Alpha and Inwood, just west of the Galleria. David J's beauti-fully decorated ice cream pies and cakes are also available, with a cake with 24 to 36 servings costing about $35.

▲ **Empire Baking Company** has caused a bread revolution in Dallas, Just a year ago Robert and Meaders Ozarov launched their high-tech bakery on Oak Lawn just south of Highland Park. Their is a non-yeast method of baking bread, based on old-fashioned bread-making traditions that results in a crustier and chewier bread. Meanwhile, Empire is a name frequently and reverently mentioned in food-loving circles. Decisions for purchases are difficult, but the Oak Lawn shop always has samples of each on hand to help in the process. The author votes for Calmata Olive bread and, of course, the Walnut Raisin bread, but also has a bias toward the Pane Paisano and several other of the flavorful varieties. This is not by bread alone, and the shop has the best rugelach we have ever tasted and luscious tarts, brownies, sweet rolls, scones and cookies, all deftly prepared by an ex-Mansion pastry chef. Meanwhile the breads are available at other places around town, including Eureka!, Whole Foods Markets, City Cafe To Go and Magnifico in Irving. The bread makes noticeable appearances at restaurants and at dinners presented by some of the city's better caterers. The shop incidentally, carries the makings of an easy-to-assemble meal, with imported pasta, sauces, Mozzarella Factory cheese, Dean & DeLuca herbs and legumes, jams and other necessities for sale. Neighbors Carté (for invitations and cards) and Botanicals (for flowers) can conveniently supply other ingredients for entertaining.

◆ **Frosted Art.** The Neiman Marcus bakery has moved to a Las Colinas warehouse location, but it continues to supply all the baked goods for the Neiman Marcus area stores, and for several hotels and country clubs as well. A Frosted Art cake is an iced masterpiece and is baked with the Neiman Marcus assurance of quality. Our readers may be interested in knowing that, in May 1993, Executive Chef Arturo Diaz was a finalist in the Ultimate Wedding Cake competition, sponsored by Christie's in New York as a form of edible art. While wedding cakes are a specialty, all the dessert and celebration cakes are wonderful. A 12 inch by 16 inch sheet cake serves 50 and costs about $35. and a 12 inch decorated round cake costs $65. Fancy wedding cakes, serving 50, start at $185. and go up to $800. for an extra fancy cake serving 300. The manager reports that chocolate raspberry truffle is now the most popular flavor for those who are celebrating. Patrons can order direct, or through Neiman Marcus stores, where there are always cakes for purchase, as well as samples for custom orders.

▼ **Häagen Dazs** is a spiffy newcomer to Highland Park Village and an easy drop-in spot for a dessert course. In addition to the fabulous ice creams and frozen yogurts, the ice cream cakes are decidedly above average in appearance and waiting to create an instant celebration. Cakes, with flavors like Macadamia Brittle and Swiss Almond Vanilla are $20. for a cake to serve eight to ten and $30. to serve 12 to 15.

● **The Humble Pie and Cake Company** is a new endeavor by Mange-Tout cooking teacher Susan Johnson and food entrepreneur Jean Crow. Together, they offer a mouthwatering array of freshly-baked pies and cakes. Items include the "So Good Pecan Pie"serving eight at $15.; "An English Trifle," made with homemade custard, fruits and their special cake, serving ten at $18.; and the "Chocolate à la Humble," an elegant chocolate lovers' delight, serving 18 at $36. Fruit tarts vary with the season. These are fabulous desserts for any occasion and one to add flavorful accents to the take-out or festive dinner. Orders must be made in advance, since each order is baked especially for you. There are optional delivery charges.

■ **Ida Mae's Specialty Cakes** in Jacksboro is a major statement on the wedding scene, not only locally but nationally. The confections are flowered and towering works of art. But, lest you think that wedding cakes are their only art, we've enjoyed owner Becky Sikes fabulous cakes, decorated with sugar flowers, fruits and vegetables, at a Les Dames d'Escoffier's annual event and at a ninetieth birthday celebration.

▲ **International Bakery & Sandwich Bar** is a pleasant "find" in Dal-Rich Village near Whole Foods Market. Fabulous looking desserts, like the chocolate mousse wrapped in a chocolate shell, and fancy pastries reveal the artistic hand of a classically trained *patissier*. In this case, the master is Vietnamese owner Hy Trong. If you are looking for a celebration cake, there are numbers of photos to choose from and prices for the very artistic cakes are reasonable, about $35. for a custom 12 inch cake to serve 18 to 25.

◆ **Judy Terrell Ebrey** of Cuisine International, who is listed above under "cooking classes" in Chapter II, was a caterer and food stylist long before representing the major catering schools of Europe. Now, she concentrates on her thriving wedding cake business. She normally will take only one order a week for her cakes, for which she uses only the freshest ingredients and decorates with either fresh or porcelain flowers. Judy reports the most popular flavors of the moment are Italian Cream or the traditional white with various fillings.

▼ **La Française French Bakery & Cafe** was the first to bring fresh croissants to Dallas almost 20 years ago. Located in Lake Highlands, they have a special place in our culinary hearts for their fruit tarts, eclairs and French authenticity. Their clientele has been faithful and with good reason. Like other bakeries, La Française has added "& Cafe" to their name and functions. A second location has just been opened on East Mockingbird near Abrams.

● **Kathleen's Art Bakery.** See listing below under "Take-Out."

■ Nancy Wilbur's **Kozy Kitchen**, "Home of Delicious Desserts," has been a going concern for 24 years and no wonder! Her custom-order baked goods are favorites for special occasions — the centerpiece for a morning coffee, lunch, afternoon tea or dinner party. With suggestions like Sour Cream or Lemon Pound Cake, the luscious Chocolate Mississippi Mud or Orange Pecan Cake, or the hand-decorated butter cookies, you can understand the attraction of keeping a Kozy Kitchen dessert on hand — or presenting them as gifts to friends and business associates. (We want to remind you that they freeze quite well for future use.) The Kozy Kitchen is now selling to various retail outlets around town, so readers will have the opportunity to sample the cakes at Borders Books, among other establishments. And look for Kozy Kitchen cakes in the '93 Neiman Marcus Christmas catalogue, an accolade to their excellence. We've been acquainted with Nancy and her baking expertise since the early days of her business. Its success is no surprise to long-time on-lookers.

▲ **La Madeleine Bakery and Cafe.** How did we live without La Madeleine? Owner Patrick Esquerré started his now 18 chain store eleven years ago at their Mockingbird-near-SMU location. With stores in the Metroplex, Houston, San Antonio and New Orleans, authentic French bread and pastries have become as accessible as your local neighborhood grocery. We have noticed that the breads introduced by Empire Baking Co. have prompted the competition to come up with their own new varieties, such as the Macadamia Raisin bread and the Mediterranean Olive bread — all the better for the Dallas consumer. Not only do we frequent their baked goods shops for staples — for baguettes, croissants, muffins and desserts for all events, but they have become our destination for bistro dining and excellent take-out. See also our listing for La Madeleine under "Take-Out."

◆ **le gâteau cakery** in Highland Park north of Knox Street, where baker Jackie Spratt has retail space for her booming wedding cake business, is one of the favorite destinations for Dallas brides-to-be. Party cakes are another specialty and are as beautiful as they are delicious. They come in a number of flavors, such as Italian cream, spice or chocolate amaretto cream, white chocolate truffle fudge and other such mouth-watering flavors. An eight inch cake to serve 15 ranges from $25. to $30, and a 12 inch for 25 to 30 people costs $35. to $40. Incidentally, a four-tier wedding cake for 200 guests cost $350. A 16 inch groom's cake runs $135. While orders must be made in advance, there are occasions when Jackie can produce a small celebration cake in a hurry.

◆ **Mama's Daughter** is a restaurant, not a bakery, on Irving Boulevard, but judging from the lines waiting to buy the mile high meringue pies, they might as well be. This is a funky place to put on your "must list" if you like home-style meals at pre-inflated prices. And, don't miss the pies to take home.

▼ **Massimo da Milano's** airy breads and rolls grace the tables of many of Dallas' best restaurants. The Italian baked goods run toward excellent biscuit-like cookies, fruit tarts, eclairs and panettone for the holidays. Unlike the other bakeries, Massimo's has extensive take-out to accompany its eat-in, particularly at its original Lovers Lane location. Massimo last year opened a fabulous new bakery/take-out/cafe in Village on the Parkway and now still another at Hillside Village. Word has it that Massimo will become to Italian bakeries what La Madeleine is to French bakeries.

● **Morgen Chocolate, Inc.** Owner Rex Morgen has one of Dallas' most unique specialties — that of a European-trained chocolate maker. His truffles — the perfect sweet ending to a special meal — are on a par with the very best. And, we can't imagine Easter without his special molded and truffle-filled baskets and bunnies, or Valentines Day without his hearts. Morgen sells his chocolates at his West End Brewery retail location and through such specialty shops as Marty's, Simon David, The Coffee Company in Preston Center, and during holidays at Korshak's and other fine emporiums.

■ **Neiman Marcus** has full bakery services at NorthPark and Prestonwood. See Frosted Art above.

▲ Two European chocolate-makers have a presence in Dallas, the well-known **Godiva Chocolatier**, with now just one shop at The Galleria, and **Neuhaus**, which now has five shops and cafes serving and also selling cakes and home-made ice creams in area malls, including both NorthPark and the Galleria. During 1993, Neuhaus opened a larger cafe, **Neuhaus Chocolate Cafe** at Preston and Royal (near the always bustling Borders Books and Music). The new shop has an enlarged menu in addition to the homemade ice cream and low-fat yogurts.

▼ **Out of a Flower** is one of Dallas' real food treasures. Michel Bernard Platz, former chef of the Anatole's L'Entrecote Restaurant when it was at its culinary zenith, and partner Jose Sanabria saw an opening in the niche for superb quality ice creams and sorbets — an how they are filling it!!! French-born and trained, Platz had a passion for edible herbs and flowers. Sanabria loved to grow the same things. Now, in only the second year of their operation, Out of a Flower took FIRST PLACE in the dessert category at the 1993 New York Specialty Food Trade Show, the nation's premier trade market-place!

Their winning sorbet was "Peach and Champagne with Mint," made from Texas peaches and the spearmint they grow themselves. Ice cream and sorbet flavors vary seasonally, depending on what is in "flower." The Summer's Mango, Melon and Plum will give way to the Fall's Pumpkin with Toasted Seeds and Chestnut with Glazed Chestnuts for a total of 50 flavors in the repertoire, all made from the best natural ingredients and flavored with flowers and herbs. The next time you are serving a simple but distinctive dessert, or an *intermezzo* sorbet for an important dinner, your guests will be impressed with an Out of a Flower flavor, such as Rose Geranium Blossoms, Fresh Nutmeg or Southern Pecan Coffee with Marc de Bourgogne. Our personal ice cream favorite is Lavender, absolutely sublime and reminiscent of ice cream previously found only in the South of France. Platz is also developing frozen dessert specialties, such as Frosted Alsatian Cake and Frosted Christmas Log Cake, now being used by several caterers and available for special order. Out of a Flower is selling nation-wide at all the most famous food emporiums. Locally, we can find it at Marty's, Whole Foods, TJ's Seafood and at the new Magnifico in Irving. Williams Sonoma has already featured Out of a Flower in its catalogues and the product can be seen in the 1993 Neiman Marcus Christmas catalogue. You will also see the company's creative gingerbread house kits in the stores for Christmas sales. Not to be overlooked, Platz is one of Dallas' best chef-teachers. He is listed also under "Cooking Classes" in Chapter II.

*See the advertisement for **Out of a Flower** on page 212.*

● **Romano's Cheesecake Company** was first a bakery and now a take-out shop and catering gem on Monticello near Central Expressway Owner Linda Losee has been selling her delectable cheesecakes (in 50 flavors) to area restaurants and gourmet shops for several years. They are available at her tiny shop, where she also serves lunch and does a growing take-out and catering business. **Spirited Cakes** owner Elaine Luttrell works with Romano's shop, providing convenient pick-up for her custom-ordered and sinfully delicious cakes.

■ **Sarah Jane Francis** is the "grande dame" of chocolate cakes, having captured the premier position among grooms' cake purveyors. The cakes are absolutely sublime, and come in a variety of chocolate "flavors." We particularly like the 24 Caret Gold Cake and the raspberry-accented Ruby Mountain Cake. The impressive, chocolate-curl decorated cakes come in three sizes, the smallest serving 75 and the largest 175. Costs start at $190. and go up to $475. for the grandest Ruby Mountain. These are "experiences" — and worth every dollar! Happily, the cakes make appearances at other than weddings. We've enjoyed them as celebratory focal points at birthday parties and teas. Sarah Jane's calendar fills up quickly, so order far ahead to avoid being disappointed.

▲ **Special Affairs Catering** has a dual personality, as baker and caterer, and is also listed below under "Catering." Their notable wedding cakes can be ordered through their Lovers Lane shop, as can the conversation-stopping stacked and wrapped box cakes, which make fabulous celebration cakes for parties of all sorts. Incidentally, owner Paul Jerabek's signature stacked cakes have a two-page layout in the Tiffany wedding book. Recently, we savored another of Paul's cakes at a Fall wedding. Not only was the Southern buttermilk cake delicious, the French-pleated, buttercream icing was visual delight.

◆ **Spirited Cakes** started out mainly as a Christmas gift enterprise by enterprising Elaine Luttrell. Her luscious liquor flavored cakes, which come in flavors like Kalua-Mocha and Rum Pecan are long lasting, so we'd recommend giving them to friends who like to keep a dessert on hand for impromptu entertaining or to take along to the ranch or lake house for weekend house guests. Non-liquor cakes, such a Italian Cassata and Double Fudge Devilsfood are also on the list. As the demand has grown, Spirited Cakes takes year-round orders for the cakes and has branched into wedding and celebration cakes as well. Elaine's cakes can also be found at Romano's Cheesecake Company, mentioned above. We'd also like to remind our readers that the moist and well-packaged cakes make wonderful holiday gifts.

● **Stein's Bakery**. Like Aston's, mentioned above, Stein's has been on the bakery scene since pre-croissant days. Legions of children have celebrated birthdays with a cake from Stein's and the celebration cakes are still a mainstay of their business on Preston Road, just south of LBJ.

■ **Strictly Cheesecake.** Nadine McFarland oversees this popular cheesecake emporium located in an unlikely Forest Lane strip center just east of Central Expressway. She has long ago been discovered by restaurants and caterers who offer her creamy cheesecakes on their dessert menus. A 10 inch round cake — in any of the 50 available flavors — will cost $20. and will serve 16 to 20 guests. Other sizes and shapes are available and can be decorated with messages. The less usual flavors, such as kahlua and pumpkin must be ordered 48 hours in advance. Dallas may be the epicenter of the cheesecake world. In addition to Strictly Cheesecake and Romano's, there is also the aptly-named **Heavenly Cheesecakes**, located on North Central Expressway in Keystone Park, **Cheesecake Royale** on Garland Road, and former Dallas journalist Lyn Dunsavage's **New York, Texas Cheesecake** available by mail from near-by LaRue, Texas. Each has quite a following among cheesecake aficionados.

▲ **Sweet Endings** is a delightfully delicious "find" in Deep Ellum. Aside from stopping by to enjoy their sweets while you are in the neighborhood (and even up until two a.m.!), consider ordering their cakes for an impressive ending to your dinner parties. Since Sweet Endings will deliver in the downtown area, we also recommend they be high on the office list for office entertaining. It's hard to say which dessert we like the best, but do try the Coconut Cream Pie or the Black Bottom Devil's Food Cake. Cost for a pie that will indulge eight to ten people will cost $16. to $20.

◆ **Sweet Temptations Cafe and Bakery** should be a destination for every hostess in search of a ready-made dessert course. We are aware that many caterers do just that. Few could do better. Their cakes are European in style and so unbelievably delicious that selection is difficult. Perhaps, it would be wisest to plan a high tea to serve at least the Chocolate Indulgence Cake, the Chocolate Mousse Cake piled high with chocolate shavings and the Coconut Cream Cake. The 10 inch Indulgence Cake, for example, is $27.50 and will serve twelve. Most others, like the Lemon Mousse Cake and the seasonal fruit tarts, are under $20. British born Clare Van Loenen, former pastry chef at the now-defunct, five-star Cafe Royal, is the creator of the fabulous concoctions, pastries and breads. The adjacent bistro-like restaurant gets rave reviews, not unsurprisingly, with credit due to Clare's Dutch-born husband and chef, Hans. Sweet Temptations is on Skillman where it intersects with Audelia near LBJ. Look for a multi-storied, Mediterranean-styled shopping Center.

● **Tim Louque Designs**. Tim Louque has the unrivaled talent of cake sculptor and his reputation grows each time one of his cakes is presented at an event. In fact, a Tim Louque cake will most likely become a party's centerpiece. Tim has sculpted faces for his popular birthday portrait cakes; an entire

English village with thatched-roof homes, colorful gardens and trees, as he did for the Summer Musicals "Brigadoon" cast party; a new home, complete with yard and mailbox with the owners' name on it; even a container of Blue Bell ice cream for one customer; and scores of cars, cuddly bears and Barneys for the younger set. His most intricate project was another for the Summer Musicals, this time for the cast of "Grand Hotel." The multi-storied hotel, complete with roof tiles and window treatments, had an open, pillared lobby with marble floor and the 120 gold bamboo chairs from a significant scene in the production. At one '93 party for a dynamic duo celebrating their birthdays together, Tim capitalized on their "theme" of royalty for a day with the presentation of a bejeweled crown cake for each honorèe. The cakes, complete with a lady on a ladder climbing to the top of one crown, were the party's *pièce de resistance*, adding a sense of humor to the celebration! Tim can show you his incredible portfolio of edible art. Cakes starts at $75. and portrait cakes at $95.

A La Mode

Dallas may be on the way to becoming a frozen dessert capital.
We are home to several growing companies-

- *David J* with sorbets, ice creams and ice cream cakes.
- *La Crème*, now making gelatos and fruttas for restaurants.
- *I Can't Believe It's Yogurt*, owned by sister and brother Juli and Bill Brice. The chain has taken the yogurt world by storm, now with almost 370 free-standing stores in 37 states, and that is just the domestic U.S. total!
- *Out of a Flower*, the rich gourmet line of flower flavored ice creams and sorbets that are now selling nationwide at the most prestigious food emporiums, such as Dean & DeLuca and Grace's Marketplace in the Big Apple. First Place Dessert Winner of the 1993 New York Specialty Food Trade Show.

Take Out

Take-out for entertaining is the salvation for the busy hostess and instant entertainer. Meals can easily be built around a "main course" of subs, barbecue or chicken for a casual event. As a reminder, we have **Arnold's Texas Bar-B-Q** and **Sonny Bryan's** for great take-out barbecue. Sub shops and several deli's, such as **Gilbert's**, have the monstrously-long, piled-high sandwiches — conversation pieces as well as main course. Chicken is a treat from **La Madeleine, Cowboy Chicken** or **Chicken Chicken**, not to mention the old favorites from **Bubba's** and **Pollo Bueno**. Gourmet pizza is also a focal point for spontaneous entertaining. **Mise en Place, California Pizza Kitchen, Massimo's, Cafe Expresso**, or any number of gourmet pizza take-outs, can set the party scene before the game or for impromptu pool parties.

For more serious meals or buffets, take-out shops can substitute or supplement home-cooked meals, from starter soups at **La Madeleine**, to main courses from **Marty's, City Cafe To Go, Tommaso's** and **Pasta Plus**, to desserts from wonderful bakeries and specialty ice cream emporiums. For luncheons and teas, there are any number of options. **Marty's** and **Good Taste to Go** deliver. Pick up is simple at **Celebrity, Maudee's** and at all the delis, such as **Deli News** and **Bagelstein's**. Even the most serious gastronomes need not suffer. In this day and age, almost instant entertaining from casual to grand is a possibility. Set a pretty table and you will be ready to receive your guests.

The take-out shops listed below can be found in the "Directory of Sources, beginning on page 223. For your convenience, there is also a "Telephone Directory," which begins on page 247.

Among our best shops

▲ **Amore (To Go)**, adjacent to the Snider Plaza eatery of the same name, is a welcome entry in the take-out field and offers a variation on the usual prepared foods to go. You merely order from the dinner menu and take home their appetizing bruschetta, veal piccata, lasagnas and other pasta. The waits are not long, but, preferably, call ahead. The prices are moderate.

◆ **Arnold's Texas Bar-B-Q** offers award-winning barbecue, like barbecue is supposed to taste. Arnold's is the answer for take-out or catering. See listing for Arnold's Texas Bar-B-Q under "Catering."

▼ **California Pizza Kitchen** is the latest entry in the category of pizzas cooked in wood-burning ovens. The first of the California chain to open in Dallas is on Belt Line, just east of Prestonwood Mall, and the second in Preston Center. A third is slated for Plano. Pizzas range from traditional to the unusual, such as Burrito, Caribbean Shrimp and Tandoori Chicken. Pasta, salads and sinful-sounding desserts round out the menu, all available for take-out and home delivery.

● **Cafe Expresso** in Preston Center has been a favorite since its origin as a Lombardi's outpost. During the day, the cafe functions as both take-out and eat-in and all the prepared salads and Italian specialties are excellent. By the time the restaurant dresses up for the evening, most of the daily take-out items are gone, but there are always the gourmet pizzas to go and some of the city's best European-styled cakes and pastries from the bakery case.

■ **Camellia Cafe**, a cute eatery in Snider Plaza, is one of the better places for Cajun take-out, sold in quantity — red beans and rice, jambalaya and gumbo are among the cafe's best bets. The restaurant will also cater.

▲ **Chicken-Chicken** may develop into a take-out chain. Meanwhile, the Old Town prototype provides excellent chicken specialties for the nucleus of an impromptu dinner. Whole rotisserie and wood-grilled chickens are the favorites, accompanying potatoes, vegetables and salads are also available.

◆ **City Cafe to Go**, located on Lovers Lane near the Tollroad, is perhaps Dallas' best and most extensive take-out emporium. City Cafe To Go, reminiscent of New York famed Silver Palate, has a mouth-watering display of prepared foods at all times. The daily variety is impressive and the menu, like its next-door parent, City Cafe, changes monthly to keep up with the freshest foods on the market. On one recent evening, we feasted on the crab and crayfish cakes with red tartar sauce at $14. per pound, pork loin filled with spinach and apricots and served with Madeira sauce at $13. per pound, and black bean and rice salad at $7. per pound. Don't miss the desserts, which include delicious fresh fruit tarts, crème bruleès and chocolate pecan brownies. In case you have forgotten your own platters, to make the offerings look like they have come straight from your own kitchen, there are earthenware platters available, as are wine and other sundries to complete the entertaining scenario. Your guests will applaud you. It is understandable why City Cafe to Go is consistently rated tops in take-out. They will be happy to fill picnic hampers and ice chests for the trip to the farm or to the athletic event. Also, take note that City Cafe To Go also caters, earning high marks by those who have used them.

■ **Eureka!**, in Preston Center East, is the newest entry in the take-out field. Lisa Kramer, owner of the-missed Bravo on McKinney Avenue, and former Over the Rainbow owner Joanne Levy have teamed up to create an eat-in, take-out, heart-healthy establishment that has been an instant success, especially with the lean and fit among us. Eureka! has on hand the ready-made and healthful components of the spontaneous dinner, prepared by chefs who have had training in Canyon Ranch's famous kitchen. Available also are sandwiches, food trays and box lunches to meet the demands of the busy hostess. The retail area is filled with the best epicure on the market – sauces, rices, pastas and a line of coffees as well – all for self-indulgence and gift-giving. This is where you can have your cake and eat it too!

▲ **Fit-Kit Cuisine.** With the launch of fully-prepared, chilled meals, the prestigious dani group merges five-star dining, convenience and heart-healthy eating. Chef Nick Barclay has developed complete packaged meals, perfect for both dinner parties and fitness programs. We've already savored a birthday luncheon à la Fit-Kit. Soups include Spicey Tomato with Basil Cream; entrèes with side courses include Cinnamon-Flavored Breast of Chicken with garlic mashed potatoes and green beans and Salmon Galantine with yogurt dill sauce and fresh greens. Ordering and delivery are direct from the dani group. Several shops around town, such as Fresh Start Market on Oak Lawn, have been carrying the flavorful meals.
Please see the advertisement for the dani group on page 213.

◆ **Going Gourmet**, at Northwest Highway and Midway Road, which debuted in early 1993, has already doubled its size. A few tables had been available for the crowds who discovered it as soon as it opened. Now, the owners, chef Ona Settembre and husband Ettore, have already expanded to the adjacent space. It may now be that the emphasis is on the eating-in aspect of their business. Nonetheless, the food cases are always filled with casseroles to go, including beef stroganoff, chicken and dumplings, chicken enchiladas, cottage pie, lasagna, paella, pastas and vegetable accompaniments. Prices range from $7.50 to $12. in servings for two. The shop also carries Allegro coffees and other food items.

▼ **Hernandez Mexican Foods** and **Luna's Tortilla Factory**, each on the Northern fringe of downtown, make interesting grocery shopping for Mexican food aficionados. Here, the shopper will find homemade tamales, tortillas and fresh tortilla chips straight from the stove, as well as several off-beat items. Luna has a second shop in Oak Cliff.

● **Highland Park Cafeteria.** Dallasites may think that take-out started on Knox Street, so popular had been the habit of stopping by to pick-up dinner, or to order an entire Thanksgiving meal-to-go, long before take-out was a culinary concept. While food styles constantly evolve, the popularity and prices of HPC's home-style food is still served to many a guest, especially over the holidays and when the menu calls for one of their popular pies. Speaking of pies, we have to remind non-natives that the four restaurant chain also makes wedding cakes and celebration cakes and runs a full-catering operation.

■ **Kathleen's Art Bakery**, sibling to the adjacent cafe of the same name, is as much about take-out as it is about baked goods. The display cases are filled with the offerings of the day — meat loaf, pasta salads, crab cakes, eggplant parmigiana and, of course, cookies, cobblers and cakes. There are always casseroles available — three-pesto or chicken lasagna, Greek lamb and chick pea casserole — all about $54. for servings for 12. Chess pie and carrot cake always seem to be on hand. The food is what mother would make, if she were a good cook, and your guests will love it. Kathleen's can accommodate the at-home dinner party with a menu of your choosing, either for take-out or catering.

▲ **La Madeleine French Bakery & Cafe** is a major entry in several food categories. Foremost a bakery, but also a cafe and take-out favorite, La Madeleine has changed the city's eating habits. Now that marvelous herb roasted chicken (at $7.95 a whole chicken) is available, as well as hard-to-beat soups and quiches, there is everything here to serve for a dinner *chez vous*. The Caesar salad and dessert complete the meal. Only the wine, flowers and candlelight will have to be supplied by the hostess. There are now six La Madeleines in Dallas, making them convenient to many of us. See also the listing above under "Desserts."

◆ **La Popular.** If you want Tex-Mex to satisfy the cravings of your guests, head to La Popular, on Columbia near Fitzhugh. Owner Jesse Moreno has several varieties of freshly-made tamales (at $5. a dozen) and tortillas every day. The crowds come on weekends when the family specialties are available – *menudo, carnitas, guisos* (beef and pork casseroles), *guacamole* and *salsas.* By all accounts, the *barbaco* is the most popular. Prepare for a feast! During hunting season, La Popular will custom prepare your venison into tamales.

▼ **Magnifico Fine Foods**. See the write-up of Las Colinas' new fine food and take-out shop, listed under "Specialty Markets."

● **Marty's** has its origins in a wine shop, and has been covered above. The combination of the finest in food and wine make it simpler for the take-out entertainer. The word "gourmet" aptly applies to this Oak Lawn shop which is also Dallas' top-of-the line purveyor of prepared fine foods. The display and availability of prepared foods is extensive at all times and the hurried hostess will have no trouble assembling the prepared components of a cocktail party or an important dinner.

While Marty's' has pastas and salads, hors d'oeuvres and luncheon plates, one is more likely to be drawn to Loin of Pork stuffed with Shiitake Mushroom, Spinach and Garlic and crusted with fine herbs as well as accompanying dishes, such as Rustic Pasta, tossed with green beans and herbed pesto, for serious entertaining at home. For mini-events, the hostess can pick up a Pastry Presentation at $2.50 per person or a Cheese Display at $3.50 a person. Marty's has the best cheese and pâtè selection in town, as well as caviar, smoked salmon and mouth-watering baked goods. Marty's motto is "everything essential to the epicure." Believe it!

Marty's will also prepare fabulous picnic and lunch boxes, including wine, at $20. per person and offers a wide variety of catering possibilities — dinner parties and business functions among them. Not to be overlooked is the breakfast take-out, a great way to add a sense of pizzazz to the early-morning corporate seminar or the charity board meeting. Their delivery service is particularly helpful for the busy host or hostess. See also the listings under "Wine," "Gourmet" and "Catering."
Please see the advertisement for Marty's on page 218.

■ **Massimo da Milano**, the Italian Bakery/Cafe with now several Dallas locations in addition to the Lovers Lane original, has simply *magnifico* food-to-go. The specialty pizzas, hot selections, such as eggplant parmigiana, and outstanding salads are simple to select for home entertaining. Salads, such as Sollacetti (bow-tie pasta salad with ham, swiss cheese and cornichons), Risotto con Fagioli (rice salad with black beans and scallions) and Insalate de Pollo (the city's best chicken salad with swiss cheese, cornichons, peas and sweet peppers), can dress up any summer buffet table. The added award-winning bread and desserts make this a one-stop meal pick-up. Massimo's growth mode means two new bakery/take-out/eateries opening last year at Village on the Parkway, convenient for the Addison and Bent Tree crowds, and in Hillside Village at Mockingbird and Abrams, much to the delight of East Dallas fans and residents. See also our listing under "Desserts."

▲ **Maudee's**, a Lover's Lane tearoom, has a big following among those who like to pick up sandwich trays for lunches, committee meetings and teas. Trays run about $3.50 per person and box lunches about $5. for favorites like chicken salad and pimento cheese.

◆ **Mise en Place**, located in the Lovers Lane area and one of Dallas' best gourmet pizza take-outs, uses "culinary experts" to prepare pizzas and tasty salads. For guests, consider one of their up-scale pizzas topped with smoked duck or chicken, black beans or seafood. Twelve inch pizzas range from $10. to $18. They are rightly proud of having been voted *"Number One in Pizza"* by the late D MAGAZINE.

▼ **Redwine Catering** last year opened a sleekly designed shop on McKinney, just South of Knox Street, as a base for both its catering and take-out businesses. First offerings reflect the European training of Canadian-born chef Kerry Chace, who has been a chef with nouvelle exposure at Parigi's. The luncheon salad offerings are the result of exceptional cooking and an eye for the best produce on the market. We enjoyed Mediterranean Chicken and Pasta Salad with artichoke hearts, pear tomatoes, black olives, fresh oregano and Dallas feta cheese. *Provençale* pizza and Katherine's Wedding Cake, also on the menu, will certainly satisfy the take-out crowd. The Italian cream cake, made for a wedding catered by Redwine at an area ranch, has become a signature dessert. The take-out menus are available for breakfast and lunch hours. Meanwhile, there is an opportunity to order almost any dish for take-out with some advance notice. See also our listing under "Catering."

● **Tommaso's Pasta.** Tommaso D'Onofrio moved to Dallas in 1981 from Italy, bringing with him his pasta equipment and family recipes. From a small family-run operation, Tommaso's has become the area's largest pasta maker with products widely available at area markets. A full range of products — sauces, lasagnas and pasta salads — is available at their Spring Valley retail store, one of Dallas' better take-out emporiums. It's best to order ahead, and for more gracious dining, you can drop off your own containers the previous day. Catering is also available. Prices are moderate, with cheese, meat and zucchini lasagnas at $6.50 a pound.

■ **Party in a Box** defies classification and yet needs to be included in our book. The company is more of a "send-to" rather than a "take-out." Owners Sue Davis and Judi Landin have put together a concept for the party box — to celebrate everything or anything from Father's Day to new baby. An instruction sheet guides the honorèe through his or her festive occasion with everything from party hat to equipment and ingredients. The "Lone Star Roundup," for example, contains all the fixins' from the chili pot to the bandana. Themes and occasions are endless. Prices are in the $50. range.

▲ **Pasta Plus.** "Home of Dallas' best pasta" was on the cutting edge with pasta popularity. The Preston Royal and Plano stores dispense fresh pastas, savory sauces, oven-ready lasagna and cannelloni, and much more. The selection of salads, bread and Italian desserts makes this a one-stop take-out shop. In addition, Pasta Plus carries a number of grocery items, such as olive oils, Dean & DeLuca herbs and imported Italian canned goods. With the new shop at Preston and Campbell, Pasta Plus is expanding both home delivery and catering services. A new slogan has appeared in their stores: "Caterer of Fine Italian Foods," to emphasize its new role. Prices are moderate and quality is high.

◆ **Simon David** shouldn't be overlooked for take-out. A fast meal menu can be made just touring the great inventory - fresh fruits, cooked shrimp and lobster, ready-roasted chickens, cheese and wines — before even approaching the take-out counters filled with salads and baked goods of all varieties. The excellent selection of cheeses and wine are a bonus. See also our listings under "Markets" and "Wine."

A Reminder — *the addresses and phone numbers for the shops listed can be found in the "Directory of Sources," which begins on page 223.*

deli detour

Last year. we had a few newcomers on the scene — such as **Deli News** in its Crescent location and **European Market & Deli**. This year, **Soramy**, in both Plano and Preston Royal, joins the scene. Overall, there seems to be a burgeoning of the Dallas deli population, resulting in greater convenience to the impromptu take-out crowd. All have ready-prepared meats and salads, some with more extensive menus than others. Most have party trays available for casual events. Several are into full catering.

Delicatessen means "a store selling foods already prepared or requiring little preparation for serving, as cooked meats, cheese, relishes and the like." The history of the deli, likely the beginning of take-out, would be an interesting discourse, but suffice it to say, that transported New Yorkers find great comfort in the proliferation of delicatessens in the area.

▼ **The Cheese House and Deli.** We grew up on Cheese House food — take-out and sandwich trays — before such ideas were commonplace in Dallas. Many years later, The Cheese House, now in a Preston Forest location, is still going strong with a loyal following and an active catering business.

● **Deli News.** Like many other delicatessens, Deli News is restaurant, take-out and caterer. In all instances, Deli News is more ambitious and, with its second location at The Crescent, is really spreading its wings. DALLAS MORNING NEWS critic Waltrina Stovall observed that Deli News is like dying and going to New York City. The two Russian owners and cousins, Misha Fishman and Sacha Adamovsky, combine their heritage and New York delicatessen experience to treat Dallas to the real thing. All their specialties — mile high sandwiches, cheese blintzes, smoked meats, and potato pancakes are available for take-out, as are whole turkeys and hams, to name just a few more items. The owners have launched an enterprising catering operation and have now opened a charming second floor room in the Crescent location, decorated with murals of Russian fairy tales and appropriately named The Russian Room. See the listing for The Russian Room under "Restaurants."

■ **Gilbert's New York Delicatessen,** in Preston Forest, has a loyal following and a larger bill of fare than most. Its full restaurant allows for a wide selection, most of which can be ordered for at-home convenience. The party subs, incidentally, are very popular.

▲ **Henk's European Deli** is an offshoot, so to speak, of the popular Kuby's. Henk Wennbust was Kuby's original partner in their University Park venture. Henk ventured off on his own and now has a similar operation behind the old Sterling Jewelry property on Northwest Highway. Associated with the deli is the Black Forest Bakery, with some of the best breads and cakes in town. Black Forest has a real following of its own and does a considerable wedding cake business.

▲ **Mr. G's Deli** in Plano is the closest to the deli category. As part of the huge Mr. G's Beverage Center, covered under "wine," Mr. G's provides all the basics that go with deli food — cold cuts and salads, party trays and more. This is one-stop shopping with the addition of some gourmet foods, such as pastas and olive oils.

◆ **Polish Delicatessen.** Dallasites now have tow Eastern European take-out delis – adding the above-mentioned European Markey and Deli on Forest – to the Polish Delicatessen on Northwest Highway east of White Rock Lake. Lucky for us to become acquainted with Polish specialties – *pierogi,* stuffed cabbages and potato pancakes.

▼ **Soramy** in Plano is among the newest of the delicatessens, this one with a Middle eastern twist. Owners Amy and Sorin Lazar, along with chef Yatchak Sonek, are all from Israel and incorporate their backgrounds into the specialties. Plans include a second location, which is scheduled to open in Preston Royal as this book goes to press.

● **Bagelstein's, Kuby's,** and the **European Market & Deli** have been covered earlier in the chapter. Bagelstein's and Kuby's, in particular, have co-contributed considerable to our local eating habits and culture. Both are staples in the deli food arena.

pizza to go

Gourmet pizza is one of the easiest of the impromptu entertaining menus. Fortunately, the availability of "designer pizza" has changed our thoughts to pizza as a dish worthy of company. The entries in this category are so numerous we are listing only a few of the outstanding sources. *These sources are listed in our "Telephone Directory," which begins on page 247.*

Arcodoro
Cafe Expresso
California Pizza Kitchen
Campisi's to Go
Marco's Pizza
Massimo da Milano
Mis en Place
Piccolo Cuccina, at Barneys NorthPark
PoPolo's

delivery services

■ Three delivery services can be indispensable to the harried hostess who may have last-minute entertaining to handle. Both **Entrèes to Go** and its newer competitor, **Home Delivery Network**, pick up orders from 200 Dallas area restaurants. Service charges are minimal and delivery, preferably orders with sufficient advance notice, is speedy. Each service has its own group of affiliated restaurants, so be sure to ask your favorite restaurant which service they use. **Takeout Taxi**, a nationally-affiliated company, is the newest delivery service in Dallas and services 12 to 15 restaurants in the Addison and North Dallas area. Included are California Pizza Kitchen and the Key West Grill. In their case, call the delivery service with your order and it will arrive in about 45 minutes. (They blanket their area with menu books of their affiliated restaurants every 90 days.) Delivery service extends from Forest Lane on the south to Frankford on the North.

A Reminder — *the addresses and phone numbers are listed in the "Directory of Sources," which begins on page 223.*

food and wine for thought

Local publications to make us savvy to the Dallas food and wine world

Dallas Eats! Newsletter — a monthly commentary on fine food and drink by David Gershner and Rod Monger, two avowed experts in eating out! The authors aim "to keep Dallasites up-to-speed on the culinary front through restaurant commentaries, interviews with epicurean personalities and reports on newsworthy happenings. Call 890-6666 to subscribe at $18 per year.

The Wine Letter by Rick Avery — a monthly newsletter with a run down of the best values in local wine purchases, available for $15. per year by writing the author at 2152 Kessler Court, Dallas 75208.

VI
Let The Pros Do It

caterers & party planners

O nce your party plan is under way, you may want to bring in outside help. Choosing professional party assistance may add the pizzazz needed to make your party distinctive, and allow the host and hostess to enjoy their own event. Whether a caterer to handle only the food, or a planner to conceptualize and add drama, the professional can sometimes draw on sources and talents not otherwise available to the individual.

Whereas the caterer will work in your home, or at a designated "off-site" location, the party planner has a wider range of locations, since their activities extend to events held at hotels, clubs and restaurants, and include caterers when needed for at-home or non-traditional sites.

caterers

Dallas is fortunate to have so many outstanding caterers. Many of the well-trained chefs who have come to Dallas to work with the hotels and restaurants have gone into their own food businesses. European chefs, such as **Roger Buret**, **Michel Bernard Platz** and **Nick Barclay**, to name only a very few, now oversee stoves and staffs in their own catering or food companies. It is fortunate for the consumer to have such culinary talent available. Likewise, there are individuals with quite a flair for gracious living, such as Bettye Wellons of **Au Bon Goût**, Wendy Krispin of **Wendy Krispin Catering**, Rollie Anne Blackwell of **GOURMETDALLAS** and partners Andrea Whiteside Hagger and Shelly Barsotti of **Food Company**, who oversee convivial and delicious meals at the homes of their clients. Also, Tex-Mex and barbecue provide ample opportunity for casual and less-costly entertaining.

If you are looking for a caterer, we urge you to consider the type of caterer best suited to your particular needs. Some caterers shine at smaller events, but do not have the capacity to handle a large, off-site event, perhaps lacking additional kitchen help and trained waitstaff to carry off an event for 100, or even 500 or more for a large celebration, charity or corporate event. Several caterers, such as **the dani group**, **The Silver Tray**, and **Daryl's by Design** are expert at the largest events. **GOURMETDALLAS** and **Food Company** are other catering companies that expeditiously handles larger parties with creativity and élan. On the other hand, caterers such as **Au Bon Gôut** and **L'Epicurean** will awe your friends at small to medium size dinner parties where the focus is on the food and the genial setting for a limited number of friends. Just as you would choose a site appropriate for the number of antici-pated guests, so would you choose the caterer.

There is also a fine line between some caterers and party planners. Increasingly, it seems that caterers are broadening their expertise to handle all aspects of the party, from theme to decor, to music and lighting. The hostess must decide whether to choose her own florist and entertainment or rely on the choices of the catering company. You might want to consider the caterers' recommendations for other providers, since they work with and have many opportunities to observe talented people in other aspects of the entertaining community. Of course, if time is a major factor, you may be happy for a caterer to handle the entire event.

We suggest that you start with a budget — a realistic range for the dining and service part of a party — as well as the theme or style of entertaining before you start the process of hiring a caterer, unless, of course, you feel comfortable with a catering company and know that they will discuss options and their capabilities with you.

All caterers should provide a proposal in writing, with the menu, services and terms, no matter how large or small the party. Proposals for larger parties should be very explicit about the responsibilities of the caterer. On a financial note, a fifty-percent deposit is usual for a large party, with the bal-ance due on the day of the party, or sometimes, even before it commences. Depending on your personal rapport with the caterer, a deposit for a smaller party may be waived.

With these factors in mind, we are sharing the names of some of the best caterers in Dallas. Some concentrate on corporate and convention events. Still others are associated with the growing numbers of take-out and deli shops. There are also increasing numbers of caterers who work from their homes. *In dealing with any caterer, we recommend that you inquire about his or her licensing and liability insurance before you hire.*

All of the caterers immediately below have one thing in common — catering is their primary business. *Their names and phone numbers are listed in the "Directory of Sources," which begins on page 223 and also in the "Telephone Directory" on page 247.*

Because we also have so many restaurants that also cater, we have listed them in the latter part of this chapter.

▲ **A Catered Affair.** Owner Gayle Skelton is living "the American dream," so says someone delighted with her business success after only ten years. We have enjoyed her food many times and, especially this year, at a major birthday party. We can easily understand the recent award as '93 Caterer of the Year, an honor bestowed by NACE, the National Association of Catering Executives — quite a recognition by one's peers — for promoting industry professionalism and ethics. Fans are enthusiastic in support of her creative menus and her concern for pleasing clients. Gayle is busy on the wedding scene, and given the six to eight cakes a week baked by an in-house wedding cake specialist, we can believe the scale of that portion of her business. Since all events, corporate or social, are custom-designed, the price range is considerable. Her average food price for an evening wedding reception for 150 guests is $15.

◆ **Adelina's Catering** has a special niche in the catering arena, that of authentic, regional Mexican cuisine, which is little known in the Dallas area. Owner Maxine Oesterling has studied with Mexican food authority Diana Kennedy and continues to take Colonial and indigenous Mexican cooking classes, such as recent studies in Oaxaca. As she says, "Mexican food can be every bit as sophisticated and intriguing as any other national cuisine." Adelina's caters everything from weddings to trailrides in Arizona, artists' receptions in Sante Fe, housewarmings in San Francisco and New York to all types of local events and parties. She has a devoted clientele and admits to working within their budgets.

▼ **Affaires to Remember** has a real following for full event productions, particularly for weddings, where Owner Christine Garrett is able to handle multiple aspects of planning and execution. Christine even has her own rentals and facility on Marsh Lane, near Brookhaven Community College, to use for smaller events, such as bridal showers and birthday parties.

● **Au Bon Goût.** Proprietor Bettye Wellons is one of our long-time favorites, who orchestrates some of the most memorable Dallas dinner parties. We have been privileged to admire her creativity and sample her cuisine on many occasions! In fact, the author worked closely with Bettye many years ago when she conceived and produced the first soup cookbook for the Dallas Museum of Art. Her

professional career is a reflection of the care given to that enduring book. One of our recent favorite Bettye Wellons catered events was a dinner party for a young bride and groom. The visuals were award-winning, and the compliments about the cuisine and table presentations were a major topic of the evening's conversation. The happy guests were convinced they may have had their best Dallas dinner — or was it the previous occasion when the menu included smoked salmon ravioli with asparagus and lemon sauce. Our real favorite is the High Tea she has mastered for one of her clients. There may never be a more beautiful tea table laden with small sandwiches, scones, cakes, cookies and sweets. The presentation is picture perfect, a delight for both palate and palette. Bettye works hard to create new menu ideas and exciting visuals, by either a designer on her staff, or in conjunction with your floral designer. Bettye has a list of regular clients, both private and corporate. Try to get on it!

*Please see the advertisement for **Au Bon Goût** on page 219.*

■ **Boster's Gourmet Catering.** Doug Boster has great "catering genes," having worked for a lineage of our best caterers and take-out establishments

in his 14 year career — Carr's, Chow's, Marty's, Mirabelle and Daryl's by Design. Last year, Doug launched his own company, utilizing his solid catering background and creative abilities to present outstanding food. Boster's great asset is to meet (and enjoy) a challenge with a totally new idea and to excel at the unexpected, whether a timetable, a budget or a theme. He knows that for each pleased customer, there will be many

future occasions. Partly as a base of operation, Doug has a small luncheon spot in downtown's Founders' Square landmark building, convenient to many of his business clients. From here, he deploys breakfasts to please the early-morning conference set, and luncheons to keep the deals brewing. His many clients in the Design Center give him high marks for aesthetics, a real accolade from a discriminating clientele. For one Design Center client, his charming buffet was a integral part of the showroom's country French setting, integrating the surrounding antiques and fine silver into the food display. For another, a Salute to Frank Lloyd Wright, his streamlined food and setting likewise met the aesthetics of the event. This time, the food setting included verdigris copper, stained glass and mossy rocks to complement the architect's favorite materials.

Clients, however, are just as likely to be North Dallas party-givers and brides-to-be, where Doug, assisted with a few chefs, can handle, with characteristic flair, foods from home-style to classic French. Planning by the

budget is a strong point and a realistic note of the day. Doug relies on his good judgment to showcase the most interesting foods and conserve expenses on the less important. As an end result, whether for business or for personal entertaining, he wants to ensure that his hosts and hostesses shine!
*Please see the advertisement for **Boster's Gourmet Catering** on page 222.*

▲ **Carolyn Unsworth** is the caterer of choice for many North Dallas hostesses who love the home-style quality and presentation of her food. We have enjoyed many of her catered dinner and buffet parties, especially the delicious teas and luncheons that she has done for many Dallas brides and debutantes. Carolyn charges approximately $12. per person for tea service and $10. per person for a box lunch, appropriate for all those committee meetings. Carolyn uses staff very familiar to guests on the party scene and specializes in small, at-home entertaining.

◆ **Catering by Angela**. Angela Gordon is a smaller caterer with a dedicated following, particularly in the Park Cities area, with several law firms and for several charitable organizations. Angela concentrates also on social occasions in the home and small weddings. Desserts are her specialty, including an occasional wedding cake. Menus, for an "upscale Mexican" or a Mediterranean buffet start about $16. and go to about $40. for a more elaborate, seated dinner.

▼ **Catering by Arthur** is a major name on the catering scene. The ten-year-old company enjoys a "by word-of-mouth," well-earned reputation that has spread steadily. We'd first noticed their distinctive trucks, always at the "right places." The "Arthur" of the name is Lowell Arthur Michelson who, with his chef/partner John Lacritz, specializes in full-service catering and event coordination for private parties — both at your home and off-site — for celebrations of every sort, including bar and bat mitzvahs, weddings, and parties for every event and holiday. This doesn't even include the company's solid corporate business, including daily corporate lunches, which they deliver all around town. The owners love themes using food as the unifying element. Michelson, a San Antonio native, has an easy flair for Southwestern themes and excels at backyard Mexican Fiestas, when the occasion calls for something casual. Through the years, he has acquired quite an inventory of props to establish his favorite themes. Michelson also likes to add a "fun element" to any party, whether it be an action

food station, with pastas made on the spot, or some eye-catching prop, such as giant toy soldiers as the thematic take-off for a Christmas theme. Chef and Partner John Lacritz is the former assistant manager of Neiman Marcus bakeries, so you can imagine the excellence of desserts. We might mention that the house specialty is the "almond crunch cake." And, if you haven't had it, you are missing out on one of Dallas' best desserts. Regular clients run by the company's Addison offices just to pick up a cake between parties.

Catering by Arthur has no set menus and prices, but Michelson quotes a starting price of about $17. per person for a buffet dinner, excluding service, rentals or other miscellany, and $24.50 and up for a seated dinner. For those in the market for a wedding caterer, Catering by Arthur does its own wedding cakes — which is no surprise considering the in-house baking talent. Another distinction is an associated company, **Simcha Catering** is one of Dallas' very few off-site kosher catering companies. Simcha handles a great many bar and bat mitzvahs, all with the style and professionalism of the Michelson/Lacritz team. *Please see the advertisement for* **Catering by Arthur** *on page 204.*

● **The Catering Company** is a three year venture of attorney-turned chef Greg Rankin. A former Mansion pastry chef with impressive stints elsewhere (such as the executive chef at The Buffalo Club), Greg decided to pursue catering full time. Small parties are a specialty, and yet he has done parties for up to 400. He also likes doing ethnic cuisine and experiments with innovative foods, such as lemon-grass chicken and Moroccan couscous, while shying away from Southwestern and Tex-Mex. Greg reports that business has certainly mushroomed, with work for political candidates, a few film companies and the popularity of his desserts. Chocolate-chocolate brownies and key lime tarts are just two of his deserts now being carried at Whole Food Markets and at other take-out counters around town.

■ **Catering by Don Strange** has name recognition throughout the state and the U.S. The San Antonio-based caterer keeps an office here, ably managed by Kathy Phillips. Emphasis is on large events, such as the Cattle Baron's Ball, which Don Strange catered nine of the Ball's eleven years, one of the gala's for the 1991 Texas Fest at Washington's Kennedy Center and the October 1992 State Fair Gala. While the image is of ranch-type food, the company has a much wider spectrum. There is a $3500. minimum for their services, which comes as a full per person package, including staff and rentals.

▲ **Chateau Magdalena Caterers.** Classic cuisine is the trademark of the established Chateau Caterers. Chef/Owner John Santi was Executive Chef at New York's Waldorf Astoria before starting a Dallas business with his wife, Fredericka. The Santis cater anything from luncheons for a dozen in your Cowboy Stadium Box, to gourmet dinner parties at your home, to corporate cocktail buffets for 2000 — all with style! The Santis report that they have been catering a great many weddings. Daughter Magdalena Santi has joined the business to supervise the corporate business. Dinners start at $18.

◆ **Chef's Shadow** has a split personality as a wholesale supplier of salads and baked goods to some of Dallas' best take-out shops and as a caterer. Owner Betty Ablon actually "backs up" a number of caterers with her specialties and handles a good number of corporate lunches. And what Betty will do happily for her clients is "drop off" catering, although she has superbly handled many a wedding and bar mitzvah. So, for those of you who are looking for food preparation with the finest ingredients, using your own help and finishing touches, this may be an exciting source. A chicken salad, accompanied by a vegetable ratatouille and one of her fabulous desserts can be had for about $9.50. This would be a great luncheon for friends, for the committee or for the office meeting!

▼ **City Market Catering Company.** City Market, the eat-in/eat-out restaurant in the Trammell Crow Center, has another persona in the food world. Kathy McDaniel, owner also of The Grape, has an ambitious catering business as well. A convenient downtown location is advantageous for corporate business and their savory food makes frequent appearances in the more food-conscious boardrooms. Being located in the midst of the Arts District, City Market also caters for the several non-profit organizations, including the neighboring Dallas Symphony. City Market specializes in very fresh foods, well-prepared by Chef Jennifer Forte, a graduate of the Culinary Institute of America and City Cafe's original chef.

● **the dani group** has created a special niche in mastering the large "off-site" catering sites with both the finest cuisine and exacting service. If hosting a spectacular party at the Dallas Museum of Art, where they are now the preferred caterer, or a large at-home wedding or celebration, the dani group would add the distinctive ingredient. The assurance of near-perfect execution may come, in part, from the principals' combined years of experience. David Mock, with a hotel food and beverage background, and former Plaza of the Americas, British-born chef Nick Barclay are a formidable duo, with admirable planning assistance from Tina Harlow. The litany of their accomplishments is impressive. They have catered, with some of Dallas' finest cuisine, for many of the city's most prestigious events — patron parties for the Crystal Charity Ball, the recent gala openings of the Catherine the Great exhibit and the Greer Garson Theatre, the October '92 Wildflower Festival at the LBJ Ranch beside the Perdanales River. The most recent and most impressive credential is the September

Hors d'Oeuvres

Smoked Canadian Salmon Croquettes
Roasted Lamb Loin Slices on Tortilla Chips with Guacamole
South American Empanadas with Spicy Beef
Chicken Roulade with Portabella Mushrooms on Black Bread

Cakebread Cellars Sauvignon Blanc 1991
Piper Sonoma Champagne Brut 1988

Dinner

Texas Gulf Crab Salad with
Red Chili Aioli and Arugula Pesto
on a bed of Peppered Zucchini and Squash

Cakebread Cellars Chardonnay 1990

Roasted Beef Tenderloin with
Cognac and Raisin Sauce
Nutted Wild Rice
Tomatoes with Spinach and Morels

Cakebread Cellars Cabernet Sauvignon 1989

Late Summer Field Greens with Oregon Blue Cheese
Stone Ground Mustard Dressing

A Celebration of Desserts

Brazilian Love Cake
Apple Tart
White and Dark Chocolate Tulip
with Green Peppercorn Ice Cream & Trio of Sauces

Piper Sonoma Champagne Brut 1988

Coffee

'93 "Celebration of the Americas" opening of the Hamon Building. It is difficult to conceive a more beautifully executed four course dinner for 850 guests. Beyond quality of cuisine, style and presentation, each of the above-mentioned events demonstrated the company's versatility of food genre from Czarist Russian or ranch elegant to American nouvelle. As always, the guests applaud the group's latest and finest event. Yet, there is always another great challenge and unique environment to master and menu to conceive. On the subject of challenges, we hope you will refer to the dani company's latest venture, Fit-Kit-Cuisine, which is discussed on page 84 under "Take-Out." The dani group is now preparing fitness foods with all the taste and style that you would want for a dinner party at home, not to mention as a convenience for very everyday fitness foods. Another new challenge and success is taking on all the special event catering for the Dallas Stars, our new hockey team. Our focus will soon be on a new sport and it is comforting to know that the VIP spectators can have special parties and outstanding cuisine to complement their evenings' athletic adventures.

But lest we leave the impression that the dani group caters only grand balls, we have enjoyed some of their most impressive dinners in the homes of many satisfied clients. The polished service and five-star cuisine are available for private parties in the intimacy of your home.
Please see the advertisement for the dani group on page 213.

■ **Darrie Hinson Catering & Co.** Owner Darrie Hinson is artist-turned caterer with an end-result that is visual theatre. Darrie, once chairman of the Greenhill School Art Department, started giving summer cooking lessons to kids in her home. Her reputation for style and good food grew so rapidly that she is now celebrating her 16th year catering to corporations and individuals. Understandably, her specialty is "the total table," a visual display incorporating food, theme, flowers and props, usually with an able assist from Grassroots talented floral designer, Rick Harris. Added to her artistic flair and sense of organization, Darrie Hinson employs local chefs to create luncheons that start at $8. and dinners that start about $18., although an elegant dinner would average in the mid $30. range. That possible menu could be a grilled hors d'oeuvres selection of lamb chops, her trademark pizza and potato skins, followed by a fabulous buffet of poached salmon, beef tenderloin brochette, vegetable primavera (a fresh vegetable confetti salad), Empire Bakery bread and a chocolate terrine for dessert.

▲ **Daryl's by Design** has been voted the most popular caterer in Dallas, by last year's People newspapers' poll — one who can flawlessly handle outstanding food, presentation and service for both large and small events, such as major celebrations and fancy corporate parties. There is, unquestionably, a sense of drama in his fantastic displays of food and flowers, inspirations for still lifes on canvas. Daryl has a litany of good clients. We see him frequently at Neiman Marcus events and at cocktail parties in the homes of our friends. We were happy to enjoy his tasteful and artistically arranged food at a recent party at the Hall of State. He likes to incorporate food ideas from the start of the party — to be evolved with the theme and the decor. He may suggest covering the buffet table with Balinese blankets and serving Indonesian food to treat your guests to a new experience. He is equally adept at doing amusing box lunches for the corporate jet. Receiving a proposal from Daryl Richardson is in itself impressive, and he is one caterer who breaks down the cost for every component. He quotes $14. a person as a starting point for a cocktail buffet. On another occasion, we received a proposal for an off-site buffet dinner for 600, complete with all rentals and staff for $50. per person, exclusive of beverages, which were supplied by the host.

Daryl owns his own facility for entertaining — the Dallas World Aquarium, the not-to-be-missed, spectacular West End facility, which is covered in more detail under "Special Sites."
*Please see the advertisement for the Daryl Richardson's **Dallas World Aquarium** on page 219.*

◆ **Ethel MacIntosh** has been preparing comforting food for now two generations of Dallasites who know and love her style, nostalgic of food served by mothers who cooked very well!!

▼ **Food Company** run by Shelly Barsotti and Andrea Whiteside Hagger has been a mainstay of Dallas entertaining for many years. Theirs is always outstanding food, leaning toward Southwestern, always well-prepared with the best of ingredients. Presentation is a strong point. Hors d'oeuvres are innovative, and tray and table displays of food, flowers and props are exceptional. Their young, attractive staff is part of the pleasant experience. On average, the buffet menus run about $22. per person and a seated dinner about $30. to $35., which could include hors d'oeuvres, an appetizer of polenta with fresh corn and home smoked salmon, an entree of roasted leg of lamb stuffed with garlic, sage and black olives, or grilled beef tenderloin on a bed of roasted peppers and onions, plus a sinful dessert, as mere examples of their always pleasing food. Their strong suit is the dinner party, but The Food Company is equally apt to be the caterer of choice for a major corporate reception at the Meyerson Symphony Hall or a community awards' dinner at the Hall of State. We personally enjoyed their food at two of Dallas' more spectacular weddings this year, one a seated dinner for about 250 people and the other an outdoor wedding for about 500 with varied and visually dramatic food stations.

● **Gil's Elegant Catering** is run by Belgian-born Mr. Gil and his food is reflective of his formal background. Presentations are outstanding, and his service and food always excellent. Mr. Gil has done a good many parties at the Hall of State, in private homes and for party planners. Recently, we enjoyed his catering at a high-profile North Dallas wedding, where the formality of his food was a perfect choice for the special day.

■ **GOURMETDALLAS.** Rollie Anne Blackwell's successful catering business has really taken off from its quietly but methodically planned beginning in 1985. Quoting the owner may be the best description that we can give of the company that seeks "... to provide interesting and creative cuisine, using the freshest quality ingredients in unusual and fun presentations.

At GOURMETDALLAS, we not only provide catering, but are a full service caterer, offering party decor, entertainment, flowers, service staff, rentals and go out of our way to find unique locations for a functions, including yachts, museums, private galleries, atriums, gardens and ballrooms."

Rollie Anne concentrates on creativity in every facet — from theme to food to arresting presentations. Her dinners can be small affairs for 25 or major productions for 2000. In between, she favors the parties for 100 to 200 where she has an opportunity to shine on presentation. Last year's Italian Renaissance theme for a client was wondrous with all the sumptuous suggestions of Florence or Venice in another era. Antique tables were draped with Fortuny-like fabrics, classical urns filled with flowers, and bounteous foods arranged in huge wooden bowls and a hand-painted backdrop were all reminiscent of an Italian master painting. Adding to the ambiance was the carefully selected menu and appropriate music. Lest we leave the impression that GOURMETDALLAS menus are only formal, a recent party on a boat on Lake Texoma provides an appropriate contrast. Thanks partly to a wide exposure through traveling, Rollie Anne can draw upon her travels to come up with endless themes — Latin, Russian or anything to vary the anticipation of her faithful clients. Rollie Anne also has a good team with Chef Carlos Araujo, able assistant Tonya Farrington and floral designer Randy Davis, with whom she often works in concert.

Please see the advertisement for GOURMETDALLAS on page 214.

▲ **L'Epicurian.** One of the best catering companies in town, L'Epicurian is co-owned by Roger Buret and Karen Cassady. Buret, French-born and charcuterie-trained, was a chef at New York's Côte Basque, and then at Marty's, where he established Marty's reputation for fabulous pâtes. Since 1983, Buret has catered for his own company and continued with his pâtés and terrines, available through L'Epicurian and at several retail outlets, including Marty's, the Wine Emporium and Simon David. Buret and Cassady have a very ardent clientele who appreciate their expertise, their use of the finest ingredients and the quality of their service and presentation. One of our recent parties included Buret's unsurpassed ballotin of salmon, chicken farci, rosemary roasted potatoes, and chocolate decadence cake. On another occasion, we fell in love with Buret's red pepper polenta as an accompaniment to a simple roasted chicken. For the important dinner party, or an event where the guests will be impressed with outstanding cuisine, we enthusiastically recommend L'Epicurian.

Cassady and Buret have other ventures important to the entertaining scene. They own **Dragon Street Dinner** in the Decorative District, where you can order for take-out fabulous box lunches containing their pâtés and excellent desserts. Dragon Street is also available for parties on weekends when it is normally closed. New this year is a gift basket service featuring the famous pâtés, great for corporate and Christmas gift-giving! Package prices are $35., $50. and $75.

◆ **Nancy Beckham**, former chef-owner of Brazos and Main Street News, is a familiar name both on the restaurant and the catering scene. Nancy will bring her chef's jacket and whisk to your home or party site to handle any number of guests. Her menus vary, from the Southwestern Brazos style to more eclectic offerings. Nancy's academic background was in design and performance, and a natural flair is revealed in her presentations and impromptu arrangements. We've been real fans ever since Nancy rescued a large party we were hosting, along with some friends, at a Deep Ellum venue that closed just two days prior to the scheduled party. We've enjoyed her creative cuisine for parties many times since — under less hectic circumstances. Starting menus without service are in the $15. to $20. range. When not catering, Nancy consults with restaurants.

▼ **Redwine Catering** is in an attractive McKinney Avenue location south of Knox Street that also serves as a facility for take-out. Ron Redwine is the event planner/business partner while chef duties go to Kerry Chace. Kerry, a Canadian native with serious training in Switzerland, was formerly with popular Parigi's Restaurant and is now creating simple but innovative food for the new venture. Ron oversees the arrangements and the important staffing of each party. If the take-out food is any indication — simple, well-prepared and very flavorful food with European and Oriental influences — the enterprise is a winner. As a postscript, there is something very comforting about being able to sample the cuisine of a catering company before a major commitment. The take-out shop is an interesting extension of their catering activities.

● **Silver Tray Catering & Outrageous Affairs** is a five-year success story. Owners Ron Timberlake and Tom Beene have impressed their clients with good food and a real sense of savoir faire. Theirs is a multi-faceted company that can provide the elegant dinner party for a few, a simply beautiful wedding, and

 mastermind a corporate party for 2000. To quote the owners, "celebrations come in all shapes and sizes" and they have helped folks successfully celebrate all of them. Silver Tray bought out Outrageous Affairs last year, giving them the added dimension of full party planing. Outrageous Affairs

functions as the Special Events Division of Silver Tray Catering. Business Partner Tom Beene and Executive Chef Ron Timberlake make a fabulous team. Tom has overseen some of the city's largest events, such as the 1993 State Fair Gala, which filled the Fair Park Coliseum for dinner, dancing and a Clint Black performance. Ron is a kitchen pro, having taught the catering business for a number of years. Together, they can conceptualize, execute and oversee a party of any size with the ease that comes from the organization behind the scenes. We first enjoyed their food for a tea in a Preston Hollow home, prompting the immediate inquiry, "Who is catering?"

The Silver Tray food has a showbiz quality to it, whether it is the perfectly executed luncheon for the office conference or an action station at a buffet, something they do particularly well. Buffet tables are a strong point, with clever and flavorful ideas, The shrimp dip is likely to be in a hollowed out loaf of bread or the table topiary edible! Presentations are a mosaic of baskets, gourds, greenery and flowers, all used to complete the artistic still-life backdrop for fresh and delicious food. One dazzler was a chocolate tree decorated with chocolate birds nests, filled with strawberries. Likewise, even simple dinner menus always have the unusual touches that distinguish their cuisine — delicate beggars' purses filled with poached salmon for a starter, followed by beef tender with rose-pistachio cream accompanied by bundles of blanched asparagus tied with leek bows. There is always the element of surprise and detail. Not surprisingly, the duo are perfectionists.

Please see the advertisement for **Silver Tray Catering & Outrageous Affairs** *on page 217.*

■ **Some Enchanted Evening** is a new catering company by returning-to-Dallas entrepreneur Phyllis Aceto. After several years back in her native New York where she both cooked and styled for Made in Heaven, one of

New York's and South Hampton's premier catering companies. Regional Italian cooking is her forte — including treasured family recipes — and she loves personal parties at home (without forgetting experiences with major galas). With many friends from her previous sojourn in Dallas, Phyllis expects to find a ready-made clientele.

▲ **Special Affairs Catering.** Owner Paul Jerabek is both caterer and celebration cake maker. Mainstay of the business is the fabulous cake selection that can be seen at his West Lovers Lane shop. We originally tracked down Special Affairs because we were so impressed with their stacked cake, decorated to resemble gift-wrapped packages, which had been a conversation piece at a birthday party. Only then did we realize the multiple dimensions of the business. Special Affairs is one of the Arboretum's recommended caterers and caters regularly for Junior League functions. We also noted his food at a recent Chanel/Crystal Charity Ball patron party. To complete the food scenario, Special Affairs does a take-out luncheon business from that same shop.

◆ **Spice of Life** is well-known on the catering circuit with full service catering. With the experience of 14 years, owner and chef Ricky Baldwine oversees a staff of chefs. Spice of Life can handle a luncheon for 10 or a corporate reception for 3000 with gusto. During the past year, there have been changes, with the accidental death of co-owner Jim Warburton and, now, a new business manager Ted Vottler, who will bring a new dimension to the business. Assisting are coordinator Veronica Olivera and wedding consultant Colleen Warburton. Spice of Life has its share of weddings and garden club and ladies luncheons. They are regulars at the major off-site facilities, such as the Hall of State and the Dallas Garden Center. Chef Baldwine personally oversees the kitchens for the Dallas Woman's Club.

▼ **Today's Gourmet.** Owner Cynthia Cathcart was treating Washington D.C.'s Texas State Society to barbecue and Tex-Mex before returning home to Texas some years ago to abandon politics and to take up catering full-time. Cynthia is always ready for a party and certainly sets the mood with costumed characters who hand deliver invitations right through to the last good-bye. She loves the labor-intensive details, like decorating cookies or luncheon baskets with flowers. We've loved any number of her parties, such as the Japanese-inspired birthday luncheon for a crowd. We are sorry to have missed the dress-up Academy Awards dinner and the Caribbean party with Calypso music and dancing. Holiday deliveries are a big part of Cynthia's business. The costumed pilgrims driving around on Thanksgiving delivering dinners are certainly from Today's Gourmet. Mother's Day breakfast is another specialty — and order early. If Santa comes to the door, he may be delivering an invitation. Lunches start at $20. and dinners start at $25.

● **Wendy Krispin Catering** has made a real impact on the Dallas party scene in just a year or so. Owner Wendy Krispin is a real pro in the trade, with years of previous experience with Chow, as Director of Catering for Simon David and with Daryl's by Design. A background in food styling and event planning round out her resumé. Her multiple talents add significant dimensions to her blossoming catering business. Wendy likes simple food with unique touches — with style that is important to clients like the Crystal Charity Ball, several Design District showrooms and high-profile regulars. Wendy has gotten raves from a number of weddings catered during the year, especially one at the Arboretum where guests delighted to the food stations of the couple's favorite dishes, including stir-fry in one location and quesadillas in another, all embellished with the Krispin flair for presentation. Another lakeside wedding featured cuisines representing the international backgrounds of both bride and groom. In price range, Wendy quotes $16. and up, per person, for cocktail party food and a similar starting point for a simple seated dinner. With so many friends in the community, coupled with her experience, we suspect that Wendy Krispin will be a catering name heard with increasing frequency.

Wendy has also refurbished the Dallas Design District space formerly occupied by Daryl's by Design, now renamed Krispin — the restaurant. This also means that the curious catering customer can sample from the lunch menu to help judge the quality of Wendy's cuisine. See also the listing under "Restaurants" in Chapter VII.
Please see the advertisement for **Wendy Krispin Catering** *&* **Krispin - the restaurant** *on page 221.*

■ **Vick's** is a recognizable name in Dallas for food and entertaining. Vick's clubs were downtown staples for business lunches long before sky-scrapers were topped with prerequisite private clubs. Vick Clesi, Jr. runs the family's restaurant on Greenville in Energy Square and oversees its catering business, still popular with business clientele. This is a sixty-year enterprise, making Vick's Catering perhaps the oldest catering company in Dallas.

▲ There are a number of other caterers who are adept at small dinners and luncheons. **Constance Muller**, several of whose meals we've enjoyed, gets high marks from discriminating clients. She has an artistic background, revealed with her plate and buffet presentations. Partners Ann King and Peggy Zbinden own **Just Delicious** and likewise cater many smaller parties. We've enjoyed their cocktail party food on numerous occasions. Another caterer and, coincidentally, sister of Ann King, is **Joan McIlyar**, in demand for her excellent box lunches, which make frequent appearances at committee meetings and athletic events. Another duo, **Jean Ann Cheatham** and **Betsy Lawson** have been making a name for themselves in catering corporate lunches and small dinner parties. **Très Bon Catering**, run by Don Ardoin, is one of the newer catering companies of which we take note. Don's parties, including several gallery openings, have been getting applause from those acquainted with his efforts. All of these caterers have real fans.

◆ *And do remember*, a number of chefs, delicatessens and take-out establishments, mentioned in other sections of the book, also cater or deliver party food and trays.

For your convenience, there is also a "Telephone Directory," listing the sources by chapter, which begins on page 247.

Restaurants and take-outs that cater

The tendency for restaurants and even hotels to supplement or complement their businesses with outside catering is commonplace in this city. Often, it is easy dealing with a restaurateur/caterer who has a both equipment and staff to handle outside events. Sometimes, these are restaurants you already know and feel comfortable in dealing with them, particularly if you are not a regular with a catering company. In addition to the restaurants that cater, many of the take-out shops likewise cater. Regretfully, space does not allow the listing of all restaurants and take-out shops that cater. We are listing a few that have outstanding reputations and experience.

▼ **Arnold's Texas Bar-B-Q** takes its barbecue on the road — to the many cook-offs where they are frequent winners and to your home or other site for an authentic touch of our Western roots. The food is great, and Arnold's can add authenticity and decor to the party with a few Texas-type side shows, Western props and outrageous characters. Based on 100 guests, Arnold's can do three meats for $11.50 per person, with salads and garnishes. Arnold's has been the caterer of choice for the annual Hockaday Parents' Club fund-raiser, done in Western style, and had been the caterer of choice for Neiman Marcus back when the annual Fortnights brought celebrities to Texas. Service is also the key — plus a large dash of showmanship to make the barbecue an experience as well. As owner Arnold Sanchez puts it, "Our catering has success because we offer excellent food, an interesting theme and an honest desire to please our customers." Arnold Sanchez has just opened **Silverado City** as a private party facility to carry out his Western themes. See "Special Sites" in Chapter VII.

● **Blue Mesa Grill** in Village on the Parkway has one of the more ambitious and appreciated catering enterprises. Their Southwestern food with

a Sante Fe twist is only the starting reason for the popularity. Blue Mesa makes numerous suggestions for its catering menus, one choice being more mouth-watering than the last, creating indecision. Their Sante Fe Celebration includes Garlic Shrimp on Angel Hair Pasta with Goat Cheese Cream Sauce. The Southwestern Gala menu includes Southwest Barbecued Duck, Mesquite Grilled Cornish Hen, or Black Bean Goat Cheese Ravioli. The Blue Mesa Dinner Party sets the tone with Duck Taquitos for an appetizer. Desserts, such as the Chocolate Bread Pudding and Jack Daniels Pecan Pie, are extraordinary. It's not difficult to understand the success of their catering department. Even catering off-site, Blue Mesa brings its atmosphere along. Blue Mesa will be happy to orchestrate the entire party, providing everything from rentals to bartending, entertainment, decorations and valet parking. See the listing for Blue Mesa Grill under "Restaurants" in ChapterVII. A visit to the restaurant is a great test case for the dinner that can be served in your home.
Please see the advertisement for **Blue Mesa Grill** *on page 208.*

■ **Caliente Ranch Grill & Cantina** is a corporate sibling to the above Blue Mesa, owned by Liz and James Baron's de Nada Restaurants. While Blue Mesa leans toward Sante Fe, Caliente is firmly Texas ranch cooking at its best with everyone's favorite Tex-Mex specialties that can be catered at your home or off-site location. Specialties include mesquite grilling, such as hickory smoked ribs, brisket and chicken, great fajitas and classic Tex-Mex. Caliente has its own dedicated audience, particularly among the young crowd and confirmed Texans. Caliente can handle a seated dinner for 50, a reception for 500 and the perfect lunch to impress the out-of-town business clients. Their most popular party is the Fajita Party — fajitas and all the side orders for $7.95 a person. Other popular menus include a Quesadilla Party (their signature item and our absolute favorite) at $6.95, a Barbecue Ranch Party and a Tex-Mex Fiesta. Catering prices include colorful Fiestaware, flatware and napkins! The catering team often uses the talents of flower maestro Wesley Lujan who has winning ways with native flowers and casual assemblages to enhance buffet tables and the overall decor.

▲ **Colter's Bar-B-Q** is a favorite among barbecue fans. Colter's will do a barbecue buffet, including delivery and set-up, for $12.95 per person for 50 to 99 people. Full service catering can be had for any number from 25 to 1000 and even more. For 100 guests, the full-service price is approximately $9.95 depending on the variation and selection of meats (chicken, ham, sausage, beef, ribs, etc.), salads and the addition of mainly cobblers and pies for desserts.

◆ **Deli News**, the multi-faceted restaurant/private facility/take-out/catering business in the Crescent has been written up under the "Take-Out" section. As part of their food-blitz, the Russian proprietors have taken up catering as well.

● **Loma Luna**, of the restaurant of the same name, features Sante Fe style Mexican food. When they catered the 1992 Cattle Baron's Ball, visibility for their catering business escalated, and now the business is expanding to a ranch just north of town in Prosper for private parties. Meanwhile, their in-town catering might include an hors d'oeuvres menu of grilled shrimp, quesadillas and chimichongas for about $13. per person, with a $75. set-up fee for the outdoor grill. A 20 percent service charge covers party help, with the addition of each bartender at $75. Buffet dinners, featuring fajitas or grilled chicken, run from $10. to $15., excluding dessert. Incidentally, Loma Luna has a chuck wagon for added theme, which can be rented for $250.

■ **Marty's**. Most serious of the gourmet food shops that cater is Marty's, always a standout contender in the field of food — and even more so at the moment with a new team in place in the kitchen. Part of the new culinary team are Catering Director Warren Farmer, Chef Jeff Worthington and Food Manager Karen Joyce, who together have put new emphasis on catering. Marty's already has a built-in and appreciative audience. In years past, catering has been geared to the lovely small dinner party at home — and this is still the major part of their catering business, but the scope is definitely broadening. Recently, Marty's has catered several large events, including a lunch at Children's Medical Center for 2,000. We'll also put in a good word for their breakfast catering. Now, there is the opportunity to look forward to those early morning meetings, or surprise the work-out group with an occasional well-earned reward. *Please see the advertisement for Marty's on page 218.*

▲ **Newport's**. Fish-fanciers are usually well-acquainted with the background of owner Jack Baum, owner of the original Hampton's seafood market and restaurant near the Farmer's Market and later in Preston Center. With this experience, he brings a solid background in knowing the seafood product and its best sources — always a great recommendation. As caterers, Newport's can be counted on to stage some of the best clambakes and luaus. Chef Travis Henderson can prepare a real feast for your guests, at your home or other site, with a lobster "clambake" ranging from $35. to $65. per person. This could include cold oysters, clams and mussels on ice and the entire crustacean fantasy — not a bad treat for a special occasion or for nostalgia of the Northeast. A colorful luau — a popular theme at the moment and always in vogue for the summer — costs $20. to $40. per person, excluding rentals. Newport's and Sam's share the same ownership, and so Sam's Catering Director, Laura Boozer, will lend her expertise to the occasion. *Please see the advertisement for Newport's on page 215.*

◆ **Sam's Cafe** has always met the catering needs of their devoted clients, many of them neighbors in the Crescent complex. Now, with the addition of a second Sam's Cafe in Preston Center, Sam's will be even busier on the off-site catering scene, taking their food to any location, from a pre-concert party at Starplex to your Labor Day lakehouse party for friends. Sam's Southwestern food, always served with style and flair, can be made as casual or elegant as

the host and hostess desires, to suit the ambiance of patio party for the newly-weds-to-be or the party for the law firm summer recruits. For the rehearsal dinner or birthday party, Sam's can dress up the occasion with all the embell-ishments — fancier menu, decorations, and entertainment. Experienced Catering Director Laura Boozer brings to her position a wonderful "black book" of sources to make the occasion unique. The cocktail menu is sufficiently mouth-watering to plan an immediate party — choices such as shrimp tamales, spicy crawfish cakes, assorted quesadillas and fajitas — and all at reasonable prices. A four course dinner including an appetizer, an entree, such as grilled chicken with black bean relish, and one of their fabulous desserts, such as the cinnamon bunuelo served with seasonal fruits and warm vanilla sauce, comes to about $20. A mere $1. per person includes the colorful fiesta ware, glass-ware and cutlery. Incidentally, the Sam's Cafes also have a "Send for Sam's" delivery available, if your party should be impromptu.
Please see advertisement for **Sam's Cafe** *on page 215.*

▲ **Sonny Bryan's Barbecue.** In the realm of barbecue, the name of Sonny Bryan has instant recognition. The new owners of the 80 year old Dallas institution have expanded into "big time" catering, and will do both full and "drop off" catering. A per person charge for a meal with two or three meats, beans, potato salad, bread and fried pies will run under $8. For full catering and a minimum of 50 people, Sonny Bryan's will present the food in chafing dishes and provide all set-up and supplies, adding $30. per helper for a four hour minimum. A bartender is $45. for the first three hours. Otherwise, for a $20. fee, Sonny Bryan will drop off and set up your order.

◆ Other restaurants that cater include **Casa Domenguez** and **Uncle Julio's** for Tex-Mex, and **Deep Ellum Cafe**, which began its existence as a catering company and has maintained its toehold in the arena. **Five Star Catering** is part of Tony's Wine Warehouse and Bistro, which has become a favorite for bistro food. Fortunately, their cuisine can be enjoyed *chez vous.*

▼ Meanwhile, do not overlook the many Take-Out establishments that cater — beyond merely providing drop-off services. Please refer to the write-ups of **City Cafe to Go, Goodies from Goodman, Kathleen's Art Bakery** and **Pasta Plus**, as well as the delicatessens under "Take-Out."

a check list for caterers

❑ FORMAT OF EVENT
   dinner, brunch, tea, cocktail party

❑ THEME
   while not necessary, this element will influence the menu,
   decor and entertainment and, perhaps, even the place

❑ PLACE
   home or off-site

❑ FOOD
   type of menu — Southwestern, nouvelle, etc.
   menu selection
   hors d'oeuvres — what and how many per person
   meal — number of courses, how to be served:
      buffet, plated or butler passed
      presentation of plate or buffet
      tasting, if the party is large or the caterer
      is new to you

❑ BEVERAGES
   reception — what drinks, quantity and brands
   wines with dinner — selection, amount, how to be poured
      supplied by the host or the caterer

❑ SERVICE
   ratio of bartenders and waiters to guests
   extra service for kitchen or other location

❑ RENTALS, IF NEEDED
   tables, chairs — size and style
   dinnerware and glassware — style
   linens — color and size, undercloth, if needed
   additional serving equipment
   number of guests to a table

❑ TABLE DECORATIONS
   responsibility of host or caterer

❑ ADDITIONAL CONSIDERATIONS
   car parkers
   music or entertainment

❑ EXTRAS
   floor plan
   table to hold place cards or for check-in, where applicable
   coat rack, if needed

❑ FINANCIAL TERMS
   cost per guest
   additional costs of service, taxes, etc.
   written proposal

Dallas has party planners and party designers who rate with the best in the country. The city's reputation for great entertaining, as we have previously noted, is legendary — and much of it thanks to the creativity of the numerous individuals who have specialized in the fine art of creating drama and fantasy. Essentially, party planners conceive and orchestrate events to provide a host or organization with pizzazz and impact. With their expertise, they select specific talents and resources to best execute their ideas. Some have their own in-house staffs for assistance in the overall concept and coordination and, perhaps, even for design, decor and lighting.

Whether party planner or uniquely designer, all may help with suggestions about the other aspects of the party, anything from invitation design to big name entertainment. These talented and experienced individuals can create the setting and orchestrate the details that will make the difference between an ordinary and a memorable event.

Planners and Designers

▲ **Affairs Extraordinaire** is a young business that has rapidly gained the attention of the party planning community. When faced with starting a new enterprise, owner Gloria Solomon opted to do what she did best — plan parties! With a reputation of hostess *par excellence*, she utilized her talents to plan for others. Now dozens of young people benefit from her creativity and organization in planning bar mitzvahs and bat mitzvahs and, more recently, scores of weddings. Private and corporate parties are part of her expertise as well.

◆ **Bill Reed Decorations.** Bill Reed has been in the party planning business for many years and can be credited with doing memorable stagings for debutante and charity balls. He has the creativity — and the inventory after such a long career — to put together almost any conceivable theme. Bill Reed also rents his props to other party planners and caterers, and his Fair Park area warehouse may be the closest we have to a Hollywood prop shop. It is a real fantasy-land and a historical tribute to parties of the past and his role in them.

▼ **Gale Sliger Productions** is credited with so many recent extravaganzas, one more creative than the last, that it is difficult to keep track. With theatre-trained partner Jim Monroe, event impresario Gale Sliger conceives, designs and executes the most original and memorable parties, balls, weddings and charity extravaganzas. They've assembled a good crew of talent and resources and a warehouse of accessories to back up their magic wand. We've been awed by Carnival-themed birthday parties, Russian-themed Opera Balls, Renaissance-themed Museum Balls, dozens of memorable debutante balls and even a backyard party or two. Gale has also masterminded some of the most spectacular weddings, including a large-scale wedding at the Meyerson last summer and several at the Dallas Museum

of Art. Dallas is still taking about one June outdoor wedding designed and executed by the Sliger team. If the bride is cherishing memories of her storybook wedding, Gale was the Fairy Godmother. The pristine white tents, gloriously decorated with vines, twinkle lights and an abundance of summer flowers, only gave the first hint of the ambiance of the nuptial setting. Incidentally, they have started doing all their flowers in-house. Gale and Jim can assure you that all will run flawlessly, with never a fret to the host and hostess. This is a credit to the tireless details that are executed behind the scene and a real expertise in knowing what will work. Just a tour through Gale's meticulous warehouse conveys a message. No wonder the company functions like clockwork. It is part of their everyday organization. We have worked with Gale and Jim on a number of occasions and can attest to the creativity and the originality of their projects. The real bonus is the pleasurable experience in dealing with the Gale Sliger team, all of whom are pros.
Please see the advertisement for **Gale Sliger Productions** *on page 220.*

● **Jed Mace** developed a specialty for party design and concept from his background as interior designer *par excellence*. His design projects have been a mainstay through the years with the Junior League and Crystal Charity Ball and for his favorite clients' family weddings. Recent extravaganzas have been the transformation of the Fair Park Coliseum into a dramatic forum for the '93 State Fair Gala and knock-em-dead staging for Clint Black, the performer of the evening. For many years he has designed the annual Crystal Charity Ball, and the '92 "A Southern Christmas" at the Loews Anatole Hotel was memorable. Understandably, he has legions of friends and admirers.

■ **Kaleidoscope Decor** is an offspring of Kaleidoscope, Inc., a full service "destination management company," successfully run by Betty Calloway for 17 years. Now, the next generation, Shelly Calloway Orsinger and Sue Calloway, are overseeing an offshoot directed toward private parties, charity events and prop rentals — all backed up with the experience, full time staff and 20,000 square feet inventory of parent **Kaleidoscope, Inc.** Kaleidoscope Decor already has kudos in executing the decor for TACA's 1992 Grand Hotel featuring Tommy Tune at the Meyerson and the 1993 and 1994 Cattle Baron's Balls. Added to the list are fund-raisers for Ursuline, Jesuit and SMU and more than a handful of deb and charity parties around town. Kaleidoscope excels at Southwestern motifs, having the city's largest inventory to add to the spirit of the Old West. Kaleidoscope Decor is full-service in its new thrust, from invitations, with their own in-service designer, to full execution.

▲ **Life's a Party**. We were happy to make the acquaintance recently of attractive Patty Traub Menter who has been overseeing party arrangements for more than six years now. Her specialties are bar and bat mitzvahs, birthdays and anniversaries. Patty has carved a niche in murder mystery parties, quite the rage at the moment. With her party savvy, we suspect she will be well-versed with themes as they come into vogue.

◆ **Liland's Special Event Productions**. With a background as a floral designer and the experiences of countless weddings and parties, John Liland and his sister-in-law, Delene Bell, have launched a full-scale event business to better serve their growing clientele. Through years in business, Liland has accumulated some of the city's nicest prop inventory, especially cut-out scenery, another indication of the quality and direction of his work. The 1992 Idlewild Ball, introducing the year's debutantes, is an example of the beautiful props used by Liland. A backdrop of cut-out, art nouveau panels, fronted with balustrades and dripping with the look of wisteria, provided a courtly staging for the annual, prestigious event.

▼ **Party & Event Designers** relies on 30 years of experience with Howard Eckart at the helm. Howard was a well-regarded Dallas florist before broadening his business design to include the total ambiance of an event. Obviously, the floral component of his work remains a strong element of the company's extensive work, enjoyed by brides and party givers. Recently, we heard tales of the fabulous wedding Howard created at a near-by ranch, truly the stuff dreams are made of and, in this case, made into reality for the bride.

● **Russell Glenn Floral and Event Design**. With increasing frequency, proprietor Rusty Glenn designs the entire party, not solely the floral components, although he frequently works in conjunction with the party planners and designers mentioned in this section. Rusty has a background in fine arts and utilizes his artistry in conceptualizing and executing large-scale events. He excels at overseeing complete visual details of weddings and deb balls and, instantly, we can think of smashing examples of each, such as one of

1993's loveliest summer weddings and a deb ball a few years earlier for the same bride. We are also happy to know that we are sharing his talents with Fort Worth. This year, he will be designing the Steeplechase Ball, one of that city's major debutante cotillions. To appreciate the range of Rusty's talents, please read the entry for Russell Glenn Floral Design under "Flowers" in Chapter VIII. *Please see advertisement for **Russell Glenn Floral Design** on page 218.*

■ **Steve Kemble Event Design**. Party and event planner Steve Kemble has had a meteoric rise on the Dallas event planning scene in the last three years — after several years of behind the scenes groundwork in public relations, political campaigns and promotions for the Dallas Chamber of Commerce's Convention Bureau. As a result of his experiences with the city, he knows its area well and has made contacts in other cites, where he exports his event talents frequently. In fact, Steve is equally at home planning parties in Atlanta or Washington, D.C. as in Dallas. As an example, the accompanying photo was taken at a corporate President's dinner at a Boston hotel overlooking the Boston harbor. Steve uses off-site facilities, such as the Hall of State and the Science Place, with ease and imagination and works with caterers, florists and other specialists, to use his words, " in the role of general contractor."

He is in demand for parties and charities, such as FOCAS, the Weekend to Wipe Our Cancer, and Easter Seal's "Lights, Camera and Action." (We, for one, ran right down to the Fairmont Hotel to see the balloon Eiffel Tower for an "April in Paris" party — one of Steve's light-hearted additions to the annual FOCAS party featuring Dallas chefs.) Steve has a lot of "show biz" to contribute to events, everything from conceptualizing an in-town Western Town for one recent

event, to small but effective ideas for others, such as tuxedo-wearing strawberries for a dessert, to the fuse-like tube invitation that created the dynamic anticipation of another event. You can be certain that Steve will come up with something that will add impact to the theme and the occasion.

One of the greatest accolades from his peers is chairing — for its inaugural and now its second year — the annual fund-raiser staged by his fellow professionals in Meeting Planners International. Steve Kemble is Dallas' greatest cheerleader and his vivacity is contagious. As a result, his clients know in advance that his parties will be smashing successes.
*Please see the advertisement for **Steve Kemble Event Design** on page 206.*

▲ **Winn Morton** is a dean among designers. Fortunately for all us Dallasites, University Park-born Winn Morton returned to Dallas after a successful Broadway and television career as a set and costume designer.

The Parsons School of Design graduate designed for such shows as "Shenandoah," "Where's Charlie" and the Guy Lombardo Productions. Spectacular costumes for the Ringling Brothers Circus are also among his credits. In more recent years, Winn designed the 75th Lady Bird Johnson Birthday at the Crescent, the star-studded AIDS Benefit at the Loews Anatole, a stunning Fern Ball for the Dallas Museum, a memorable Phantom of the Opera Ball for The Dallas Opera, the Cattle Baron's Ball and so many more! Suffice it to say, Winn is in demand for events like the Texas Tycoon Gala and the Mayor's Ball.

We loved his March '89 costume retrospective at the Trammell Crow Center Pavilion, an accolade to a fabulous career. Annually, Winn has created the costumes for the Tyler Rose Festival, and his designs the 1993 Ball, with both stage set and costumes, was outstanding. With an 1870's theme set in four great cities — Paris, Vienna, New York and St. Petersburg — Winn was able to draw on a full range of his best design talents. Once having worked with Winn, many a debutante is anxious for him to set the scene for her romantic wedding. We were particularly impressed with a '93 outdoor wedding, one of the city's more spectacular. One tent, luxuriant with tree and live love birds, accommodated the service. The reception tent was breath-taking with its draped ceiling of blue fabric and ribbons and focal point of painted trellis, which was repeated on the dancefloor below. Grapevine chandeliers and silk-covered tables overlaid with *point d' esprit* were only some of the additional elements. What a sight for the guests and memories for the bride and groom!
*Please see the advertisement for **Winn Morton Designs** on page 205.*

◆ **Wolf & Company.** Owner and impresario Peter Wolf has been a vital component of the creative event scene in Dallas for many years. His expertise led him to multi-media and other productions in recent years, and away from the Dallas party scene. We were so happy to savor his return two years ago at a fanciful Sherwood Forest deb ball, one of the most splendid in some time. It was nostalgia for those who recall the many debutante cotillions, charity balls and private parties he orchestrated through the years.

▼ **Yellow Rose Touring & Special Events,** like Kaleidoscope, started out providing transportation and tours for city visitors. Through handling that facet of the business, owner Dorrit Turner has learned the city inside-out and has launched a full-fledged event business with estimable credits among the business community. Yellow Rose events increasingly reach into the non-profit community, specifically as sponsors and organizers of the annual SPCA Mardi Gras fund-raiser. Another of their community events is the "Dallas 100" awards to recognize the fastest growing companies in the Metroplex. Yellow Rose's forte is showing Dallas at its best.

party planners and social secretarial services

● **Party Service.** There was a time when Ann and Jim Draper, then proprietors of Party Service, coached every Dallas debutante, and coordinated the entire Dallas social "season" and scores of weddings and parties. As most Dallasites then knew, rules for "the season" were established and our children grew up knowing their social "p's and q's." Sandra Dingler has been the owner of Party Service for a few years now and continues to plan the private parties and weddings of the Drapers' former clients, as the service has always done. She has also gone on to make many new conquests in the event arena, now handling corporate and out-of-town events, based on a rapidly-established reputation. Party Service has reported on its more recent activities, including parties for clients in Los Angeles, St. Louis and Houston, and even a major fund-raiser for the children's cancer fund in Houston's Astrodome. Party Service will oversee everything from guest lists to caterer selection and hiring the band. One of the real services that can be provided is access to the extensive sources carefully cultivated through the years. If there is a talent to do it, Sandy will know about it! Party Service has also become more active in its subscription calendar for all the city's social and charity events, a must for those scheduling activities. While Party Service may be devoting less time to social secretarial work, their invitation business continues strong. Please see their listing also under "Invitations."

■ **R.S.V.P.** will also be happy to direct any and all aspects of your social projects. R.S.V.P. owner Barbara Paschall, an ex-deb herself, orchestrates both the Idlewild and Symphony debutante seasons. And, through her intense involvement with the deb seasons, Barbara knows the young set and their preferences in entertaining and being entertained. Her office oversees a good many parties and weddings for clients, also relying on her reliable sources for everything from invitations to florists to photographers. R.S.V.P. also keeps a community calendar, so if you are planning a large charity event or a wedding, we recommend before going any further, that you check with R.S.V.P. to find out what is already scheduled on the city's social calendar.

entertaining for a cause

Raising money for charities by staging events is a fine art in Dallas, and the charities involved gain far more than dollars in the process. These fund raisers become the vehicle for gaining community visibility and attracting others to their cause. We've often mused that the balls, luncheons, auctions, rodeos and more are also good for the city's economy, and for the caterers, party planners and designers who have the opportunity to showcase their talents before large audiences. Many of the volunteers who work on and chair these events could successfully run large corporations, so demanding is the work involved. Some of them have now gone on to use their expertise for a changing community scene..

▲ **Community Connection** is the creative idea of two very accomplished Dallas community leaders who, between them, have forty years of experience in chairing major events, including the Crystal Charity Ball and the Junior League Ball, and who have sat on countless community boards, most of which raise funds through events. Recognizing that, in today's world, the volunteer who can devote full energy to fund-raisers is rare, partners Gail Madden and Linda McFarland have stepped in to fill the gap. So considerable is their flair for organization and knowledge of the Dallas community that their event planning business has spilled into the private sector as well. Increasingly, corporations are utilizing them as outside event planners for both corporate functions and seminars.

◆ A number of the city's public relations specialists plan events for corporations and for charities, or will add their own expertise in the formative stages. There are a special few, such as Julia Sweeney of **Julia Sweeney and Associates**, Martha Tiller of **Martha Tiller & Company** and Brooke Stollenwerck and Terry Van Willson of **Resource 3**, who have a great deal of savvy in helping organizations, corporations and individuals maximize their audiences and visibility. These are the pros who see a "big picture" and know the city's resources and audiences well. Frequently, they are able to assist charities just by knowing what will be appealing to potential supporters and to the press.

VII
The Right Place
hotels, clubs, restaurants, & specials sites

There are occasions, whether by sheer size or appropriateness of event, for which an off-site location is the best venue for either the special private or corporate party and, of course, for the charity endeavor. It can be a simple and casual graduation fiesta given at a Mexican restaurant, or as grandiose as a sixtieth birthday celebration at the Adolphus' French Room. It could be an impressive corporate dinner in the Great Hall of Fair Park's Hall of State or a debutante ball at a country club.

Overall, as a guideline to entertaining away from home, there should be several considerations — budget, size and ambiance, to name only a few — and each should be weighed according to it's significance to you, the party-giver. These factors can be applied to all forms of entertaining, but particularly to entertaining that is away from home and subject to less control by the hostess.

Obviously, the budget is a major consideration, and a factor in assessing whether you want to consider a party at a non-home site. In some cases, the party away from home may actually cost less than the party at home, if the home party requires large rentals, catering, parkers and decorations. Last year, the author gave similar-sized luncheons for two brides a week apart. One was at home, a usual preference for the author, the other at a restaurant with a private room. On a comparative basis, the at-home luncheon for twenty four guests was more expensive. The

author has a well-stocked home for entertaining. Nonetheless, there were rentals of outdoor tables and chairs as well as serving help, parkers and flowers for the house and tables. None of these were additional expenses at the restaurant. The cost of a lovely restaurant lunch with wine and service was actually less. While the author prefers the personal and relaxed ambiance of her own home setting, the two events so close together were an easy price comparison.

On the other hand, if your event is an evening event, where there will likely be larger consumption of alcoholic beverages and where you have greater options for controlling the cost for food and service, the expenses could be less in a home setting. Alternate spaces can also be expensive in terms of decor, in addition to beverages.

The size of a party is another factor in determining the location. Few of us can accommodate a large crowd at home, although some of us can utilize the out-of-doors when the variable Texas weather co-operates. Not to be overlooked is the convenience of using a venue where the services and expertise provide enticing options for the hostess. There is also the subjective factor of finding a festive site which allows the party giver to experiment with a new theme or ambiance.

hotels

The city is fortunate to have outstanding hotels with excellent chefs and facilities, well suited for large events such as charity balls and luncheons, large weddings, bar mitzvahs and corporate meetings. Not only do the hotels' have varying facilities for events, they have the experienced and full-time staff to execute the demands of large events. Not to be overlooked, some of the hotels have more intimate spaces that work exceptionally well for personal entertaining, such as the smaller rooms at **The Mansion on Turtle Creek** and at **The Adolphus Hotel**, to name only two.

▲ **The Adolphus Hotel** is always on the list of nationally-recognized hotels — by such discriminating publications as CONDÉ NAST TRAVELER, which in 1992 selected the hotel as one of the United States' top ten hotels. Dallas' grand turn-of-the-century hotel, built by beer-baron Adolphus Busch, is one of the city's most elegant facilities for entertaining — from the opulent French Renaissance Grand Ballroom with 5,000 square feet, seating 350 for seated dinners and more for receptions, wedding and balls, to the cozy French Room lounge accommodating 25 or 30 for a seated tea. A new addition to the Ballroom level space, adding another 4500 square feet, is The Century Room, a great joy to those who want to use The Adolphus for larger balls and wed- · dings. We've enjoyed momentous balls there, including a deb ball that utilized the entire first floor and Ballroom level as well, as did one Christmas-themed TACA ball a few years back. The hotel's elegance was the perfect setting for the Italian-themed '93 Dallas Opera Ball. On a more intimate scale, one friend has an annual, festive Christmas tea for her friends there, and the lovely, landmark hotel with its decorations provide all the ambiance that is necessary. And what bride-to-be has not assessed the richly-appointed hotel without envisioning her storybook wedding. Centerpiece of the hotel (and one of Dallas' and the nation's premier restaurants) is the exquisite, fresco-ceilinged French Room, available for luncheons, dinners and receptions when not open to the public. A malachite-colored marble floor and an updated menu, christened "neoclassic," are part of recent changes. Some of our fondest memories are of special events at the Adolphus. Their extraordinary staff and Executive Chef Kevin Garvin will make the planning and experience a pleasure. We enthusiastically recommend the Adolphus for every event. The location alone will make it significant.

Count on dinners costing about $35. per person in the ballroom and meeting rooms and about $50. in the French Room. Lunches are about $25. The sumptuous lobby tea is $15. and is a gracious way to entertain out of-town guests and brides-to-be. Gratuities and alcoholic beverages are additional. See an additional listing on the award-winning French Room under "Restaurants." *Please see advertisement for* **The Adolphus Hotel's French Room** *on page 218.*

◆ **Hotel Crescent Court.** Superior service and quality distinguish Rosewood Corporation's Hotel Crescent Court. The monochromatic, art and flower-embellished Great Hall gives immediate importance to events and parties. The ambiance on entering, graciousness of space and exemplary cuisine under Executive Chef Jim Mills make the Hotel Crescent Court special to your guests. A 3000 square foot ballroom provides luxurious dining space for 250, and 350 for receptions. Two smaller rooms and the 1200 square foot glass walled Garden Terrace, overlooking a courtyard, are available as pre-function rooms or for smaller luncheons, dinners and parties. Incidentally, there is also a small wineroom that will seat 14 guests for very special dinners. The Conservatory, the hotel's top-rated restaurant, is one of the city's most attractive settings for a sumptuous private dinner party.

▼ **Fairmont Hotel,** "a Texas kind of a hotel" according to hotel literature, is used extensively for personal and corporate entertaining and for charity events, particularly with its two grand ballrooms each accommodating 1200 and more for balls and luncheons. The versatility of the downtown Fairmont Hotel is another feature. The Banquet Level Gold Room can accommodate about 400 and some 20 other rooms on both the Banquet and Terrace Levels can seat anywhere from 20 to 200, or provide overflow Ballroom space. The nightclub-style Venetian Room, which can accommodate another 400, and the award-winning Pyramid Restaurant are both available on "dark nights." The hotel's catering staff, under Executive Chef Roger Hyde, gets high marks for professionalism. The food is always outstanding, even for large numbers. Food and beverage prices are in line with other luxury hotels, but selections are so broad that working within a budget is realistic.

● **Doubletree Hotel at Lincoln Center.** Poised at the carrefour of LBJ Freeway and Dallas North Tollway, the Doubletree Lincoln is at the epicenter of Dallas' population, making it one of the area's most convenient hotels. Sleekly modern and attractive, the hotel has a drive-up, courtyard appeal that adds instant caché to your entertaining events. This, coupled with one of the area's largest and most gracious lobby spaces, also confirms immediate impressions. A raised lobby area, surrounded by columns and planters would make an ideal afternoon tea or reception area. The ballroom, like the entire hotel, has recently been renovated, and the nicely scaled and wood-paneled foyer is now embellished with significant chandeliers. The 9300 square foot Lincoln Ballroom, including dance floor and orchestra, is perfect for 650 guests, making it one of the most comfortable-sized rooms for charity events, wedding receptions, proms and bar mitzvahs. The ballroom can seat up to 900 for luncheons and up to 1200 for receptions. Charity mavens should take note of the series of connecting rooms opposite the ballroom, perfect for simultaneous auctions and activities. Not to be overlooked is the hotel's distinctive **Crockett's** restaurant, which is available for private parties on Sundays and Mondays. We've enjoyed a fabulous wine society dinner there as well as an AIWF champagne tasting, both on a Sunday evening.

■ **Four Seasons Resort and Club**, in Las Colinas, is our close-to-town 400 acre resort that hosts a great many Corporate 500-type conferences. At the same time, the hotel has made friends among the neighboring business community who also look to the hotel for social and business entertaining. Fine food is a given. German-born Executive Chef Bernard Mueller enjoys recognition, and pastry chef Randy Gehman is a Culinary Olympics winner. The hotel will benefit from the addition of Clive O'Donoghue, former co-owner of the much-missed and prestigious Actuelle Restaurant, as Director of Food and Beverage. Spaces for private parties are comfortable and very well-appointed indeed. There is the Wine Room for groups of eight to 18 off the Cafe on the Green, and two comfortable small ballrooms for groups of 200 to 300. The Gallery, seating about 40, is perfect and pretty for rehearsal dinners and parties with friends. The Byron Nelson Room in the adjoining Sports Club is available every evening and weekends for private entertaining, plus a pre-function area and covered terrace for expansion of numbers. Decor all through the hotel is tasteful and luxurious with fine wall coverings and patterned table skirts to armorial plates and botanicals in the Cafe, for example, and elegant fabric wall coverings in the smaller ballrooms. Slated for Spring '94 completion is a party-perfect pavilion, overlooking the well-tended greens and home of the Byron Nelson Classic, *just* for private parties. (Dallas' own Tavern on the Green with a more casual air!) Nearby will be a large, free-form pool with lush and expansive surroundings that we imagine will be the setting for some of the area's best pool parties.

▲ **Grand Kempinski Hotel**, on Dallas North Parkway north of Beltline, is another hotel with great entertaining potential. Its 20,000 square foot Crystal Ballroom is frequently the site of many high-profile events, such as the '92 Flora Awards Luncheon, the "92 Dallas Opera Ball and the annual Dallas Cowboys kick-off luncheon. The handsome Malachite Room, nightclub in origin and in configuration with stage and permanent dance floor, seats up to 550 for dinner dances and weddings. In addition to six smaller, second floor rooms, there is the new Garden Court Ballroom, surrounded by lattice work and plants and adjacent to the lobby. The Grand Kempinski maintains a complete kosher kitchen, making this a desirable location for bar mitzvahs and bat mitzvahs.

◆ **Hotel St. Germain,** Dallas' first serious small hotel, more like a small *maison particular* in the Parisian quarter of its namesake, provides a number of opportunities for small scale and luxurious entertaining. Teas, dinner parties and receptions are frequently booked in the restored 1906 Maple Avenue Victorian home across from the Crescent. Afternoon tea for a minimum of seven, at $30. per person, is a very special treat for one's lady friends — perhaps for a birthday, for an out-of-town guest or for a bride-to-be. Seven-course, *pre-fixe* dinners, with Southwest-influenced French cuisine, are $65. The entire dining facility is available and especially popular for rehearsal dinners and weddings. An adjacent Garden Court has a special charm of its own and adds enjoyment for cocktails or dinner, when weather permits.

▼ **Loews Anatole Hotel** provides the city's greatest mix of hotel spaces: the gigantic 28,000 square foot Chantilly Ballroom, suitable for the grandest balls and charity lunches for up to 2,000 guests; two smaller ballrooms, the Grand and the second floor Kymer Pavilion each seating up to 1500; the Wedgewood Ballroom for 400 and the still smaller Peacock Terrace, both in the "new wing," and close enough to the main ballroom to provide auxiliary space. We've enjoyed parties in all of them and miraculously the Anatole has perfected the execution of mammoth-sized events, with very credible food, especially the show-stopping desserts. Most enjoyable have been the parties in the hotel restaurants on their "dark nights", especially the top-rated L'Entrecote, with a recently revamped, lower-priced Mediterranean menu, and the Nana Grille, now presided over by chef Marty Cummins. The Anatole also owns the adjacent Veranda Club, where occasional private dinner parties with visiting chefs and a few dinner dances have been held. There is a space at the Anatole for every size party. See also the Veranda Club under "Clubs."

● **The Mansion on Turtle Creek** has its very own category of luxury as the flagship of Caroline Rose Hunt's Rosewood Hotels and Resorts. Fortunate are Dallasites to have the nation's premier hotel, with the lovely Italianate King Mansion as its hub for an entertaining venue. An invitation to The Mansion conjures up the image of luxury and perfection. The Mansion Ballroom is small for a hotel, accommodating only 150 for dinner and 350 for receptions, which keeps all events there very special. Our own experiences have been memorable, whether for a cocktail party, dinner dance or wedding reception. A luncheon or dinner in the gracious Garden Room, off the reception hall of the original mansion, is comfortable for groups of 12 to 24. Maitre d' Wayne Broadwell will help with a menu and oversee any additional needs, such as flowers and placecards. This is one of the premier spots to honor a bride, a friend for a birthday, or visiting Dallas guests. Luncheons will average about $40 per person, including beverage and service. Dinners, of course, will be more. Two other rooms round out The Mansion's primary entertaining spaces. The Shepherd King Suite above the main dining room, approached by a gracious and dramatic stairway, is appropriate for groups of about 50. Then, there is the intimate and wonderful wine cellar. For a peak behind the scenes, don't forget about the cooking demonstrations by the amiable and talented Mansion chef, Dean Fearing.

■ **The Melrose Hotel.** Renovations are near completion at the venerable Melrose to restore the hotel to its former grandeur. New owners and managers of Thailand's Dusit Hotels and Resorts have augmented the "old style" charm of the 1924 landmark site. There is a renewed emphasis of quality of both food and service with the hiring of former Mansion sous-chef Kent Rathbun and numbers of The Mansion service staff. Rooms for party use lend themselves to elegance, including the 2400 square foot ballroom which is comfortable for seating of 100 to 125 and more for receptions. The space has been particularly popular for wedding and rehearsal dinners. There are several smaller rooms for seatings of 20 to 80. There is no doubt that the combination of style, service and good food has resulted in increased Melrose popularity. Not to be overlooked is the new four-star status of The Landmark, the hotel's dining room, under the direction of Executive Chef Kent Rathbun. If the reader should wonder. the chef is the brother of another well known Dallas chef, Kevin Rathbun of Baby Routh.

▲ **Omni Mandalay.** Summer '92 was noted as a change in Mandalay ownership to Omni Hotels, with restoration of the Las Colinas property to its former glory. The hotel's natural ambiance is created by both architecture and site, our only hotel with a lakeside view. On entering the spacious lobby, a feeling of its tropical namesake is evoked, thanks to the lush plants, soaring skylights and mix of plush and Oriental furnishings. Huge expanses of glass are focused on manicured gardens and Lake Carolyn. The Mandalay has a great deal to offer to the private party giver and charity planner: the 10,000 square foot Las Colinas Ballroom accommodating 900 for dining and 1500 for receptions; the 5,000 square foot Mandalay Ballroom seating 450; the garden level Rangoon Room, perfect for receptions and dinner parties of about 100 and available at all times except during Sunday brunch; the four-star, luxuriously-appointed Enjolie Restaurant, available for Sunday and Monday private parties; and numerous smaller rooms for parties and meetings of 20 to 100. A final note for gastronomes: Marc Grounac, previously chef/owner of his own Provence restaurant and former chef at both New York's prestigious Hotel Pierre and the deluxe Windows on the World is chef of the highly-rated Enjolie.

◆ **Plaza of the Americas Hotel** in the complex of the same name has recently undergone a major renovation. Now completed, there should be renewed interest in the attractive facilities, owned by the well-regarded Trust House Forte chain. Aside from the ballroom which is across the atrium ice rink from the hotel, there are two smaller facilities for exclusive rental. Atop the hotel is Windows, a one-time nightclub with an excellent evening view of the city. We've staged 100-plus person parties there with ample room to circulate for cocktails around the open bar area. The ambiance is lovely, but since the kitchen facilities are limited, it is better for cocktail parties and buffets. Also available will be the former Cafe Royal, now re-christened the Cambridge Room, more conducive to private and elegant dinner parties for about 75. The aforementioned ice rink is available for parties as well. We attended a young adult party with ice skating and dinner ring-side. Covering the arena for the use of the atrium was another solution for a Dallas Opera charity luncheon. Rental of the rink runs $185. an hour.

▼ **Sheraton Park Central Hotel,** at LBJ Freeway and North Central Expressway, offers notable opportunities for private entertaining. Foremost for large events is the 15,000 square foot ballroom, ideal for a dinner dance of 900 with stage and dancefloor. A peach-colored decor provides a warm setting and a spacious pre-function area is popular with planners of large charity events. Among recent notable parties held there have been the Arboretum-benefitting Gadsby Ball and the Dallas Opera's Season Preview. A smaller venue is Laurel's, the stylish top-floor restaurant with an expansive view. Available for daytime parties — and we've enjoyed many, many luncheons there — and on certain evenings. Executive Chef David Reardon is one of the city's best, and cuisine at the Sheraton Park Central is sure to be among the city's finest. The hotel enjoys accessibility to both the Richardson corridor and to North Dallas.

● **The Stoneleigh Terrace Hotel,** the late 20's New Yorkish-looking residence hotel on the fringe of downtown, has a small "ballroom" accommodating 200 for receptions and 130 for a seated dinner and a Garden Terrace Room suitable for smaller dinner parties of 70 or so. A 7,000 square foot penthouse, with exciting views of the city, incorporates eight rooms which can be used individually, or together, for as many as 400 guests for receptions. The hotel's spaces have been popular with groups looking for a low-key, cozy ambiance. One real asset is the food, catered by Ewald's, the hotel's street level restaurant. Many of our friends choose the Stoneleigh for all their out-of-town guests because of the hotel's comfortable size, convenient location and moderate prices. The hotel has just changed hands from the Corrigan family, who have owned the hotel for many years.

■ **The Westin Hotel, Galleria Dallas** is the centerpiece of North Dallas' most popular destination and, coincidentally, the Dallas hotel with usually the highest occupancy. The secret is location in the Galleria Mall, the diversity of adjacent attractions and the excellence of hotel services and staff. Increasingly, Dallasites are focusing on the Westin's convenient location and outstanding facilities to meet their entertainment needs, be it private or charity luncheon, ball, wedding, rehearsal dinner or intimate dinner party to celebrate a personal or business event. It is particularly convenient for ladies who combine a daytime festivity with a little shopping, for the wedding party that needs a base for a weekend of activities, and for the hostess who wants to include families for their special occasions — and all with the caché associated with Dallas entertaining. The hotel's facilities are many — a 12,000 square foot regal ballroom accommodating 800 for a dinner dance,

numerous luxurious smaller rooms for receptions, dinners and luncheons of any size from 10 guests to 350, including the twenty-first floor Panorama Room where a North Dallas view provides the glittering backdrop. The hotel can even serve outdoors on the ice rink, as it did recently for the Kidney Foundation without missing a step. We particularly like the Huntington Restaurant, written up below under "Restaurants." And while the variety of venue is sure to satisfy every need, cuisine gets special attention. The Westin Hotel has always valued the quality of its kitchen. (It was they, we recall, who brought us Victor Gielisse.) Chef Andrew Edwards is in the forefront of successfully serving "Totally Texas" items, such as ostrich and game birds, which have been enthusiastically received. Your planing will be creatively attended to by members of the Catering Staff, particularly Catering Manager Cathy Frigo. On the subject of cuisine, The Westin Galleria has the pre-eminent kosher kitchen under the direction of Executive Chef LaLonde, helping to make it one of the most sought-after destinations for bar and bat mitzvahs and for weddings as well. We were enthralled by a '93 Spring wedding that utilized the hotel's various accommodations for a wedding reminiscent of another era, complete with the meaningful traditions of a European past. Last but not least, The Westin Hotel has been sending its food show on the road, catering off-site for any number of private parties, such as the annual parents' fund-raiser for the Greenhill School, weddings and corporate events.

*Please refer to the advertisement for **The Westin Hotel, Galleria Dallas**, on page 209.*

clubs

Perhaps more than most cities, Dallas has always been club minded, partly for reason of status, and partly because of our heritage of "blue laws" against public drinking. Consequently, some of the city's most prestigious parties and weddings continue to take place at the more exclusive country and golf clubs, such as the older and established **Brook Hollow Golf Club**, **Dallas Country Club** and **Northwood Country Club**, and the newer clubs, such as **Stonebriar** and **Gleneagles**.

Likewise, clubs in the downtown environs, such as the **Dallas Petroleum Club** and **The Crescent Club**, are the site of frequent entertaining, both for business and personnel events. These clubs, along with others in the downtown or commercial areas, lend themselves to easy weekend availability, particularly for large dinners and weddings. Club entertaining has many attractions, especially convenience, comfort and privacy. The staffs are generally well-trained and ready to meet entertaining needs. Also, most of the clubs are more intimate in scale than the hotels or non-traditional sites.

Most of the above-mentioned are generally available only for members' use. There are attractive clubs in the area where the use of the facilities can be arranged for special events if a member of the club acts as "sponsor," or a "room fee" or deposit may be required. In some instances, the number of people attending the event determines the fee.

high-rise clubs

Dallas has several "high rise" clubs offering truly spectacular views, providing both panoramic scenery and conversational material.

▲ **The City Club,** on the sixty-seventh floor of the NationsBank Tower, like other of the high rise clubs, affords viewing in all directions. There are a number of options available for private parties, ranging from small groups of 18 to 300 in the South dining room. The Texas Room is a private corner room which can accommodate 60 or so for dinner, a convenient size for a dinner party. The City Club is spacious, comfortable and an attractive option for entertaining. Non-members pay a $500. deposit to secure their date.

◆ **Cityplace Club** atop the sleek Aldo Cassuta-designed Cityplace Center on Central Expressway, has only recently opened to non-members and is particularly handsome in decor, with rich wood paneling, a handsome malachite bar and a fine collection of Western Art. The architecture and urbane interior of Cityplace are among the city's best. The approach to the club via the marble and brass-detailed lobby is impressive, as is the forty-second floor entrance to the club, which overlooks a four-story atrium. The club's main room, with adjacent space for reception, seats about 200 to 220 guests. ClubCorp International has taken over the club's management, thereby assuring the quality of food and service. A $6000. minimum for food and beverage is required.

▼ **La Cima.** The sophisticated pink granite interior of Irving's premier high-rise club lends itself to important business lunches, cocktail and dinner parties and weddings. The appropriately-named Skyline Room seats 200, the Lakeside Room seats 70 and the Belvedere Room seats 35, and there are several smaller rooms as well. The grandeur and the flow of space are outstanding. The views from the top of the Williams Tower are spectacular with a panorama that includes the Dallas skyline and the area's most famous sculpture, the Mustangs of Las Colinas, in the square below. Like its affiliated Tower Club, La Cima caters for its members as well.

● **The Energy Club,** atop Cornerstone Bank on Central Expressway near Northwest Highway, has entertainment areas looking out in all directions — towards downtown, North to the Galleria, West to Texas Stadium, and East to a nearby wooded residential area. Of the four rooms, the Grill is the largest, seating 75 with space for music and dance floor. The high vaulted ceiling and dramatically arched windows, combined with its fresh new decor, makes this a popular choice for bridal receptions and other entertaining.

■ **Park City Club** in Preston Center has unique features. At night, the view of the brilliantly lighted downtown Dallas, as seen from the main dining room, is quite dramatic. Spacious enough for 200 at a seated dinner and 350 for receptions, the room has a permanent dance floor. Three smaller rooms can be used individually, or combined to seat 120. For a truly intimate occasion, the Club's Wine Room comfortably seats ten guests. An "opening fee" of $350. is required if the facilities are used during other than regulation hours.

▲ **The Tower Club,** downtown flagship of Dallas-based ClubCorp, crowns the 48 story Thanksgiving Tower, allowing panoramic views of the entire Dallas area. The graciously-appointed club, enhanced with a well-selected art collection, provides an exceptional setting for dinner dances, cocktail parties, wedding receptions and entertainment of many variations. Parties of up to 260 can be accommodated for seated dinners in the main dining room/ballroom, including space for cocktail reception and dance floor. The Cumberland North and South Rooms combine to accommodate 100 for seated dinners; the Southwestern- themed Brazos Room up to 80; and numerous small rooms accommodate anywhere from 35 to 8 — all with the forty-eighth floor views and Tower Club's distinctive food and service. The club requires a $500. deposit to secure one of the main rooms for an event, followed by a 50 percent deposit 30 days in advance. Fortunately, rules allow a few occasions for non-members to use the club, normally with member sponsorship. The Tower Club has an Event Coordinator to handle details of menu selection and to make arrangements, on behalf of the host and hostess for flowers, music and valet parking — all the ingredients to facilitate planning.

◆ **The University Club,** atop the Galleria, offers distinctively traditional club atmosphere and ease of access for those who live in the North Dallas Corridor. Among the club spaces available for entertaining is the Oxford Room, English-club in decor, accommodating about 140. The somewhat-smaller Cambridge Room seats 100 and is handsomely accented with crystal chandeliers. Additional rooms seat from ten to 40 for lunches and dinners.

▲ **Veranda Club** is the city's showplace athletic club on the grounds of the Loews Anatole Hotel. The upper level is graciously appointed for formal entertaining. There are two areas available for private use: the Veranda Lounge, seating 100, with warm-toned wood paneling and a beautiful Eighteenth Century English fireplace; and the beautifully-appointed Dining Room, accented with antiques, can accommodate up to 150. All meal service is through the hotel's outstanding catering department. We should mention that Anatole Park, just outside the clubhouse, is a lovely al fresco area for wedding receptions and other large events and the site of frequent croquet matches and parties.

country clubs

Dallas and its suburbs have numerous country clubs, each with its own regulations for use by non-members. In most instances, the club's catering manager can assist with spelling out the requirements.

▼ **Bent Tree Country Club**, in Far North Dallas, is surrounded by prestigious Bent Tree estate homes. The club's spacious entry opens into the main dining room — high-ceilinged, beautifully-appointed and glass-walled — overlooking a lake rimmed by the lovely neighborhood homes. Lush, green fairways stretch as far as the eye can see. A large event at Bent Tree is well worth considering, as the club can accommodate up to 500 at a reception. Bent Tree has a Friday and Saturday night required deposit of $1500., and, for sizable groups, all food costs must be paid in advance.

● **Gleneagles Country Club** is the flagship country club of ClubCorp International, and with good reason. Both ambiance and cuisine distinguish the Plano club, east of the Dallas North Tollway. A rich, dark green color scheme is effective in the entry's inlaid marble floor. This theme is carried into the dining room, where the ceiling is vaulted with heavy beams and lighted by majestic brass chandeliers. Enormous glass areas look out over a series of small lakes and waterways — a pleasant backdrop for entertaining. The attractive main dining room seats 125; two smaller rooms each accommodate up to 40; and still additional rooms are perfect for small luncheons and dinners. There is a $4000. minimum on food and beverages for non-member hosts utilizing the main rooms.

■ **Hackberry Country Club**, in Las Colinas, is another of the newer and graciously-appointed clubs available for non-members' use. Its dining room, too, has spacious dimensions with floor-to-ceiling windows, in this case overlooking a stream meandering through the golf course. The main area, which seats 250, is bright and inviting, and affords lovely vistas for both day-time and evening entertaining. Two additional spaces, the Oak Room and the Elm Room, can each seat about 50 for more intimate events. There is a $500. fee for the main ballroom and a $250. fee for the smaller rooms. An on-site event planner is available to assist in making arrangements.

▲ **Las Colinas Country Club**, also in Irving, has new ClubCorp International management as an asset to its attractive entertaining facilities. The club's individual entertainment rooms include a Grand Ballroom seating more than 200, plus a main dining room accommodating 175. In addition, the bright, cheerful Board room and two Miralago rooms are available. The three rooms form a semi-circle and overlook a large lake, with rolling green fairways as a backdrop to the scene. Fees here depend on the number attending the event.

◆ **Royal Oaks Country Club** is in near North Dallas at Greenville and Royal Lane. The ballroom, looking out across the golf course, was recently redecorated with sophisticated teal and cranberry colors and wainscoting. The smaller downstairs Garden room has also being refreshed with new furnishing, but retains its casual character. Royal Oaks charges $750. for use of the Grand Ballroom for parties and dinners. Other fees are determined by the choice of room and number attending.

▼ **Stonebriar Country Club** in Frisco has attracted the local entertaining clientele to it's handsome tutor-styled clubhouse and gracious grounds. Available are the Grand Ballroom for up to 350 guests, The Claredon Room for up to 120 guests and The Boardroom for up to 16, ideal for luncheons and dinner parties.

● **Willow Bend Polo and Hunt Club**, a neighbor to the Gleneagles Country Club on Park Boulevard in Plano, staked its claim to the locale before the Dallas suburbs moved north. The polo fields and sporty ambiance of Willow Bend still lend a feeling of being far away in the bucolic countryside, and offer an alternative to country club entertaining. The club's Polo Room accommodates 100 for dinner and the Rafters Room seats up to 65. A delightful feature of Willow Bend is the option it affords for entertaining out-of-doors. Large tents can be rented, and reasonable fees are charged for use of the swimming pool, racquetball and tennis courts. Room fees and deposits are required for non-members. Dinner prices average $20. to $25. per person for buffet, with a $1500 food minimum. On Mondays, the entire club can be used with an additional $450. opening fee.

The addresses and phone numbers of the clubs listed above can be found in the "Directory of Sources," which begins on page 223.

restaurants

Dallas restaurants present one of the best alternatives for smaller parties and new venues. Some have separate rooms, which work the best and provide a wider choice of availability and privacy. Still other restaurants will be happy for you to utilize their entire facility on the days or times when they are normally closed. The use of restaurants has always been the author's favorite source for varied entertaining. Numbers of guests and budgets can be matched to the restaurant's capacity and price lists. It is unreasonable to expect a restaurant to perform or price an event much differently than their usual standards. But, custom menus can be a welcome challenge for accomplished chefs, anxious to showcase their expertise and to provide something not on the daily fare. Frequently, there are price breaks on wine and beverages, by charging for wines by the bottle rather than by the glass, or by a reduction in established rates.

We are presenting just a sampling of available restaurants, primarily those with private rooms or a willingness to close for private parties. In an urban area of our size, there are many, many others, so we recommend that you speak with the owners of your favorite restaurant about accommodating a private event. We would caution you to discuss their ability to turn out meals for simultaneous eating. Not all can meet the demands of serving all the guests at approximately the same time. We are not restaurant reviewers. Rather, we are trying to point out those restaurants with the best facilities or experience in handling private functions.

Another word of caution is the constant change in the restaurant world. Chefs, owners, addresses and menus change with frequency — and with no warning. The author was once the victim of scheduling a party at a new Deep Ellum club, only to have it close a few days before the scheduled event. While we were able to salvage the situation, thanks to friends in the food world, we do know the value of written contracts and working with established names. Waltrina Stovall of THE DALLAS MORNING NEWS does an admirable job in keeping pace with the changes in her Friday "Best Bites" column of the "Weekend Guide." We recommend that you make a habit of reading it for your best and up-to-date information.

The addresses and phone numbers for the restaurants listed below can be found in the "Directory of Sources," which begins on page 223. A handy "Telephone Directory" begins on page 242.

■ **8.0,** in the Quadrangle, is Shannon Wynne's enduring and ever-popular bar/restaurant. The look is artsy, with muraled-walls, and the ambiance "funky." Private parties are possible, with space for 125 and use of the patio in temperate weather.

▲ **Adelmo's.** Lace curtain in comfort and Mediterranean in cuisine, Adelmo's offers an upstairs dining room, accommodating 30 for private parties. In addition to the winning cuisine, owner Adelmo Banchetti is a former maitre d' of the Fairmont's Pyramid Room. Be assured that your evening will run smoothly and be as congenial as the restaurant. Prices are moderate.

◆ **Andrew's** in Addison has multiple facilities for private parties. The downstairs room will seat 75 for lunch or dinner, with an opportunity to enjoy the New Orleans-style Courtyard for cocktails. An upstairs loft-style room, with French doors opening onto a balcony over the Courtyard, seats 60. Three course eclectic menus, with a leaning toward Cajun food, average from $12. to $15. with the bonus of enjoying "happy hour" drink prices with all parties.

▼ **Art Bar, Blind Lemon** and **Club Clearview.** A trio of adjacent and connecting Deep Ellum bars is available for use, singly or together. Conveniently, the owners will close one or all the facilities at almost any time for private use. Each facility has a distinct look: "artsy" for the appropriately-named Art Bar and cutting edge for Club Clearview. Dinner is most easily served in Blind Lemon, the most yuppie venue among them. It will seat 80 or more for a French/Italian bistro menu. Selections might include pizzetta and tagliatella in herbed ricotta sauce, for example, starting about $10. A major attraction will be the access to the music scene, as these clubs showcase the up and coming talent. The owners will, of course, be able to suggest the best entertainment to accompany your festivities. Look forward to the concept being expanded into North Dallas during the Spring of '94. A 15,000-square-foot four-in-one concept will provide a Mecca for North Dallas party-givers in search of space. New in the mix will be **Your Mother's Hip**, with a "kitschy" 60's diner look, and **LaVaca Cantina**, a pre-50's cowboy bar and restaurant.

● **Baby Routh**, now the sole Dallas restaurant of food impresario John Dayton, enjoys the reputation of being one of Dallas' finer restaurants. For private party use, it has a very pleasant upstairs room, seating up to 40, which understandably enjoys popularity for the chic ambiance, the decidedly superior cuisine under the direction of Chef Kevin Rathbun, and the flawless attention to service. A $150. deposit will hold the room for use by a minimum of ten guests. A nice extra is the specially printed menu to commemorate the event or the person being honored. Food is creative American nouvelle — and save room for dessert, such as the black bottom pecan pie with bourbon cream.

■ **Big Spur Corral** may be the answer to a Western party without leaving town for one of the surrounding ranches. The Big Spur Corral, east of Stemmons at Commonwealth, is a dinner theatre with the entire Western story to tell. For birthdays, graduations, bachelor parties, or just entertaining the out-of-town guests, Big Spur can even custom-script a show to include your honoree. The corral accommodates up to 250 or 300. Dinners of barbecue chicken, ribs and all the fixins' are $29. including wine and beer and the Western show. The Big Spur Corral is in its second year and its popularity is growing. One of Dallas' more creative party planners recently augmented the built-in theme with Western town props outside and a dressed-up dinner that included chocolate oil derrick desserts. The Big Spur owners, incidentally, also own the **Medieval Inn**, another thematic dinner theatre on Greenville Avenue, where the King's private dining room for 25 provides private space to "eat, drink and be medieval."

▲ **Blue Mesa Grill**, in Village on the Parkway, is Sante Fe style in food and decor. Blue Mesa has it all when it comes to entertaining: six attractive private rooms seating up to 400 in all; modestly priced with innovative food — Duck Taquitos, Chicken and Cheese Adobe Pie and Sante Fe style Honey Flan; and special services for decorations, entertainment and the like. With signature dishes so unique and flattering to any palate, the reasons for its success as a party venue are

all the more understanding. For smaller parties, there is an upstairs room for 40; two of the more inviting rooms combine to seat 150. Off-site catering is another dimension. See the write-up under "Catering" on page 105. *Please see the advertisement for **Blue Mesa Grill** on page 208*

◆ **Calluaud's** Classical French cuisine has returned with the reincarnation of Calluaud's. Fans of stellar chef Guy Calluaud will remember his mark on Dallas with the introduction of a small *traiteur* (take-out) years ago in the Quadrangle and ultimately with the proprietorship of one of Dallas' best haute cuisine restaurants, on McKinney Avenue. Now, with the able assist of wife Martine, Guy is back, in the renovated Le Caviste space on Lovers Lane. The 50 to 60 seat restaurant is available for private parties at lunch on Saturdays and Sundays and for dinner on Sunday evenings. Guy's classic greats are on the menu, including the signature Souffle au Hommard.

▼ **Capriccio**, in the former San Simeon space in Chateau Plaza on McKinney at Routh Street, benefits from having a labyrinth of small, wood-paneled dining rooms, some with fireplaces to augment the cozy atmosphere. The very home-like setting is certainly conducive to a variety of occasions. The seating numbers in the private rooms vary from 12 to 50, or 75, if combined. A three or four course dinner averages between $28. to $35. per person before extras, and the congenial owners, Claire and Jean Rubede, will print a special menu as a momento of the occasion or the honorèe.

■ **Chamberlain's Prime Chop House** has opened in the space vacated by Del Frisco's near the Addison Town Hall. Star Chef Richard Chamberlain has joined up with Sfuzzi-ex Ric Levit to launch a steakhouse with flair. Chamberlain's background as chef of San Simeon, at Little Nell's in Aspen and, more recently, at the Crescent Club have firmly established him as one of the city's best. His special talents come through with appetizers and side orders, and the emphasis on meat is sure to please a great number of your guests. A small back room can seat up to 45 for a private party and the entire restaurant is available at lunch time and on Sunday evening for private functions.

▲ **Chez Gerard**. This popular 50 person bistro with patio on Upper McKinney is available on Sundays and for weekend lunches. The country French atmosphere is unpretentious and the surroundings are cozy and inviting. Owner Pascal Cayet is familiar to many since his days with Guy Calluaud.

◆ **City Cafe** on Lovers Lane has enduring charm and always outstanding American bistro food, thanks to savvy oversight by chef /owner Mardi Schma. There is small upstairs room, which can accommodate up to 65 and is in frequent use for luncheons and dinners. An average luncheon menu runs about $12. to $15. and a dinner menu about $30. to $35. The seafood is always exceptional, and the Louisiana Crab and Crawfish Cakes are a popular favorite. Never pass up the desserts which, depending on the season, might include Lemon Blueberry Cake or Nectarine Plum Crunch with vanilla ice cream and custard sauce. They are consistently outstanding!! Menus change weekly and, of course, can be tailored to your party. Chef Brian Glover is presently at the helm in the open kitchen.

● **Dakota's** enjoys big city sophistication with its below ground level location at the triangular intersection of Akard and Ervay Streets, adjacent to the Lincoln Plaza. The contemporary American grill has a private dining room, seating 15, that is booked constantly. Alcoves and a second level, seating 20 to 40 provide additional private places during open-to-the public hours. The latter is particularly popular for rehearsal dinners. Use of the entire space, including the charming below ground-level patio,is possible on Saturday and Sunday for lunch and on Sunday evenings, when the restaurant is closed to the public. The bonus is enjoying the exceptional cuisine of CIA-trained chef Jim Severson and his concern for pleasing his clientele.

■ **Deep Ellum Cafe**, a SoHo-like bistro favorite in Deep Ellum, draws an "artsy" crowd and offers a brick-walled private room with a New Orleans-style adjacent patio. The room is a great size for about 40 and the food, a blend of Southwestern, Thai and classic cuisines, will delight your guests. Deep Ellum plans a Belt Line expansion, and, keep in mind, the Deep Ellum was a caterer before a restaurant. Catering is still one of their specialties.

▲ **Dovie's**, World War II hero Audie Murphy's former home on Midway Road near Alpha, does non-stop private party business. The 1930's home, now amidst office parks and tall buildings, was once in the Dallas countryside and retains its country house charm. There are four downstairs rooms for private use, accommodating from 18 to the largest, The Courtyard, for 90. Upstairs, there are two additional rooms. Dovie's offers two menu price selections for the myriad of showers, rehearsal dinners, company parties, and weddings held there — one at $15.95 and the other at $18.85. Use of the entire restaurant for up to 250 guests for a reception is possible at all times.

▲ **Ferrari's Italian Oven** enjoys a thriving private party business, especially since its move from Market Street in the West End to its present Brewery location. The handsome interior benefits from a second floor that can seat 80 to 100 comfortably for parties at any time. Rehearsal dinners and weddings are frequent and the calendar fills up quickly for the Christmas season. The entire restaurant can also be closed to accommodate larger parties. Owner and Italian native Francesco Secchi has been in Dallas for 12 years and brings with him a hotel school and chef's background. A four course dinner runs about $20. to $22.

▼ **The French Room.** The Adolphus Hotel's four-star, Mobil award French Room is mentioned under "Hotels," but how can we resist the reminder that The French Room is "... indisputably the most striking and sumptuous restaurant in Dallas," according to THE NEW YORK TIMES. The French Room offers the most beautiful setting for a special dinner at any time, and, fortunately, there are many private party opportunities for brunches, luncheons and Sunday evening dinners. And, although Executive Chef Kevin Garvin will customize your personal event, for up to 80 or so for dinners and 120 for receptions, we can mention a few tempting suggestions from the new menu, such as Chilled Vegetable Terrine with artichokes and portabella  mushrooms or Lasagna of Shrimp and Scallops — and these just for starters. The neoclassic cuisine, part of the restaurant's new menu and new image, is a winner.

*Please see the advertisement for **The French Room** on page 210.*

*Please see the advertisement for **The French Room** on page 210.*

▲ **Huntington's** in The Westin Hotel, Galleria, a name that conjures up images of fine dining, has taken the lead in presenting "Totally Texas" food, with all items grown or raised in the state — a nice treat especially for your out-of-town guests. Acclaimed chef Andrew Edwards has introduced menu items that alone will be the reason for settling on the restaurant, with Longhorn beef medallion, Ostrich, Quail and Pheasant among the specialties. *Please see the advertisement for **The Westin Hotel** on page 209.*

◆ **J Pinnell's** is one of the new entries this year that is particularly suited to private entertaining. The attractive Maple Avenue restaurant, housed in a restored 1902 home, has the feel of its former grandeur, complete with comfortable rooms and fireplaces. Owner/manager Paul Pinnell adds to its popularity (the "J" is for partner and restaurateur Johnny Walker). Paul Pinnell has garnered a loyal following as maitre d' at Dallas' best restaurants — including Laurel's and Cafe Royal — during his 16 year career in the restaurant business. That experience guarantees smooth oversight for parties. The arrangement of rooms in the two-story building lends itself particularly well for the individual host — a wine room that seats 10, the entire upstairs that accommodates 60 in three rooms with great flow and ambiance, and the main downstairs room that accommodates 40 with the adjacent patio available for pre-function drinks and seating depending on the season.

▼ **Javier's**, on Cole Avenue north of Knox Street, is a popular cantina for private parties. Even though the restaurant is open seven days a week, it has a series of rooms, allowing for private parties. One room, decorated in the cantina style with the look of Old Mexico, can seat about 60. Another handsome room with a bar provided a cozy Colonial setting for about 40 guests for a friend's birthday dinner. The chef specializes in exotic Mexican fare, such as the delicious chicken mole and carne asada. An average dinner runs about $35. per person for three courses including drinks.

● **Juniper**, a French Provincial restaurant, radiates special warmth in its renovated house on Fairmount Street. Two separate dining rooms, each accommodating 30 to 40 guests, and bar area allow for easy private dining. The small bar area and patio are especially comfortable for pre-meal gathering. Recently, the restaurant is open for dinners only, leaving the charming venue available for private luncheons in addition to Sunday evenings. The author has enjoyed entertaining there on several occasions, since the restaurant's ambiance and size, plus Chef Christian Gerber's exceptional French cuisine are as warm a setting as one would want for good friends. Incidentally, Juniper has been voted Dallas Best French Restaurant in the latest DALLAS

OBSERVER poll — and no surprise to regulars. The space was perfect for a bride's luncheon, a brunch for the season's debutantes and a wine-tasting dinner, all typical of the private functions held at the cozy restaurant. Each was different and each a culinary success. The menu for the bride's luncheon included fresh tomato and basil soup, a marinated chicken breast entree and the chef's signature hot apple tart. Chef and co-owner Gerber is highly regarded in the world of fine cuisine and taking advantage of his private cooking classes (which, incidentally, make great parties), special wine dinners and celebrations for holidays will make your entertainment special.

■ **Krispin — the restaurant** offers a unique opportunity and one of Dallas more attractive settings for private entertaining. The new, chic facility is restaurant by day and private party facility by evening and weekend. It is one of those rare sites that offers particularly attractive ambiance for birthdays, anniversaries, rehearsal dinners and the like. In the Design District space formerly occupied by Daryl's by Design, caterer Wendy Krispin has refurbished the club-like facility. Highly-regarded interior designer Barbara Vessels has created a sophisti-cated, monochromatic-in-color space that accommodates about 120 for seated dinners in the restaurant and up to 425 for

receptions, utilizing the bar and surrounding spaces. Because of its attractive decor, outstanding food and unique availability, Krispin — the restaurant should be on the very short list when searching for private party spaces. *Please see the advertisement for Krispin — the restaurant on page 221.*

▲ **Lady Primrose** is a charming place to plan a High Tea for a bride-to-be. The English-oriented antiques shop in the Crescent complex has an upper level where luncheons and teas are served with all the ambiance of the English countryside. The teas for up to 30 reservations are "seated" and cost $12.00, including tax and gratuity, for the praiseworthy tea sandwiches, tarts and scones. Wine and champagne are extra. Please refer also to the listing for Lady Primrose under "Kitchenware and Table Accessories."

◆ **La Tosca**, an enduring Northern Italian restaurant on Inwood Road across from Inwood Village, has a new upstairs room for private parties with a bar and all necessary facilities. The room seats 60 and is decorated in the same sophisticated black and white scheme of the lower level.

● **Lombardi's 311.** The Back Room at Lombardi's in the West End is one of the more attractive private rooms in Dallas. The 1000 square foot room is sleekly designed, leaving only a hint of its warehouse origins. With bar in one corner and area for drinks before dinner, the room can comfortably accommodate 40 to 50 for dinner. In addition to the gracious space, Lombardi's dinner will be a pleasant experience of traditional Northern Italian food, with an average dinner in the $25. to $35. range for three courses. Be sure to include the Tiramasu, their light ricotta cheese dessert.

■ **Main Street News**, the chic bistro in Deep Ellum, will close for private parties, and would be a good choice if you can fill the 60-seat house to qualify for the closing. The Mediterranean-styled food will be noteworthy, the service flawless and the atmosphere very *au courant*. We entertained there more than once and could not have been happier with the results and the reaction of our guests. And, do take notice of the small details, such as the *trompe l'oeil* touches around doorways, another indication of the attention to finishing touches. The new owners promise to keep up the tradition established by former owner Nancy Beckham.

▲ **Mario's Chiquita Mexican Cuisine** in Travis Walk is one of the favorite, modest-priced private party destinations in Dallas. Its private room can accommodate up to 90 or so with colorful surroundings and a built-in theme. A dinner will cost under $10. and drinks, such a margaritas, sangria and beer, can be served by the pitcher. Owner Mario Leal, a reliable name on the Dallas restaurant scene, suggests including Mexican music to add some flair. Book early.

◆ **Mediterraneo**, a new sibling of the prestigious Riviera Restaurant, is a venture by Franco Bertalasi and highly regarded chef David Holben in the Triad complex at the juncture of Preston and Frankfort. Holben has left The Riviera kitchen to take over as both chef and *patron* at the new offspring. The new endeavor, debuting as we go to press, may become THE North Dallas location for private parties, not only because of the suitable divided areas of the attractive Palazzo setting, but because of the style, attention to cuisine and detail of The Riviera offspring. Mediterraneo will be open for both lunch and dinner but, no matter, thanks to the restaurant's room arrangement and the adjacent Triad atrium, it can be utilized for private events both evenings and weekends. To applaud his credentials, CIA-trained David Holben, for those who are not acquainted with his top-rated, nine year stint at The Riviera, has served serious "sous-ships" under both Roger Vergé and Paul Bocuse, at the venerable George V in Paris and, finally, at the Plaza of the Americas before arriving at The Riveria.

▼ **Mercado Juarez**, at locations on Northwest Highway near Las Colinas and at Belt Line Road, is also a popular, Tex-Mex party destination. As the name implies, the restaurants feature market areas with Mexican pinatas, sombreros, dresses and pottery. The market and the weekend live music create a festive "south of the border" atmosphere at all times. The Northwest Highway location lends itself to large private parties and is available when normally closed to the public. The Belt Line location has a private room that can seat up to 200. Dinners start around $8.50.

■ **Momo's Pasta** on Knox Street has two separate rooms at their popular pasta eatery which work well for private parties. An adjacent front room can seat up to 36, and a smaller rear room is perfect for pre-dinner drinks. Dinners of salad, entree and dessert start about $18. Even though a liquor license has been added, the party-givers can still bring their own wines, resulting in considerable savings.

▲ **Nero's Italian.** Basic Italian and a private party room to boot! Nero's on Greenville Avenue across from the Arcadia Theatre can handle a private party for 50 in a comfortable room lined with wooden wine bins. The food is commendable and the ambiance is New York's Little Italy, complete with red-checkered table cloths and opera on the sound system. There are those who will be nostalgic for this atmosphere! This is the place to invite the transplanted New Yorker.

◆ **Newport's.** An August '93 review of Newport's referred to the seafood restaurant as an "in" place — especially to those who know where it is located, close to a downtown freeway and in The Brewery, Dallas' major beer-making vestige from the 1880's. Now, the beer-maker's legacy is the 31 foot-wide cistern that serves as the restaurant's focal point and adds to the historic building's character. The seafood specialty restaurant serves its purposes for private entertainment as well as fine dining. The multi-tiered and semi-private arrangement of three distinct sections is perfect for parties of about 40 in each area — and bookings reflect the popularity! Additionally, the entire facility is available for day parties on both Saturday and Sunday. Fanciers of the menu will want to know about their catering services as well, and we encourage you to refer to the write-up of Newport's other persona under "Restaurants That Cater" in Chapter VI.
See the advertisement for Newport's on page 215.

▼ **On the Border.** Texas memorabilia and cantina-style add flair to Tex-Mex cuisine. The menu leans toward "mesquite-grilled specialties from the land of the Mexican vaqueros." That means beyond Tex-Mex, to include chicken and steak fajita specialties. The Knox Street original has a private room, accommodating 80 to 90, at inexpensive prices and happy hour beverage tariffs up until seven o'clock. Because of the number of private parties held here, the restaurant has a Special Event coordinator to work out plans for you.

● **Opus** is the in-house restaurant at the Meyerson Symphony Center and is entirely in keeping with the refined environment. Previously, entertaining at the Meyerson meant events of a major scale. Now, the new restaurant, nestled among greenery and umbrellas (!) on the west side of the lobby, can comfortably accommodate from 50 to 200 for brunches, lunches and dinners when the symphony schedule allows. We enjoyed a dinner party there when it first opened and the dramatic architecture and city view were added amenities. Depending on number and access to the rest of the Hall, rentals fees for the Meyerson will apply. And do not forget to consider the facility when entertaining a few friends before a symphony performance. At this writing, $23. covers the tab for a pre-concert dinner buffet. Chef de Cuisine Tom Schroeder provides superb cuisine and Becky Miller handles the party arrangements. Applause to the Sheraton Park Central Hotel which operates the restaurant.

▲ **Pappadeaux Seafood Kitchen,** in the old Lucas B & B site on Oak Lawn, is a Cajun stage set and well arranged for private parties. There are two separate rooms on a lower level, the larger seating 125, and the smaller a convenient gathering place for pre-dinner cocktails. The charge is $150. for the large and $75. for the smaller. The main upstairs room can be separated from the remainder of the restaurant by pull-down glass doors, creating a private space, usable early in the evening or on off-evenings. It accommodates 250 with a $35. per person minimum, excluding service. Guests will leave well-fed from huge portions of oysters, andouille sausage, seafood gumbo, Red Snapper Ponchartrain and sweet potato pecan pie. The owners also run Pappas Catering, which can transport their food *chez vous.*

◆ **Pomodoro** and younger sibling **Arcodoro** on Cedar Springs have carved a niche for Italian food very well done indeed. Pomodoro, a cheery trattoria, with a few traits of its former days as a seafood restaurant, won so many fans and demands for private use of the restaurant that the addition of Arcodoro, the casual but trendy next door gourmet pizza/light meal/bar proved to be a happy solution. We've had a party there so we can testify both to the food and the fun. Bellinis to start and pasta, pizzas and dessert made for happy guests. These, incidentally, are no ordinary pizzas that come from the open hearth near the entrance. A lunch in Arcodoro will run about $15. per person before service and drinks, and carafes of wine keep the tab under control. Now, an additional room has been added to keep up with the growing demand. The new room, used for everything from rehearsal dinners to awards banquets seats about 45 and holds perhaps 100 or more for receptions.

More traditional Pomodoro has a separate front room, also available for parties, that looks out on the cheerful faces of mammoth and Mediterranean-suggesting sunflowers (the motif, incidentally, of the tiled wall ovens in adjacent Arcodoro). With Pomodoro's Italian meals, which might include the particularly good risotto, you will be certain to have a successful party where both food and atmosphere are concerned. Pomodoro is also available on Sundays for private use.

▼ **Quadrangle Grille,** owned by savvy restaurateur Tom Stark, will accommodate private party arrangements. With friends, we once hosted a memorable brunch for a capacity 150 guests in the handsome two-leveled room. The "casual American" food is always top-notch and reasonably-priced; the hip and mural-walled setting provides agreeable ambiance. Wine enthusiasts should note the Quadrangle's frequent wine-tastings, wine dinners and celebration of an annual Texas Wine Fest in September and October. Tastings can also be done for private groups.

● **The Riviera**. Few restaurants are as charming in country French decor and as matchless in food and service. Franco Bertalasi effusively greets guests in the flower-filled small front entrance. The private party-goer can enjoy aperitifs in the cozy bar and proceed to the dining room which can seat 75 to 80. Chef Lori Finkelman Holben had training in the South of France, and the *Provençal* influences are obvious. Whether you take the entire restaurant on a "dark night" or for a luncheon, for a personal celebration or a business occasion, this will be memorable.

■ **The Russian Room** is the upscale and upstairs component of the Deli-News, our favorite and authentic deli, owned by Russian émigré cousins. The party room above the Crescent complex deli is perfect for private soirees and is particularly popular for anniversaries, rehearsal dinners, and bar and bat mitzvahs — and any other event that you can imagine! The food is pre-Revolutionary and worthy of Russian royalty! The real charm is from panels of Russian fables that line the room — enlarged renditions of treasured Russian lacquer boxes that relate the country's fairy tales. The food, the decor and the ambiance — not to mention the owners and the chefs — have managed to create a corner of Old Russia for our entertaining fantasies. The upstairs facility, overlooking the restaurant, will seat 130 for dinner and has a bar and a piano.

▲ **Sam's Cafe** in the Crescent complex has long been a magnet for the "in" crowd and a very popular place to entertain for both pleasure and business. It's location in the handsome Crescent complex has been a draw for the business crowd who have made the spot their favorite place to entertain in their leisure hours. Adjacent to the popular bar area is a private room that can accommodate up to 50 for lunch or dinner and up to 90 for a cocktail buffet. The casual Southwestern Grill cuisine, which can be dressed up as the occasion warrants, is particularly popular for rehearsal dinners when the host couple want to show off the local cuisine to their out-of-town guests. Menu  items include Maria's Shrimp Tamales, Southwest Grilled Salmon and Grilled Beef Tenderloin with red onion marmalade. Average prices are about $20. per person. The opportunities to alter the ambiance within the colorful setting are endless — elegant flowers or music, perhaps a mariachi group, can add a festive air. A second Sam's Cafe has just opened in the former Hampton's Grill space in Preston Center, transformed with wooden beams and adobe colors into a convincing Sante Fe look. Here, the opportunities for private parties are even greater. The two-level eatery means a convenient, second level available for private parties at almost any time. Sam's Cafe is also among those that cater and can be found in Chapter VI in the section "Restaurants That Cater." *Please see the advertisement for Sam's Cafe on page 215.*

▲ **Sfuzzi**. The McKinney Avenue original Sfuzzi makes entertaining a joy in its " newish" Tuscan-decor private dining room that will accommodate up to 50 for a seated meal and 100 for a reception. In addition to the food, your guests will delight to the restaurant's cozy ambiance, provided by *trompe l'oeil* architectural ruins and hues of Palladian villas. An experienced catering director will assist you in every phase of planning, from menus within your budget to ordering flowers or arranging for music, should you want them. The only difficulty will be in narrowing the extensive menu selections. A recent dinner was in the $20. to $30. range before tax, service and beverages. We've also gone to a few afternoon ladies' parties there. The frozen Bellini, Sfuzzi's signature drink, and hors d'oeuvres guaranteed success. Not to be overlooked, the Addison Sfuzzi has a wine room for small dinner parties with similar selections and pricing. A new Plano Sfuzzi extends the hospitality Northward.

◆ **Star Canyon**. Stephan Pyles, one of the country's better known chefs, formerly chef and co-owner of Dallas' star-studded Routh Street Cafe, will be opening his new restaurant in the Oak Lawn area in January of '94, after we go to press. We will be anxious to discover the opportunities for private entertaining.

▼ **Tolbert's Chili Parlor**. Tolbert's has several locations, the most unique being at One Dallas Center. Its uniqueness comes from the dinner theatre format, featuring "Mornin' Dallas," a lively review poking good-natured fun at local and national celebrities. The dinner show accommodates 100, with an additional bar area.

● **White Swan** is a great find on Abrams Road in the Lakewood area. Cuban in influence, with Spanish, Mexican and Italian dishes as well — and more comfortable than haute — it has been growing to meet the demands of its clientele. Recently added are two adjacent rooms, a bit dressier than the original. One will seat up to 30 for a private party, the other up to 80. Perhaps the smaller could be used for the reception since it has its own entrance to the street. The food is excellent and moderate in price. Classical guitar players Graciela and Carlos perform on Thursday, Fridays and Saturdays in the restaurant. They are available for private parties on the other evenings. White Swan has a small take-out and bakery case, which the East Dallas neighborhood knows about. The flan is habit-forming. The White Swan is taking over the former Mario's space in Turtle Creek Village as this publication goes to press. Considering the configuration of that venue, it is likely accommodations for private parties will be available there as well.

▲ **York Street**. Available Monday evenings and at lunch, East Dallas' York Street is charming and offers classy food and wines for only 13 tables of diners. This is a prime candidate for a party with an intimate feel and the anticipation of chef-owner Mike Shaw's enjoyable cuisine.

■ There are numerous other recommended restaurants with private party potential, and, once again, we urge you to be on the look-out among the new restaurants for spaces that work particularly well. Kay Agnew's **Cafe Margaux**, a pleasant Cajun eatery on Travis near Knox, has a private room overlooking the atrium entrance to the restaurant and building complex. **L'Acenstral**, across the street in Travis walk, is one of our more delightful restaurants with a real French feel and food to match. Owner Alain Pierre Vuilleret is very amenable to working with private parties in his 80 seat charming restaurant. **Alessio's** in Highland Park, a charming Northern Italian eatery, works well for cozy parties of 30 to 40, with an adjacent bar area for pre-dinner gathering and drinks. The comfortable and original **J. Pepe's** in the Quadrangle, where the food is Tex-Mex, has a private room that can accommodate 35 to 40. As in many other restaurants, "Happy Hour" prices for beverage apply until seven o'clock. We would be remiss in not mentioning **The Wine Press** and **Ristorante Savino** as popular places to accommodate private parties.

additional restaurants with great private party potential

Addison Cafe	Bombay Cricket Club
Casa Domenguez	Eduardo's Aca Y Alla
Highland Park Cafe	India Palace
Jennivine's Restaurant	Mattito's Cafe Mexicano
Mi Piaci	No Place
Swan Court	Tillman's Corner

special spaces

Dallas does not abound with non-traditional sites for entertaining, though the situation seems to be improving. Fortunately, we do have our share of public and cultural facilities, such as the **Dallas Museum of Art** and the **Hall of State** that can be rented to provide the host with a location of unique interest. At the same time, the monies from rentals help those civic organizations defray costs of operations and offset on-going budget cuts. There are also a few, grand older buildings, such as the **Belo Mansion** and **Aldredge House**, which have a personal and historical charm and offer a change from the more conventional environment. In addition, some of the area's best alternate sites can be found at numerous farms and ranches, now put to use for thematic entertainment. These are particularly appealing for large groups and for out-of-town visitors, who savor and expect the Western atmosphere.

▲ **Aldredge House** appeals with turn-of-the-century charm in the historical Swiss Avenue District of East Dallas. One of Dallas' loveliest homes, now the landmark headquarters for the Dallas County Medical Auxiliary, is available for teas, luncheons, dinners and weddings. A large central hall, mahogany-paneled living room, banquet-sized dining room, enclosed conservatory and accompanying gardens provide gracious rooms and space for entertaining on a near personal level. We have enjoyed teas and garden parties there, reminiscent of another and grander era. Guess Who's Coming to Dinner provides all in-house food services. The house comes equipped with china, silver and glassware to make arrangements easier.

◆ **Belo Mansion**, the landmark, Ross Avenue residence of the founders of THE DALLAS MORNING NEWS, is now home to the Dallas Bar Association and provides a pleasant home atmosphere for special events. A number of rooms work for parties of differing sizes, including the grand, paneled dining room and gracious living room of the original home. The new addition of dining room/ballroom, will seat close to 200, without allowance for a dance floor, and even more can be accommodated for reception. An adjacent foyer makes a convenient pre-function or cocktail space. Rental fees start at $450. for fewer than 100 people and increase to $750. for additional numbers. The in-house caterer is Culinaire International. Sponsorship by a member of the Dallas Bar Association is required.

▼ **The Carpenter House**, a historical 1898 Plano house and now a bed and breakfast, is one of several new properties on the market available for special occasions, such as intimate weddings, showers and parties. Catering and other services can be arranged by the owners. **Schimelpfenig Showplace** is another new addition for private entertaining space. Housed in a recently restored home in downtown Plano, the Showplace offers a private dining room accommodating about 25 and up to 125 for receptions in the home's downstairs rooms. A veranda adds to the charm. The rates for usage are moderate and the facility has many of its own needs, such as table, chairs and some china. We suspect that the historic uniqueness will add to the popularity, especially for weddings. **The Reichenstein Manor,** on Cedar Springs in the Springs apartment complex, is another new venue available for small parties from 40 for dinners to about 125 for receptions. The 1930's Tutor-style and well-furnished house was the original centerpiece of the property. Rates start at $75. per hour, with a three hour minimum.

● **Cityplace Conference Center,** on Central Expressway just North of downtown, benefits from its location in a building designed by one of the nation's best architects, Aldo Cassuta. The Conference Center is divided on either side of the urbane marble and brass-accented lobby, with theatre and meeting rooms on one side. On the South side of the lobby is the 4000 square foot Turtle Creek room, which can be used for up to 250 guests for a seated dinner, or be divided into three rooms. The adjacent Lakewood I and Lakewood II rooms can each accommodate 100 guests for dinner or be combined for one room for larger party with ample room for orchestra and dance floor. The party giver can find almost any size space for dances, dinners and receptions. The Catering and Sales staff report that the Conference Center is popular for proms, class reunions and weddings. Meanwhile, ClubCorp International has recently signed on to handle management and catering for both the Conference Center and the forty-second floor club. Conference Center lunch menus average $10. and dinner menus range from $15. to $18. per person, with a variety of other reception and buffet formats available.

■ **D-Art Visual Art Center,** an exhibit center in the Wilson Historic District, has space available for meetings, receptions and other special events in a gallery setting. The 24,000 square foot building features local artists' works, and the exhibits will vary. Care must be given for the art work in scheduling any event. This is for art lovers and for a completely different experience.

▲ **Dallas Alley,** in the historic West End, is a popular spot for private parties, particularly for the young set, be it a graduation or deb party. Dallas Alley has eight clubs under one roof, of varying sizes and "motifs." For example, "Bobby Sox," one of the clubs, accommodating up to 350 people, has a 50's theme. The $175 an hour rental fee includes the facility, with a dance floor. Entertainment can easily be arranged. Other clubs in the complex include "Take 5", with a sleek and sophisticated look, the New Orleans-themed "Froggy Bottoms" and the prerequisite "Roadhouse Saloon" — providing a potentiality for everyone's taste and size. Dallas Alley has a preferred list of caterers, including Sonny Bryan's for barbecue, or, should you prefer, you can bring in your favorite caterer. Marlene Andre, the very accommodating Event Coordinator, can arrange for decorations and live entertainment.

◆ **Dallas Arboretum and Botanical Garden,** on White Rock Lake in Northeastern Dallas, has one of the loveliest locations in Dallas. The surrounding floral profusion, not to mention the rare lakeside view, make the facility unique for entertaining. The site's comfortable 1930's Camp House has first floor rentals at $175. per hour, with a four hour minimum and a $1000. security deposit. (A security deposit is usual for the city and organization-owned properties.) The space, with sizable living and dining rooms, terrace and catering kitchen, will accommodate 60 for a seated dinner or 200 for a reception. We've also attended several lovely luncheons on the extensive lawns overlooking the water's edge. Once a date has been selected, the rental coordinator will assist with an approved list of caterers and other needs.

Happily, the Camp House has its own tables and chairs, which means a savings on rentals. The adjacent Spanish Colonial-style DeGolyer House, also part of the Arboretum property, is available to supporters of the Arboretum. As appealing as they are, both facilities are understandably popular and booked far in advance.

▼ **Dallas Civic Garden Center**, another of the city's institutions, this one in Fair Park, has the built-in ambiance of a garden and is popular for ladies' luncheons and weddings. The center hall seats 175. with a $525. rental fee and a $300. deposit. A still larger room will seat 450 and the fee is $800. for four hours.

● **Dallas Communications Complex** has a soundstage, which could be rented for your fantasy party, and we do know of some interesting parties that have been held there. This is a consideration for an ambitious undertaking.

■ **Dallas Museum of Art** offers one of the most exciting opportunities for entertainment in Dallas — from hosting a few friends for a tour and lunch in the Gallery Buffet, available to anyone, to small lunches and dinners in the Founders Room, to a wedding reception or grand corporate party in the Museum's center Barrel Vault or Sculpture Garden. The opening of the new Hamon Wing in the Fall of 1993 affords additional and exciting space in the three-storied Atrium. There are restrictions, certainly, to the use of the Museum for these special events — normally when it is closed to the public and for those who are Associate or Corporate members of the Museum.

The DMA has also perfected "the fine art of entertaining," partly as a means to supplement their operations budget. They have their own preferred in-house caterer, the dani group, one of Dallas' most sought-after catering companies with large-scale expertise. The menu choices are innovative and the price range is considerable, from $7.50 to $35. for cocktails and $24. to $43. for a dinner menu. The cocktail buffet format works well, particularly if the guests are not familiar with the Museum. They have the opportunity to wander and enjoy the opulence of their surroundings. Or, for the truly grand event, the space allows the imagination to soar. A $1500. deposit is required for security and operations fee to cover costs associated with opening the museum after hours. Ed Chance is in charge of Special Events and Catering. He can also work with you to arrange flowers, parking and music. The Special Events Department knows what works best to complement the extraordinary surroundings. Obviously, the museum setting can provide one of the most dramatic scenarios in the city of Dallas for that very special event.

▲ **Dallas World Aquarium** in the West End opened in late Fall of 1993 with anticipation of one of Dallas' most unique private party facilities. The result does not disappoint any visitor! Caterer and amateur diver Daryl Richardson has restored a 1924 factory at the corner of Hord and North Griffin in the West End and created a space that is totally unique. The entire concept is fascinating, and, understandably, the space is being booked far in advance for everything from rehearsal dinners and bar mitzvahs to corporate celebrations.

The 4400 square foot, first floor restaurant and bar level houses 11 wall-size aquariums — 65,000 gallons worth — filled with underwater sea life from the world's major dive areas, including a walk-through tunnel tank featuring an open ocean exhibit. The major dive areas of the world are represented — Indonesia, Mexico, the Caribbean, etc. There is another "tank" housing a trio of crowd-pleasing penguins. The exotic and endlessly fascinating underwater fantasies and their tropical residents add an incredible backdrop for the lower level restaurant and party space. The sea-life filled aquariums are the cue for

around-the-world menus and themes that embrace the Caribbean, luaus, Mexico and the entire gamut of Jacques Cousteau's world. Upstairs is a large attractive space that can accommodate 360 for dinner and dancing. A roof deck for cocktails and downtownviewing is on the horizon. Plan on themes to complement the decor.

First floor rental is $500. and both floors rent for $750. Cocktail buffets range from $10. to $20. per person and dinners from $14. to $25., exclusive of beverages, staff and some rentals. Daryl has been building up his inventory, including handsome cloths to complement marine themes and colors, to reduce the need for outside rentals. Incidentally, the space at North Griffin and Hord can't be missed by the three sculpted, jumping fish on the roof and the green-lighted outline of the building..
Please see the advertisement for **Dallas World Aquarium** *on page 219.*

▲ **Ellum Beach Club.** Aside from the beach at Stonebriar Country Club, the Ellum Beach has a near-monopoly on sand. For beach parties and luaus, Ellum Beach has a 3000 square foot outdoor area with bandstand and full serving facilities. (It also had a volley ball net at last viewing.) Inside, there is a 2000 square foot facility of two adjacent and unmarked Elm Street store-fronts, complete with a bandstand and equipment for suitable themes. The facility is run by the nice folks who own the Park Lane Cattle Company, so they know how to handle parties.

◆ **Granada Cinema** can be a "fun" facility for entertaining. We attended a birthday bash there, with dinner, an on-stage orchestra and a screen version of the of the honorèe's life. (We hope this is not the only occasion she will see her name on a marquee.) Rates for the use of the theatre vary, depending on the night of the week and the number of guests. For simpler fare, such as pizza and hors d'oeuvres, the food is done in-house and costs about $15 per person. For a dinner, or more complicated menu, outside caterers have access to the on-premise catering kitchen. The theatre will seat up to 500 for a show or film and up to 350 in the dinner format. Rental of the theatre for use by an outside caterer runs about $3000. and includes all set-up of tables and chairs, use of the A-V equipment and the clean-up.

● **Hall of State,** showpiece of the 1936 Texas Centennial, and one of the country's most acclaimed Art Deco structures, may very well be one of Dallas' most beautiful sites. The Fair Park facility, run by the Dallas Historical Society, has been the choice for events honoring many official visitors, including the 1991 visit by Queen Elizabeth. The Great Hall — and it is truly magnificent — will seat 300 or more for dinner and up to 750 for receptions and dances, utilizing the semi-circular Hall of Heroes antechamber. Two smaller rooms are each comfortable for groups of 50 to 100 for dinner. Rentals start at $200. per hour for the Great Hall, with a three hour minimum, and $75. per hour for the smaller rooms. The staff will be very helpful in everything from advice for catering and rentals to ideas for music and sound. We've happily used the facility many times for memorable charity events. The marble Great Hall, with epic murals depicting the history of Texas and golden seal of Texas, is so impressive in itself that decorations need only focus on tables. Caterers and menus should be chosen with care, since the kitchen facilities are limited.

■ **Krispin — the restaurant.** Wendy Krispin's Design Center facility is more accessible for use than most restaurants, since it is available every evening and weekends as well. Consequently, it is worth noting among "Special Sites." *Please see the advertisement for Krispin — the restaurant on page 221.*

▲ **La Botica Mexican Cafe.** Pete Vaca has run La Botica, on Haskell just four blocks east of Central, as a store-front, private party space for 13 years now. Many of us have seen his brightly painted bus, the Tijuana Limo, which is available to pick up party patrons at a designated home or parking location. Mexican dinners for up to 50 guests, plus an all-weather, tented pavilion for another 125, is the format. The $14.50 dinner, excluding taxes, beverages and gratuities, make La Botica a favorite and moderately-priced destination for young and old alike. The facility comes with a piano and a jukebox, filled with records from the 40's and 50's.

▼ **McKinney Avenue Transit Authority** is a nostalgic adventure for anyone old enough to remember trolleys in major cities. Phil Cobb's brainchild makes a party place in its own, for children with parents in tow or for all those adults who party on the trolley or use the trolley for progressive dinners and transportation en route along McKinney Avenue. Conveyances are the fleet of cars dating from "Rosie," the 1906 Brill car to "Petunia," a 1920 car which served Dallas from 1920 to 1947. A restored Interurban, air-conditioned no less, will be next on line and, in the near future, will be a Ross Avenue extension, to the West End. The ideas for the use of the trolleys— starting at $95. an hour with a two hour minimum — are endless. Almost anything, from a wedding to a fiftieth birthday celebration can be planned.

● **Morton H. Meyerson Symphony Center.** In keeping with the use and support of our city's best public facilities, Dallas' world-class, I.M. Pei-designed Symphony Center has become an increasingly popular entertaining milieu. In fact, available dates for the hall's rental are spoken for quickly when the symphony announces its season and confirms its use of the hall. Savvy party planners reserve well in advance. The Center has both hall and lobby spaces available. The Eugene McDermott Concert Hall, seating more than 2000, is used primarily by churches and other arts organizations, such as the 1992 Shakespeare Festival and TACA's Tommy Tune event. The marble lobby, with soaring dramatic spaces and glass walls "portraituring" the city, provides an uncommon experience. The East Lobby has 24,000 square feet that can accommodate 1000 for dinners and 3000 for receptions and weddings. A 3000 square feet West Lobby now has a full restaurant, called Opus, and the use of the adjacent Betty B. Marcus gardens. Please refer to the listing under "Restaurants" for information regarding Opus.

Fees for the facility vary, depending on use and group. Base fee for the entire building for a non-profit organization starts at $1650. for six hours; fees range up to $3300. for other groups. Lobby rental alone for three hours starts at $450. and goes up to $750. The Sheraton Park Central Hotel is the exclusive caterer. Insurance is mandatory.

■ **Sammons Center for the Arts** is located in the historic 1909 Turtle Creek Pump Station, used as a water pump station until 1930. Restored in the 1980's, it is still owned by the Dallas Water Utilities and is available for rentals when it is not being used by the resident arts organizations. Sammons has several spaces suitable for parties, dances, and concerts as long as the events are arts related. Its main room with 35 foot ceilings lends importance to the space and can seat more than 200 for dinner and is adjacent to a commercial kitchen. The facility rental fee is $850. which includes chairs and tables, and there are linens to rent. We caution that car parkers are a necessity when the guest list goes beyond a certain number, and we recommend mailing a map or giving very precise directions to negotiate the sharp turn off Harry Hines Boulevard going North to enter the premises.

▲ **Silverado City**. The Wild West of our hallowed past has been recreated behind a deceiving storefront on Industrial Boulevard near the Design Center. Fastidious and creative in assembling his Western atmosphere, owner Arnold Sanchez has launched a winner with a private thematic party facility, the likes of which have been sorely lacking in Dallas. Sanchez has established his theme with touch-of-reality Western storefronts wrapping around his party space and enough authentic Western frontier brick-a-brack to lend atmosphere — moose heads, saddles, cactus, chuck wagons. The town folk — can-can girls, barkeepers, cavalry officers, sheriffs, miscellaneous cowboys, and a bandito or two — all wear carefully researched and often authentic

costumes from the 1870's to 1890's. Head Honcho Arnold is of Arnold's Texas Bar-B-Q fame, so arrangements for food are easy. The Silverado crew will be happy, however, to work with your caterer or party planner, which is a plus for being able to alter the space and cuisine to suit the party givers' fantasies. The uses for the facility are endless. Think of the party for the out-of-town wedding guests who expect to find a Western City, or the birthdays, anniversaries, graduation parties and more. The space, with dancefloor and bandstand, can accommodate 350 and comes with many built-in basics. Packages vary, depending on number and choice of food and entertainment. About $35. a person will provide a fairly complete package, with action gunfighters, can-can girls and good country music, often Scott Hoytt from Austin. See also the listing of Arnold's Texas Bar-B-Q under "Catering" in Chapter VI.

Please see the advertisement for Silverado City on page 216.

◆ **The Studio on Hall** provides a unique opportunity for dinner party and reception space. In addition to 23 foot ceilings, tract lighting and skylights, the personal art collection of artist Chapman Kelley hangs on the walls. Joan Kelley now oversees the low profile facility at Hall Street and Oak Grove. A year ago, we urged using the space quickly for fear its use was only temporary. We are happy that it still available. It's perfect for seated dinners of about 60 and buffets of about 100.

▼ **Texas Commerce Tower Skylobby**. We don't know any other skyscrapers with holes in them, so, understandably, the fortieth floor, greenery and fountain-filled atrium Skylobby in the Texas Commerce Bank Tower is an attractive party site. Managed by building owner Trammell Crow Company, the Skylobby has its own list of preferred caterers, some of Dallas' best. There is a $600. rental fee for the space that can accommodate about 225 for a reception and 150 for a seated event. Needless to say, the views are dramatic and truly panoramic. The Trammell Crow Company also has its twin Pavilions on Flora Street, in front of the Trammell Crow Center, available for use for arts-related groups.

● **Texas Stadium Club** is still a popular party place, even when the Cowboys are not playing. The spacious club, which overlooks the playing field, can hold up to 800 for lunches and dinners and more for receptions and is available for private parties, alas, when THE TEAM is not playing. Rates for use start at $100. per hour. Before the Cowboys take to the gridiron, four small rooms are available for perfect "tailgate parties" of 40 to 100 guests. Football fans will love the environment, as will out-of-towners. A renewed interest in the club may come from both the team's fortunes and Donna Wright, Catering Sales Manager of the Texas Stadium Club. Incidentally, if you have enough friends to fill the playing field, the Stadium will rent it as well. The club has its own catering company and has recently expanded to catering off-site. Texas Stadium Catering is one of the up and coming catering companies of the area.

■ **Three Teardrops Tavern.** It's not surprising that the DALLAS OBSERVER has just voted the two-year-old Industrial Boulevard tavern "Dallas' Number One Honky Tonk." It's as authentic a pre-70's Country & Western hang-out as Dallas has, complete with vintage C&W music and enough mem-orabilia to make it believable. Among the "charm" is a 30 year collection of photos, record albums and posters from Hank Thompson's drummer, old photos of the legendary C&W greats, some miscellaneous stuffed animals and the musicians themselves who drop by to catch the best of the Austin music scene. "This is a Bob Wills sort of place," as neighbor Arnold Sanchez of Silverado City says. For our readers, the establishment is available Sundays through Wednesdays for private parties. Owner John Bailey gets a good citizen award for changing the complexion of his neighborhood and transforming it into a budding C&W strip.

▲ **The White House,** an imposing Greek Revival colonial mansion on Forest Lane, owned by the adjacent community church, is now available for private parties. The unfurnished 2,500 square foot ground floor of the 1940's former home can accommodate about 60 for a seated dinner and up to 300 for an indoor-outdoor reception. Use has been mostly for weddings, dinners and corporate seminars. The caterer of your choice can be brought in, and the house comes with a limited number of chairs and rectangular tables. Beer, wine and champagne are permissible.

◆ We have any number of other publicly-owned facilities, such as the **Aquarium,** the **Dallas Zoo,** the **Science Place, Union Station, Plano Convention Center** and our very unique **Old City Park,** where private functions are pos-sible. Pairing size and ambiance to your entertaining ideas is significant. By all means, if you are hosting a party for an avid fisherman or scuba diver, look into the Aquarium. Likewise, the local historian will thrill to a country supper at Old City Park's period Brent House, which can accommodate 60 for dinner. Cocktails on the porch, with the city skyline as a backdrop, is Dallas' best scenery.

the country and western theme

The Texas myth certainly lends itself to the popularity of the Country & Western theme, particularly for our out-of-town visitors. Besides, we occasionally need to reconfirm our Western roots or adoption.

Most of the ranch and C&W facilities are large and frequently enjoyed by conventions and corporate parties. A few, such as **Bill Bates' Cowboy Ranch**, **Circle R Ranch** and the **Park Lane Ranch & Cattle Company** can be comfortable for smaller groups as well. The barbecue menus generally offered mean a modest tab for entertaining and are great for reunions, graduation parties, rehearsal dinners and company get-togethers. If need be, all can be dressed up with decorations, live music and creative food additions — as far as the budget and the imagination will allow. For those destinations, you should consider optional bus or mini-bus transportation for your guests or, at least, very specific maps and driving time estimates.

▼ **Austin Ranch,** Grapevine, just two miles north of D/FW Airport, can accommodate from 35 to 2,500 guests at their convenient facility, the first of the area's dude ranches. Several rooms of varying size help tailor the party to the size of your guest list. The "Round-Up Room," for example, holds up to 350 people and has a dance floor and stage. Charges are on a per person basis, with costs declining with larger numbers. The barbecue dinner, the most popular choice, is $17.50 for 150 to 250 guests, with beer, wine and soft drinks adding another $7. The mixed drink package is $12. Pat Stenson, Director of Sales, knows the property well and is resourceful for all your needs, from decorations to Country & Western dance lessons. We recommend you take a look, if you are considering a Western-themed party.

● **Bill Bates Cowboy Ranch.** For a genuine Texas experience, ex-Dallas Cowboy Bill Bates has recently opened his 346 acre ranch to the public. In wide open spaces, just north of the Dallas city limits, longhorns graze in lush pasture land next to city folk fishing in one of the five lakes, or riding horseback across gently rolling hills. Bill's air-conditioned and heated party pavilion will seat 800, including room for dancing. The ranch provides full bar service, catering and transportation, as well as packages which include trail rides, hayrides, swimming and games such as volleyball and croquet. Food prices vary, but average $21. for a picnic for 50 and $36. for an evening dinner. The food staff specializes in barbecue, steak and Mexican dinners, but they are flexible and can satisfy the preferences of their guests. Among the area ranches, the Bill

Bates Ranch atmosphere and facilities are first rate. This is frequently a top choice among those who have researched the local ranch scene.

■ **Billy Bob's Texas** is tauted as the world's largest honky-tonk and a must-see for area visitors. Located in the Fort Worth Stockyards area, Billy Bob's has two private party rooms. The public areas provide the spectacle of big-name Country & Western bands, dancing and bull riding in the indoor rodeo arena. Pre-set menus range from $10. to $20. per person for dinner, with full bar service available thoughout the complex. Hire a bus or a van for this jaunt!

▲ **Broken Bow Ranch.** Loma Luna, popular Tex-Mex caterer and restaurant, is now branching into the ranch business. Owner Stuart Jacobsim has purchased a working ranch in Prosper, about 10 minutes north of Plano. Plans are underway for flooring in an arena for outdoor parties, and an adjacent building will accommodate about 400 indoors. Catering will be provided by Loma Luna and neighboring barbecue maestro, Warren Clark of **Clark's Outpost** in Tioga. The ranch is debuting its business with Christmas parties and a patron party for the '93 Cattle Baron's Ball. Because of its somewhat smaller size, we suspect the facility will lend itself to more intimately-scaled parties than other of the ranch properties.

◆ **Cedar Canyon Dude Ranch,** just ten minutes south of Downtown in Lancaster, is perhaps the most accessible of area ranches. Cedar Canyon, with a 39 year history of pleasing its patrons, has everything in sports and games primarily for family or company outings, weddings, graduations and reunions. Johnny and Frances Landers, chef and manager respectively, have been on the scene since the day the operation started! Prices for the barbecue menu range from $17.95 per person for 100 or fewer guests to $12.95 for parties of 500 or more and this includes use of all the facilities for a six-hour period. Arrangements can be made for hayrides (at $150. for four hours), carnivals and live entertainment, to name only a few available extras.

▼ **Circle R Ranch.** If the image of the Texas dude ranch is manicured rolling hills, expanses of white wooden fences and grazing long-horns, this is it, just minutes West I-35 in Flower Mound. The Powdermaker family is into its second generation of congenial Texas hospitality, complete with rodeo area and air-conditioned and heated Western-style pavilion, with accommodations for up to 5000. Smaller groups of up to 200 can use the Chisholm Lodge. At Circle R, the hay rides are drawn by Belgian horses, the rodeo is animal-friendly, and the food and entertainment first-rate. This is a facility in great demand for everything from convention to corporate groups, as well as rehearsal dinners and sorority parties. Numerous charity groups have held their fundraisers there — including the Kidney Foundation, the American Cancer Society and the Tejas Foundation. All parties are "custom," but the base package starts at $24.95 for grilled steak and chicken. Singing cowboys, roller-ropers and, of course, the full rodeo are extra.

● **Cowboys**, our very own, big-time Country & Western honky-tonk, drawing major talent, is "in" at the moment. Large enough (Texas-sized!) to accommodate a crowd of 3200 in their Old West setting, Cowboys is closed to the public on Mondays and Tuesdays, and regularly hosts private, charity and corporate events. The minimum for private use of the facility is a guaranty of 500 guests, with a bar minimum of $10. per person. Catering can be arranged by the club, or the party host can make their own arrangements. Of special appeal is the music talent from Nashville that can be brought in for your party — anyone to suit your budget, all the way up to Lee Greenwood at $15,000. If a big name is not in the budget, Cowboys has its own ten piece band, Bobbie Smith and the Country Blues, available for $1500. to $3000. depending on the calendar. Cowboys will also close their club for private use on other occasion with certain guarantees. Incidentally, the club is located near White Rock Lake in East Dallas.

■ **Mesquite Championship Rodeo** is one of the area's greatest treasures and should be on the "must list" when entertaining out-of-town visitors. The Mesquite Rodeo has developed into one of the country's best; in fact, Governor Richards has proclaimed Mesquite the state's "rodeo city." According to all reports, rodeo attendance has been on the upswing, and no place could it be more visible than at the Mesquite Arena, where the ownership has seen a major increase since 1991 — partly a result, perhaps, to their weekly coverage on TNN. The Mesquite rodeo is owned by new Rodeo

Hall of Famer Neal Gay, who with his son, Don Gay, an eight-time bull riding champ, partner Don Carter and President Jack Beckman see that the Mesquite crowds are treated to one of the nation's best shows. The excitement is great for all the individual ticker-takers, but the facilities make the Mesquite rodeo a great place for entertaining as well. Luxury air-conditioned boxes are available during the season for up to sixteen people and include the rodeo plus dinner, bar and parking passes for $850. Any number of alternative packages can be assembled — from entertaining at a private rodeo for groups of 300 or more at $50. per person, to any number of people using blocks of grandstand seating. For the latter, prices range from $14. per person, including a barbecue dinner, to a $30. per person package, which includes not only their great dinner but Country & Western music and a private tent for the festivities. An adjacent party pavilion is in the works which will greatly expand the opportunity for private entertainment. Incidentally, in-house caterer, the **Great American Food Co.**, has even taken its chuck-wagon to the White House and is available for off-premise catering. Owner Floyd White is a pro and will make your event at the Mesquite Rodeo, or elsewhere, a success.

The Mesquite Rodeo also takes its show on the road and has presented mini-versions of its rodeo on the grounds of area corporations.
*Please see the advertisement for the **Mesquite Championship Rodeo** on page 220.*

▲ **Old Fort Dallas** may be one of the area's best kept secrets — although it was the site of the 1992 Cattle Baron's Ball — on 250 isolated acres just 15 miles south of downtown. This is not a dude ranch, but an 1880's Western town with 24 authentically reproduced "Old West" buildings, many available for different-sized parties from the largest cantina accommodating up to 2000 down to an old-time bar and casino that is comfortable for 150. The nice planners at Old Fort Dallas (in business since 1980, and now with new ownership) will customize a party for you with dinners starting about $23., live bands, gun fights and all the expected thematic touches. This is certainly one of the more unique properties where your guests can experience the "feel" of the "old West." Just for the record, some six movies have been filmed there. Their sets are also the Western backgrounds for many a Dallas Cheerleader calendar, as well as popular Dallas Cowboy and Texas Ranger posters We can envision the perfect company picnic, with petting zoo and donkey rides for the youngest guests, to graduation and Valentine parties at the Ice Cream Parlor. Adjacent **Big D Dude Ranch**, once part of the same property, can supply the rodeos and string of horses to co-venture a party with Old Fort Dallas, or for its own for dude ranch parties.

◆ **Park Lane Ranch & Cattle Company** has moved to a 640 acre turn-of-the-century ranch just 15 minutes East of downtown, still within the city limits. Park Lane has everything for company picnics, children's parties and Western extravaganzas. Guests will be amused with everything from hay rides to volleyball and softball courts to a cowhands' rodeo. Whether it is a trail ride breakfast or a "Western Spectacular" with dinner and live music, all will be planned with expertise. It's an impressive operation — and "pure Texas." Food at Park Lane is more authentic than most of the area ranches, with dutch-oven, cooked over open-fire menus, like the cowboys used to make, that include sage potatoes and apple crisp desserts. Presently, the party facilities include numerous outdoor sites, a small lodge to accommodate about 100 and a large, covered pavilion adjacent to sports activities. On the horizon is an all-weather pavilion to extend the use of the attractive site.

▼ **Quarter J Ranch,** just four and a half miles East of Central Expressway on Dublin Road in Plano, lends itself to a variety of events. It is immensely popular with those in search of a convenient and congenial facility for a company or family outing, and great, too, for graduation parties and reunions. Event

Coordinator Jutta Bush draws on party planners for unusual props and, when the occasion warrants, on local chefs for more haute cuisine. Otherwise, food and services start at $18.75 for barbecue. This is one facility where the host can bring in his own beverages, which can result in a savings for many parties.

● **Silverado City.** See listing above under "Special Spaces." *Please see advertisement for the **Silerado City** on page 216.*

■ **Star Brand Ranch** in Kaufman is a premium property owned by the seventh generation of the same family. There is a retreat center on the property, accommodating up to 40, with full tennis, fishing and skeet shooting facilities. Cleverly, several groups have used the property for weekend parties for any number of occasion — family reunions and birthday parties. The ranch was also the site of a spectacular wedding a year or two ago.

▲ **Southfork Ranch** is back in business with a new owner and sprucing up. The name conjures up the image of our fair city and it is still a very desirable location for visiting fireman and large size corporate parties. There is a full rodeo arena to add to the expansive facilities.

◆ **Reunion Ranch**, thirty miles due East in Terrell, is rated by several party planners as one of the prettiest of area ranches. Natural beauty is the feature here with three lakes and cedars galore. Though we know of one very unique wedding here, the facilities — rodeo area, stagecoach and riding — lend themselves primarily to family reunions and large company picnics. A pavilion can accommodate 1500 under cover and a new Conference Center has a banquet room to seat up to 400.

▼ **Wagon Wheel** in Grapevine has been in the party business for ten years now. With three properties and 300 acres, they offer a variety of packages, from corporate picnics, weddings, breakfast rides and dinner for anywhere from 15 to 1500 guests. They do their own barbecue and will bring in caterers for other menus.

tips for judging a party space

- ❏ How attractive is the site and does it fit the theme?
- ❏ Will the location require extensive decorations to suit your purposes, and, if so, how will this affect the budget?
- ❏ What is the quality of food and service?
- ❏ Is the cost of the facility within your budget?
- ❏ Does the site include tables, chairs, china and most of the requirements for entertaining, or will most of the necessities have to be rented?
- ❏ Is there a sound system and adequate lighting?
- ❏ Is the location convenient, or will your guests need directions or even transportation?
- ❏ Is there adequate air conditioning and heating?
- ❏ What about rest room facilities, and a checkroom or place for coats, if the weather should warrant coats or rain gear?
- ❏ Is the parking adequate?
- ❏ Is there insurance and security; should these be significant factors?

VIII

Decor And Theme
flowers, party supplies and more

*I*deas for decorating are limitless, from small nuances for sheer pleasure, to the extravagant ball with major props – and everything in between. Suffice to say, be it flowers, pinatas, balloons or major stage set, the decor of a party can pull together the elements of a theme, and give focus to menus, entertainment and the overall statement. The host and hostess can put imaginations to work with accessories to reinforce the Valentine or Christmas motif, and add gaiety to the luau or the baby shower. This is perhaps the most enjoyable and creative aspect of entertaining.

Not all parties need a theme, but a "look" or mood is easy to evoke with flowers, accessories or color. For a suggestion of Spring or Easter, for example, the baskets of tulips and hyacinths can add emphasis to the invitation, event and table settings.

flowers

There are few cities with as much creative talent engaged in working with flowers, and each designer has a different talent and style. The "right" flowers for a party vary and will be determined by the place, the theme and the space — from a fiesta burst of color on a patio to elegant monochromatic colors for formal dinner parties. For bloom fanciers like ourselves, we are delighted that flowers are most often the centerpieces of choice. They add personality to a space, can warm up the most Spartan room and enhance the charm of an already cozy environment. We invite you to explore the extra dimension flowers can add to your entertaining and to the pleasure of your guests.

The names and addresses for the businesses listed in this chapter can be found in the "Directory of Sources," beginning on page 223.

▲ **Apples to Zinnias**, popular Oak Lawn flower shop, has a faithful clientele for their bright and cheerful arrangements. Their wedding business is booming!

◆ **Atelier, A Work Shop**, with Don Hathorne and his sister, Nancy Hathorne Sheets, at the helm, is the home of the perfect flower in the most beautiful container. For the impact of a single rose, no one can present it better than Atelier, who imports incomparable roses direct from France. Flowers not used are dried for very special arrangements, topiaries and door wreaths. These are masters — and the shop, on the West side of the Quadrangle, is sheer visual delight.

▼ **Botanicals**, a two-year old Oak Lawn shop adjacent to the new and popular Empire Baking Company, makes a stylish statement. The shop always has lovely arrangements to prompt new ideas, topiaries, wreaths, containers and a cooler of superior fresh flowers. Owner Tyler Sweatman is an Oklahoma native who has come to Dallas via San Francisco and a stint at In Bloom in Plano. His recent success has been noticeable, which he credits to being "incredibly service-oriented." Obviously, this and his design talents have not gone unnoticed. Botanicals has just been voted Dallas' Best Florist in the 1993 DALLAS OBSERVER poll. Tyler and staff do lots of house visits, some of the most select weddings and an increasing number of high profile charity events, such as the '93 and '94 Walt Garrison Rodeo and Ball. Tyler is a direct importer of roses; consequently the selection is choice. Stop by for the Saturday half-price specials, a good way to get acquainted.

● **The Charles Stephens Co.** Partners Stephen Smith and Chuck Bard have been mainstays of the Dallas scene for some time. Chuck Bard has been a designer for about 30 years now, drawing on experiences since his early days at Harry Bullard's, THE Dallas florist for many years. During that time, he has designed dinners and balls galore and puts his expertise to work on countless parties, bar mitzvahs and weddings. Stephen and Chuck maintain an Addison studio for their constant activities.

■ **Dr. Delphinium Designs.** Luit Huizenga and his wife, Jamie, are Dallas treasures. Dutch-born Luit comes to Dallas with a flower grower's blood in his veins. After stints with a local wholesaler and then the flower buyer for the one-time Flower Country, Luit has zeroed in on direct purchases of flowers, passing over the local wholesalers. In addition to part-ownership of a Latin American rose-growing concern, the Huizengas have started raising flowers at their East

Texas farm, and encouraging their neighbors to grow flowers as well. As a result, Dallas' freshest flowers can be found at the convenient shop, Lovers Lane at the Tollway. In addition to one of the city's best supplies of cut-flowers and blooming plants and excellent delivery service for flower gifts, Luit can be counted on to have numerous outstanding designers to keep up with the shop's growing reputation in the area of weddings and special events. We know that their wedding business is thriving. There are also designers who make "house calls" for site-specific installations. Inshort, they can do it all! We are real friends and fans!!! On a personal note, we especially like their fabulous long stemmed rose specials, twenty-five roses for $24., which can make a house look very special for any entertaining occasion.

See the advertisement for **Dr. Delphinium Designs** *on page 208.*

▲ **Flora Verde.** Owner Charles Alexander is a popular designer for charity events and weddings. With a presence at the Grand Kempinski, we have seen a number of parties at the hotel embellished with Flora Verde's classical look. We can understand the enthusiasm among traditional brides and hostesses as well!

◆ **Flowers of Oak Lawn.** Designer/owner Terry Inman has been on the Dallas flower scene a long while and always orchestrates a beautiful party. He has a wealth of talent and experience to enhance a setting. We admired a recent wedding where Terry gave a new look to an oft-used club with a fresh use of columns and greenery, adding dimensions and architectural lines to the familiar ballroom. Terry also has nice props and tablecloths, acquired through the years, available for rent.

▼ **Flowers on the Square**, Fort Worth's most prestigious floral designer, is also popular with Dallasites. Owner Bill Bostelmann can create magic with an abundant floral atmosphere, much as he did with the 1992 Sweetheart Ball.

● **Grassroots** is Las Colinas' most distinctive flower shop with large scale design capacity as well. The shop's natural looking style can be recognized at the neighboring Omni Mandalay, just across the street, and at the nearby Four Seasons, as well as major charity functions, including the '93 Kidney Foundation Mother-Daughter Luncheon at the Galleria and the Zoo-To-Do.. The shop is managed by personable Rick Harris, who has considerable floral experience.

■ **I Love Flowers** is a favorite with many North Dallas hostesses and brides. Conveniently located at Northwest Highway and Midway, the shop consistently turns out charming arrangements for home parties and weddings. Like several florists, their wedding business is blooming, with the recognition of their pretty and lush style.

▲ **La Jardinère.** Owner Frances Rain has a loyal Park Cities and wedding following. Her flowers are English garden-like, natural and lovely.

◆ **Liland's Flower Fashions** has been a mainstay of the Dallas flower scene for a number of years and has moved from its Lakewood location to Mockingbird Lane across from the old Dr. Pepper site. John Liland, a protegè of Pete Harris, Dallas' premier floral designer, has enhanced many a party and wedding with his tasteful, classical style. We've admired numerous large wedding parties he has done, one in which he very effectively used only an abundance of roses in classical urns on tall pedestals to create elegance and impact. For a recent sixtieth wedding anniversary, he reinforced the feeling of celebration with a mix of flowers and balloons. His look for the last two Arboretum-benefitting Gadsby parties has been a dramatic play of black with white flowers. Like other large-scale floral designers, he has also gone into the full event business with a coordinate company, Liland's Special Event Productions, headed by his sister-in-law Delene Bell.

▼ **Mille Fleurs,** owned by two art-trained German natives, has been in Village on the Parkway, the former Sakowitz Village, since the center opened ten years ago. Designer-partners Friedhelm Schnitzler and Heinz Reifferscheid clearly have a flair for an Old World elegance. Their following is a faithful one and their arrangements are often seen at Prestonwood Neiman Marcus and at The Westin Hotel. Corporate parties, weddings and private parties in Addison and Bent Tree are their domain, but they make "house calls" everywhere in Dallas. Located just at the Belt Line Tollway exit heading North, their is a convenient shop to pick up flowers if you are heading home in that direction.

● **Petals & Stems** has a home base at LBJ Freeway and Montfort, plus convenient shops at four of Dallas' hotels. Their repertoire is complete — pretty at-home arrangements and scores of weddings, bar mitzvahs, social and charity events. Of interest, Petals and Stems is the designer of the Dallas Museum of Art's permanent floral displays, a generous gift of a Dallas arts patron.

■ **The Potted Palm.** Very gifted Lee Fritts, one of Dallas' best floral designers, and partner Nancy Segers can put together the nicest of arrangements to enhance any setting. Lee is particularly good at "house calls" and gets to know your house and what works best in it for your parties. The duo have always excelled at potted baskets, and Lee's simply exquisite jewel-box small arrangements are a joy for the beholder. Lee and Nancy can think "big" as well and should be kept in mind for the large charity events and special weddings. During the years, Lee can be credited with some fabulous work on balls, such as one Beaux Arts Ball we fondly remember. While Nancy and Lee have had numerous retail locations, they have worked out of Nancy's home studio in near East Dallas in recent years.

▲ **Russell Glenn Floral Design.** Rusty Glenn, a noted floral designer on the scene for a number of years, creates some of Dallas' prettiest parties — with flowers as a central motif. The list of balls, weddings and at-home parties would require an entire book to relate and describe. Last year, we said that his last party was always the best. In that instance, it was the September '92 gala opening of SMU's Greer Garson Theatre. Post-theatre dinner was set on an adjacent stage, dramatically darkened upon entering and emphasized with black moirè tablecloths and black chairs to complete the scenario. Focus and illumination came from spotlighted five-foot high candelabra embellished with roses, lilies and greenery. The peripheral setting was accentuated and defined with floor to ceiling, garlanded Louis XV mirrors. The effect was worthy of one of Dallas' most special evenings. During the past year, he designed two simply fabulous weddings, among his many. One was a Thanksgiving-themed evening wedding with the most elegant and elaborate displays of all the foods, flora and fauna of the season. The bounty created a sensational impact. We also loved the pristine summer white wedding in one of Dallas' prettiest outdoor settings. Tent poles were masqueraded as birch trees and the branches traced the spines of the tent structure. Huge urns filled with white flowers on lacy white tablecloths continued the white motif. Rusty is also responsible for the 1993 Steeplechase Debutante Ball in Fort Worth. But lest you think that Rusty only does major events, his shop will be happy to do pretty arrangements to add charm and elegance to your at-home parties as well. We are also happy that one of the city's more talented designers, Tracy Hamblen, remembered from David-Thomas Designs, has joined his staff.
Please see the advertisement for **Russell Glenn Foral Design** *on page 218.*

◆ **Strictly Top Drawer,** a flower and antique shop on Oak Lawn, has developed a following for it's luxuriant floral style and well-embellished tables for dinner parties and larger events. Top design honors are now in the able hands of Ginette Medlock.

▼ **Zen Floral Design Studio**, part of the Rosewood Corporation domain, consistently outshines the competition with their lavish and creative arrangements for the Crescent Court Hotel and The Mansion on Turtle Creek. To continually create such beautiful and varied looks is a challenge and certainly well met. The lobby flowers at each hotel always make a major statement. While Zen is the "official" florist for those entities — and most use their talents when entertaining at either hotel — they are also on call for anyone and provide some of the nicest floral embellishments in town, for homes, for parties and for weddings. Judy Cocke Blackwell is in charge. Incidentally, Zen has moved to Turtle Creek Village to the site previously occupied by The Cakery. This means greater convenience for walk-in trade and window browsers.

Designers to keep your eye one

Dallas has several talented floral designers who work in studios, rather than walk-in shops. Many of them focus on their regular clientele and on special events, such as at-home parties and weddings. Many of them have regular accounts, such as area shops and offices where there work can be assessed.

● **Bret Driver**, another Zen-ex, is back in Dallas after working with the well-known David Jones in L.A. for a few years. While there, he worked with the "stars" and for the Reagans and Betsy Bloomingdale. Personally, we're delighted that he worked with Rick Duren on the extraordinary center-pieces for the 1992 Catherine the Great Gala and, more recently, for the opening of the Dallas Museum's Hamon Building. Bret's now a regular working for "the dani group" and for many Dallas Museum events. Otherwise, he freelances and specializes in parties and events. His style is much like friend and fellow Shreveport native, Kendall Bailey, who set the style in Fort Worth for many years — elegant and luxe.

■ **Carol Garner** is one of the designers to watch and to patronize. Her plaudits continue to grow, as does her faithful customer following, which includes some of Dallas' most recognizable names. Some of you may remember her retail stint in Highland Park Village. Carol moved her business, **Flowers**, back to her Holland Avenue home-studio. Her look is English country garden or, sometimes, a tight French style, accentuated with French ribbons. When not handling a full schedule of parties, bar and bat mitzvahs, and lots of weddings, she jets to places like Palm Beach and Aspen to lend her talents to their parties and weddings. Carol also reports that her wedding business is "growing like crazy."

▲ **Chris Whanger** is a designer who loves his metier and it shows. A free-lancer, Chris works on private parties and his regular accounts, such as Stanley Korshak in the Crescent and Highland Park Village's Polo Shop, where the floral displays speak for his natural style and well-chosen flowers. Chris has a background in landscaping and is sought after to work on small gardens, patios and balconies.

◆ **Dode Martin**, a Fort Worth native, SMU alum and talented flower designer, is back in Dallas after a few years in Chicago with the city's top floral design firm. Dode has commenced floral design free-lancing and, happily, he has friends from years past who know the beauty of his work. Dode prefers simplicity, not liking to combine more than three floral elements into his work, and then always including a fruit or a berry. The result is elegant simplicity, seen in a few special weddings at The Mansion and a number of private parties. We will be hearing more about his work. Dode frequently teams up with Donald Hill, written about below.

▼ We particularly like **Donald Hill** who is as pleasant to work with as he is talented. Donald has a growing clientele who faithfully entrust their home floral decor, patio and terrace plantings and party flowers to his company, simply called Flowers. Donald is in demand to help other designers on major events, such as the recent "Celebration of the Americas," marking the opening of the Hamon Building of the DMA. As for weddings, we can personally vouch for his flair. We know of one small wedding where the flowers were the loveliest ever. The selection and subtle shadings were masterful. The elegance of Donald's floral work certainly contributed to the overall ambiance of the special day, not to mention the happiness of the bride, who was our own daughter-in-law.

● **Doreen Ravenscroft** has a very special talent in arranging dried flowers. The look of the naturally-dried flowers and grasses is always wonderful and particularly suitable to the Texas look. While Doreen holds forth in a Waco shop, she makes frequent visits to Dallas and is occasionally represented locally.

■ **Fleur Adel** is a new endeavor by Eileen Adel Carver and her husband Bo who have instantly found popularity with their clients. Designer Eileen Adel utilizes her theatre background to quickly envision a total scope to the work, be it wedding or private party. It is not just a wedding or a party but a theme that makes the work different. The team gets raves for both their work and their ability to stay within the budget.

▲ **Luther Menke**, official florist of the Adolphus Hotel, has gained such acclaim for his superb lobby displays and tasteful floral designs for Adolphus events that his free-lance business has mushroomed. He works from his home studio.

◆ **Marilee Mallinson Martinez**, an affable free lancer, enjoys doing small private parties and weddings. It's not surprising that her full floral look would appeal to brides! Marilee's work can be seen regularly at Dakota's Restaurant, at La Cima in Las Colinas and occasionally at Gleneagles Country Club.

▼ **Rick Duren** is one of the area's outstanding designers, who enjoys a reputation far beyond the city limits. He may just as often be overseeing a party in New York or Arizona as in Dallas. Among his many credits, Rick was Zen's originator and went on to found Zen in California and Hawaii for Rosewood Hotels. Rick can be counted on for his intelligent application of theme and enhancement of design beyond the fabulous flowers. Rick's designs can be ultra-luxe and formal, or very natural with field flowers and grasses. Among his more recent undertakings was the July 1992 Gala Opening of the Catherine the Great exhibit, which left patrons and Russian dignitaries abuzz over the lavish flower-filled silver containers and candelabra, worthy of an Empress' fete. Rick was the designer for the much-heralded '93 opening of the Hamon Building of the Dallas Museum of Art. The so-called "Celebration of the Americas" was one of Dallas' most memorable charity parties of recent years, and Rick's sensitive but spectacular treatment of the flora and fauna of all the Americas was admired by all. Rick is a Sante Fe resident when not designing in Dallas. Sante Fe home owners need to keep him in mind for their vacation entertaining.

● **Todd Greer** uses a great deal of the personal approach in working for his many clients. For the most part, he is familiar with their homes and can easily integrate his flower enhancements with the hostesses' favorite objects. He also loves to utilize flowering plants and work with objects to create centerpieces. We've admired his work many times at the home of a friend, where his embellishments often extend to the display of flowering plants around the pool and in their natural settings.

■ **Wesley Lujan**, a Zen-ex who worked under Rick Duren, is another talented designer. Now he enjoys expanded work space in Deep Ellum for such events as last year's Heart Ball, numerous corporate parties and design for caterers and restaurants. Wesley works with Blue Mesa and Caliente restaurants and Silver Tray Catering, just to mention a few. Apropos of an entertaining philosophy, we can quote Wesley, "Good taste extends to flowers and table styling." His work can be described as unrestrained and is often exciting with use of natural flowers and grasses, as one would expect from a New Mexico native. He also says he does "lots of weddings."

▲ **Michael Sambogna** of **Valhalla** has a studio on Shorecrest near Love Field. The greatest accolades are from his peers, who praise his very beautiful work. Ex-music teacher (hence the Wagnerian Valhalla name), Michael has an exciting and rather unsubdued environmental style that he puts to work on parties, which he loves, and weddings. To check up on his style, look at Neiman Marcus in NorthPark. The floral displays are his. His four year old business has certainly caught on.

Flower shops to keep in mind

◆ **Arts District Flower Market** has several downtown locations and has the advantage of serving the business core easily for both parties and gifts.

▼ **Biggerstaff** in Plano has garnered much of the local Plano business for flowers -- for private parties and for weddings. Its Eighteenth Street location puts it in the "heart" of Old Plano.

● **Gunter's Greenhouse and Florist** in Richardson has many fans for Gunter's European-styled arrangements. We know that his reputation has spread. Several caterers attest to the charm of his high-styled work.

■ **In Bloom** in Plano is a five-shop chain enjoying popularity and increasing visibility for its high-styled design work. The Plano shop at Coit and Park Blvd., in the former Flower Country location, has a thriving business for Plano events. Other shops are located in Lakewood, in Lincoln Center at LBJ and the Tollway, in Carrollton at Josey Lane and Trinity Mills and in Arlington.

▲ **Marco Polo** has four flower shops in the North Dallas and Plano area, where near-by residents have ready access to the freshest of flowers, green plants and design services for parties and weddings.

◆ **Nicholson Hardie**. Where would we be without Nicholson Hardie for instant color, the finest, hot-house grown potted plants and the opportunity to decorate for guests in a hurry! Horticulturists and owners Linda and John Bracken, in addition to their serious nursery business at their location near the Tollway, always have on hand the nicest of seasonal flowering and green plants — lilies, hydrangeas, tulips, caladiums and more. And for the basket-less among us, there is a wide assortment of baskets and clay pots for instant containerization. This is the take-out of the plant world, and a boon to instant decor.

▼ **Seasonal Colour**. John and Carolyn Morelock have been doing pretty baskets to grace dining tables for many years now. Theirs is an adjunct to the interest in the country garden, a background that John knows well, with his years' experience in landscape design.

● **Orchid Gardens** is Dallas' only established orchid grower. If the statement of a single, exquisite flower is what you want for a party accent, Orchid Gardens can give you the flower, the education on its care and even bring it back to bloom after it has faded.

▲ As a reminder, the area around the **Farmer's Market** has become a center of the blooming plant world. When picking up food for the casual dinner, it's easy to load up on herbs and pot plants for quick centerpieces and patio profusion. Our favorite is **Landscape Systems of Dallas** on Central Expressway.

A reminder — the names and addresses for the designers and shops listed above will be found in the "Directory of Sources," starting on page 223.

Alternate ideas from a veteran party designer on decorating for a small party — as a reminder that not all parties need to have expensive or extensive decor

✳ *Use copious flowers and greens from the garden or pots from the patio*

✳ *Fill bowls or an epergne with the bounty of the season fruits, vegetables, gourds or Christmas ornaments*

✳ *Use a perfect flower floating in a bowl, or a few special roses, each in its own vase for a dramatic effect on the dining table*

✳ *Show off your favorite collection as a centerpiece, anything from Baccarat crystal or hand-painted Herend animals to antique bibelots.*

✳ *Arrange an ensemble of beautiful candlesticks for drama and elegant lighting.*

✳ *Put out your finest silver candelabra or Chinese export porcelain for a self-assured and elegant statement.*

other decor

Balloons

Balloons are associated with festive events from childhood on, and are instant symbols of celebrations, be it a birthday or New Year's Eve. Suffice it to say, in our increasingly sophisticated world, balloons are being used in new and interesting ways to convey both nostalgia and festivity. Several good balloon companies exist in Dallas, They do everything from centerpiece balloon bouquets, to arches around entryways, and to columns that sway in the outside breeze.

Balloons can also add a touch of elegance. Helium-filled balloons, for example, in a pearlized white with dangling, decorative ribbons, can add interest to a ceiling, or camouflage an unattractive one, even at the most elegant events. Balloons can create movement, reflect light and, in general, provide an air of festivity at lesser prices than other party decor. Balloon specialists will have dozens of ideas to help you.

▲ **Balloon City USA** decorates for many events where balloons are used to create an impact. In addition to working at several local clubs and for party planners, Balloon City is into decorating "exotics" on behalf of their clients, such as a 25 foot Eiffel Tower we saw at the Fairmont Hotel, to herald a French-themed event. We also saw their four-story tall Halloween spider in the West End Market Place. We loved the bar mitzvah backdrop with the young man's name spelled out on a wall of balloons, an idea we must credit to resourceful Gloria Solomon of Affaires Extraordinaire. Another of Balloon City's novelties is the exploding balloon, which pops and showers still more balloons on the heads of guests. This sounds great for the bar and bat mitzvah and graduation parties. Owner Eddie Heyland has become the balloon maestro, exporting his talents to Japan where he recently did a 90,000 balloon release to herald the opening of soccer season. When we talked, Eddie was headed to Disneyland to lend his expertise there. Obviously, if your party or theme needs something more than a balloon bouquet, this group will know how to do it.

◆ **Balloons Fantastique** is a another consideration for the installation of columns, arches, hearts and the like. They like to do one-of-a-kind center-pieces for parties, great for outdoors and large-scaled spaces. Also, Balloons Fantastique has a non-helium-filled balloon that floats, lasting several days and of being less expensive (and perhaps more environmentally correct) than the helium alternative.

▼ **Balloons to You** in Carrollton is one of the companies with both delivery and decorating expertise. They will fashion a nine-balloon center-piece in a mylar base for $12., effective in solid colors, especially the gold, silver or pearlized white for a "dressier" look. **Balloon Bonanza** is another recom-mended company for providing decor with impact — for a modest expendi-ture and for more casual parties.

● **Smiles Balloons** is primarily a commercial decorator and decorates many of the large convention parties, providing balloon releases and great splashes of color. We can attest, however, that owner Cary McIlyea is very accommodating with smaller events as well. We used Smiles Balloons to furnish towering, swirling balloon columns at one of our outdoor picnics.

▲ In addition to the balloon specialty companies, all the party supply shops sell balloons — about $.75 for each 11 inch balloon. **Discount Party Warehouse**, among others, rents helium tanks for do-it-yourselvers. A tank with helium to fill 125 balloons rents for $22.99 with a $100. deposit, and there are tanks for 200 and 300 balloons, the latter going for $44.99 with a $200. deposit. The variety of sizes and colors is extensive, with a gross of 11 inch balloons costing $9.99. Incidentally, we even noticed small-sized helium tanks for purchase at under $15. at **Sam's.**

Party Supplies

Party supply shops are great places to let the imagination gather momentum. And while we do not envision the family Christmas dinner with paper supplies and centerpieces, there are those appropriate occasions, such as Halloween and Valentine's Day, when the mind-boggling inventory of thematic and dispensable goods will lighten the hearts of all party-givers and goers.

◆ **A to Z** is the party supply oasis on Midway at Trinity Mills. The shop is well-stocked with paper basics, mostly by Contempo, and can satisfy the need for streamers, balloons and thematic accents for casual and children's parties. The strong point may be the invitation selection, with tasteful posted samples for wordings and styles to get any party off the ground.

▼ **Michaels/MJ Designs** and **Zaks** are duo craft design emporiums, each with multiple locations in the Metroplex. It's hard to believe we once existed without access to all the baskets, beads, ribbons and supplies to create parties and themes galore. These are particularly important sources for the do-it-yourselfers, theme-oriented and children's parties. Likely, if there is a missing component in your party assemblage, it can be found at one of these sources.

● **Paper Place** is a favorite party place with two locations in the Dallas area. The selection of attractive party goods is at the upper end of the paper product scale, primarily from Gibson and Haut Papier. Theme ideas, whether Easter or Christmas, are always good and above the norm for quality. Of course, they have balloons and the best choice of stickers to decorate invitations and packages. Refer also to our coverage under "Invitations."

▉ **Party Bazaar** on Lovers Lane has been the party paper store in Dallas for more than two generations and surely has provided paper plates, napkins and favors for more children's, graduation and pool parties than any Dallas shop. The designs represented are the market's best, and include the Metropolitan Museum Collection, Haut Papier and others. In addition, Party Bazaar always has a great selection of thematic paper products for all the holidays we celebrate — St. Valentine's Day, St. Patrick's Day, the Fourth of July and the entire year of possible party holidays.

▲ **Party Warehouse**, a national chain with multiple Dallas locations, is the Sam's of the party paper world. Floor to ceiling selections of coordinated paper plates, napkins, cups, etc. are about 20 percent off retail. We tried to count the colors of just solid ensembles but lost our place many times. If we were cutting costs on children's parties, entertaining the entire boy or girl scout troop or having a picnic for the neighborhood, we'd head here for great savings. There are also some invitations, fill-ins and a limited selection of Paper by the Pound.

▲ **Parties-R-Us**, on Royal at Webb Chapel, is a relative newcomer to the scene, but owner Ricardo Pineda has a few distinctions. Hours are seven o'clock in the morning to eight in the evening to accommodate the working crowd and busy mothers. The shop is also a source for custom-made pinatas, whether it is the popular Big Bird or Ninja Turtle, or something colorful to add to the outdoor fiesta, or your company logo. Prices range from $18 to $25.

A reminder — the names and addresses of the businesses listed above will be found in the "Directory of Sources," beginning on page 223.

IX

Entertainment

the right beat & other acts

*M*any agree that music makes a party. It can be a pleasant backdrop to set a mood for a quiet and thoughtful conversation, or it can be a major ingredient for the larger party. The music for a large party is the heart beat and sets the pace. Whether CD or combo, it is important that the music be right — that it suits the setting, the theme and the guests.

The same principles apply to other forms of entertainment. A fortune teller, palm reader or magician can add a touch of novelty, or be an icebreaker. Finding the right entertainment, be it a focal point or merely peripheral, is important.

In hiring an entertainer or musical group, it is helpful to hear and see the performer for an assessment — or to rely on someone else's good judgment. Most professional performers have "demo" recordings or video tapes for an initial assessment. Most groups will also let you know where and when they can be seen, if assessment is difficult by tape alone. And, certainly references count. Fortunately, the music and entertainment scene in Dallas is a rich one, and the scene changes constantly. The DALLAS MORNING NEWS' "Weekend Guide" and the weekly DALLAS OBSERVER are filled with the newest "in" groups, should your taste lean toward the trendy. It is easy to investigate them by catching their acts at the designated locations, many of them in Deep Ellum.

Musicians' fees fluctuate depending on day of the week, with the season of the year and, of course, with the growing popularity of the group. Our very own Dixie Chicks are a perfect example of escalating prices attributed to success. Fees also vary with the number of musicians who play with the group at a given time. It is essential to establish, in advance, both the fee — sometimes negotiable — and the length of time a group will perform. Another tip in the hiring process is to be explicit about both the music to be played and the volume. During dinner, for example, guests will want background music for conversation, as contrasted with a change in tempo and amplification following dinner, when you hope your guests will head for the dance floor.

We have also learned, after one humorous experience, to inquire what the musicians will be wearing. Unless it is a novelty act, a Country and Western band, or a "heavy metal" band, you may want to know what to expect. And, by all means, let the musicians know the event will be black tie or pool party, for teenagers or for senior citizens.

Our attempt here is to list the tried and true, primarily those entertainers who have been on the scene for a while and who have established reputations.

Their addresses and telephone numbers for the musicians and groups in this chapter can be found in the "Directory of Sources," which begins on page 223. For your convenience, there is also a "Telephone Directory," which begins on page 247.

Background Music

▲ **Abundio Ortiz** is the popular guitarist frequently recommended for private parties. Abundio can add another guitarist and a bass player to create a mini-mariachi sound, or put together a full mariachi orchestra. In fact, the mariachi sound, composed usually of violins, guitar, trumpets and the five-stringed vihuela, the authentic sound of Old Mexico, is one of our favorites. Abundio, who is frequently heard at private parties at Javier's and at Mario's Chiquita, has played recently for the Ambassador's Ball and the Cattle Baron's VIP party. His full costumed mariachi ensemble of seven pieces is $350. an hour.

◆ **Carol West** is a harpist always in demand for parties, receptions and weddings. After several years in California, the North Texas music graduate has only recently returned to Dallas. She is frequently heard at The Mansion, the Crescent Court and the Fairmont. As a member of the Dallas Harp Society, Carol is helpful with the recommendations of the area's other harpists, in case she is already busy. Carol also plays as part of an ensemble of flute, harp and violin.

▼ **Chenoweth Music Ensemble** is highly regarded in the area. Lee Anne Chenoweth, a SMU Meadows School of the Arts graduate and a violinist with the Fort Worth Symphony, assembles string trios and quartets from the musicians of the area's orchestras, including the Dallas Symphony Orchestra, the Dallas Chamber Orchestra and the Fort Worth Symphony. The popularity of her groups for weddings and receptions has necessitated the addition of a partner to assist with the bookings. In addition to a classical repertoire of Bach, Vivaldi and Strauss, the groups are adept at performing pop music from the 40's to present day hits. A one hour duet is $260., a trio $370. and a quartet $470. For four hours, the duet is $460., a trio $670. and a quartet $865.

● **Dan Deason**, a solo pianist who specializes in a classical repertoire, frequently accompanies opera divas in recital. He is equally skilled in a contemporary format, such as Broadway tunes of Cole Porter and George Gershwin.

■ **Deborah Youngblood** is a talented young flutist who has returned to the Dallas area after an absence of a few years. North Texas-educated and a former member of a Florida symphony, Deborah plays solo for parties and weddings, plays in combination with a guitarist for greater variety of sound and is a member of the five-member woodwind folk ensemble, Folk Like Us, mentioned below. Deborah's rates start at about $100. an hour.

▲ **Ken Boome Music Production.** Pianist Ken Boome can now be heard weekends at the Beau Nash Restaurant in the Hotel Crescent Court, after more than five years as the Adolphus' Music Director. The new venture has provided more opportunity to contemporize his sound with a digital piano and accompanying bass and drums. He also has more time to play events — weddings, and corporate and private parties. As he says, he's good at everything "from ballroom to backyard" and his repertoire ranges from Chopin to Cole Porter to Harry Connick, Jr. Solo on the piano is $75. per hour. A trio is $200. an hour.

◆ **La Musica String Quartet** is one of the recognized local names in strings, both for its quartet and its larger 10 piece group. The quartet can vary its musical components, using a bass and a piano for a faster-paced, danceable group. The 10 piece group frequently plays for the reception of larger dances and parties and as a lead-in and supplement for an evening's orchestra. La Musica, for example, works frequently with local maestro Phares Corder and his orchestra. La Musica, led by Ingrid and Mark Kovacs, who have impressive musical backgrounds, is often recommended by the area's leading hotels of and is the perfect accompaniment for weddings and elegant parties. The string quartet is $475. for two hours, with a descending hourly rate thereafter. The 10 man group is $1500. for the first hour.

▼ **Mark Carroll** is one of our favorite pianists who is also a vocalist and who can assemble a group of any size. Mark has an extensive repertoire of musical styles, including jazz, classical rock, Big Band, and Broadway tunes, both current and the enduring favorites, such as Cole Porter, George Gershwin, Jerome Kern and Richard Rogers. His credentials are as impressive as his sound. Engagements include the Palmer House in Chicago, the Eden Rock Hotel in Miami, Harrah's Clubs in Lake Tahoe and Reno, a number of Beverly Hills Hotels, The Plaza in New York and more. In addition to arranging specialty material for Johnny Ray, John Gary, Marilyn Maye and Jeri Southern, Mark has produced two of his own albums. Many of us remember the legendary Dallas nightclub, The 90th Floor. It was here Mark played for such stars as Marlene Dietrich and Julie Wilson. We are fortunate to have kept Mark in Dallas.

● **Mori Music** is a husband-wife violin duo, each with an impressive background in education and in experiences, including touring and recordings. Husband Michael Sellman, when not entertaining at private parties, leads Nana's Strolling Strings at the Loews Anatole Nana Grill. The repertoire of strolling musicians that is committed to memory is remarkable and versatile. Mori has been a member of several orchestras and is presently concert master of the Plano Symphony. Each will perform solo or put together groups. For a group of three, an hour fee is $325. and $425. for two hours. A quartet for two hours is $500.

■ **Music of the Harp**. Barbara Kirchhoff provides warm, tasteful background music for receptions, dinner parties, teas and the like. Her distinctive gold harp adds still another touch of sophistication to any setting. With a background as pianist and church organist, Barbara has been a full time solo harpist for more than five years now, and has the versatility to switch instruments (going to the piano) for another part of the event, or combine with an ensemble. Price is $225. for two hours and her repertoire is amazingly versatile. She is heard frequently at the Energy Club and at Neiman Marcus.

▲ **Opus Four String Quartet**, a distinguished string quartet playing together for almost ten years, provides primarily a classical repertoire for receptions, dinners and weddings, wherever the ambiance is elegant. All four women, with an estimable combined musical education, play in area orchestras. A two-hour minimum is $400.; the three hour rate is $550.

◆ **Schnitzer Productions**. Violinist Gary Schnitzer will add a sophisticated mood to reception, dinner party or business function. His background will impress you, even before you hear the first note. A graduate in Performance from Yale, a five year member of the Rochester Philharmonic Orchestra and past Concertmaster of the Richardson Symphony Orchestra, Gary now tours as Concertmaster with the acclaimed Mantovanni Orchestra. Fortunate for area residents, he is available between tours for solo, trio and quartet appearances at parties and events.

● **Serge Stadolnik** is a very popular figure on the private club and the small private party scene. A graduate of the Moscow State Conservatory of Music, Serge is first a pianist, but equally talented on the guitar and as a vocalist. (He is, in fact, a lead singer with a vocal group called Stardust.) Serge's repertoire reflects his comprehensive musical background. He plays classical, jazz, mellow rock, show tunes and old favorites, whatever the occasion requires.

■ **W. T. Greer, III**, a cocktail pianist who plays private parties, has an impressive resumé of bookings. During the Fall of 1992, for example, he played at the Algonquin Hotel in New York and in 1993 made a third appearance at the Meyerson Symphony Hall. In addition to appearing regularly at the Melrose Hotel's Library Room, W.T. has a six-piece orchestra, priced at $2500. He has three albums, which have proven to be very popular and can be purchased directly from him.

Music for dancing and entertaining

▲ **The Bill Tillman Band.** Brassy and bold, Bill Tillman's showpiece band has played at some of Dallas' premier events, such as the Crystal Charity Ball and corporate parties for American Airlines and Neiman Marcus. This is a front and center group specializing in swing, soul and the best of the top 40. Leader Bill Tillman, a Blood, Sweat & Tears ex, alternates sax and singing. Prior to his Blood, Sweat & Tears experience, Bill had toured with the music greats, such as Chuck Berry, Bo Didley, and the Duke Ellington Orchestra. The experience and the professionalism show — and we love the appropriate quote from his brochure "... For the next few hours, Bill Tillman and his orchestra are in control. That is when the audience knows that this is no ordinary event." Recently, Bill played two and a half hours non-stop at the famed Swan Ball in Nashville, and one of his most  appreciated local performances was for the birthday of a local luminary. Everyone had their dancing shoes on! Upcoming will be a CD and an appearance with the Dallas Symphony in a benefit performance for The Dallas Opera and more national and international exposure. Latest news is the addition of two female vocalists to alternate with Bill. Word has it that members of the ten-man band play with visiting big name groups and back-up for major visiting artists. Price for an evening is in the $5000. to $10,000. range.
Please refer to the advertisement for **The Entertainment Company** *on page 215.*

◆ **Buddy Brock Orchestra.** The Buddy Brock name frequently surfaces on the short list of final considerations for major balls and parties in Dallas and throughout the state. Though Houston-based, the Dallas credentials alone of the 50 year old orchestra read like a "who's who" of local events. We've danced to their Big Band sound at the '91 Crystal Charity Ball, the '90 Salute to Greece and the Dallas Opera Ball, the '89 Gala Opening of Ramses II and the anniversary of the Adolphus Hotel. They are here frequently for deb balls and weddings. Fred Hargis, director of the orchestra since 1990 and a leading saxophonist himself, cites the band's versatility — everything from Big Band to Rock 'n Roll — with their popularity. The Dallas fee, incidentally, is $6500.

▼**Cavalcade of Stars**, musical impersonators and a production of Tapley Entertainment, has made appearances before many of our prestigious organizations — the Walt Garrison Rodeo, Children's Medical Center and some of our local Fortune 500 corporations. Whether you want Elvis or Madonna, the group can convince you with their talents.

● **Dallas Wind Symphony.** If Souza is your beat and a Fourth of July party on the drawing board, keep Dallas' very own Wind Symphony, one of the nation's premier brass symphonies, in mind. Made up of the area's best brass and percussion players, the Dallas Wind Symphony makes occasional Meyerson appearances and plays for patriotic observances. But, they can also be heard at corporate parties and when the sound of brass is needed.

■ **Dave Tanner** performs usually with his trio, but he is best-known for his five piece group that plays non-stop. With keyboard and synthesizer, this group puts out a big sound. Everyone in the group is also a vocalist, so there is a lot of harmony. Dave plays ballroom to disco and is assured of getting all the guests to the dancefloor. Weekend rates for the five piece group are $1800. and lower for mid-week. The trio is $800. and the quartet $1000.

▲ **The Dixie Chicks** are local girls gone big-time with their lively sound, mixing country, bluegrass and swing. The always chicly Western-garbed young women are pretty, musically talented and write much of their own music. When one "chick" recently returned to teaching school, two guys were added as backup, but their toe-tapping music didn't miss a beat. They are now represented by a Nashville agent. Their fee is presently between $4000. and $5000. for two one-hour sets with a thirty minute break. Hearing them prior to hiring is no problem. Purchase one of their CD's or catch them at one of their many local appearances..

◆ **Folk Like Us**, mentioned just above, specializes in American and Celtic folk music (Celtic because it is the base for much of our American music). Credentials are many — from two CD's on the Northstar Label, bookings through Young Audiences and the Texas Commission for the Arts. The charm of the group, in addition to their music, is the broad age range of its appeal. The mix is bluegrass and ragtime, played primarily by bass, fiddle, guitar, flute and hammered dulcimer. The group is managed by Mark Shelton Productions in Denton. We might add that the flutist is the same Deborah Youngblood mentioned above. Mark Shelton represents another group which has played a number of big-time parties, such as the 1993 Ambassadors Ball. It is **Yes 'Mam**, an all female band, and despite the name, he is the noticeable male member of the group.

● **Hal Turner Orchestras.** It's hard to categorize Hal Turner with his many formats — he has a 11 piece big band and a smaller 8 man band that have been active in both New York and Dallas for more than 30 years, the former featuring "big Band" music with original arrangements from the era. The latter group, incidentally, has a little more jazz to its flavor. They've played the White House during two administrations, for both Nixon and Johnson, and with many high profile entertainers. He has entertained us locally at TACA and Dallas Ballet balls, many a deb party, and most recently at the closing gala for the Van Cliburn Competition. Hal was also the Mansion's first pianist for the ever-popular bar and he is frequently associated with his years there. Today, he is kept busy at a local club, but he plays privately for the legions of friends he has made during his years of entertaining. The Big Band rates for three to four hours are $2500. and the small band $1800. Hal will arrange combos at $55. per man per hour, and he is available to play solo on the piano (and don't forget that he is a vocalist too!) at $100. an hour.

■ **Jack Cannon**, with both his Glenn Miller-type orchestra and his well-known Allegro Strings group, has been on the Dallas scene for many, many years. We have fond memories of the many balls and private parties for the socially prominent where his group has played. His New York-style orchestra goes for about $3500. for an evening. His fast-paced, six-piece string group is $660. for the first two hours.

▲ **The Larry T-Byrd Gordon Show.** Dr. Larry Gordon, director of perhaps the area's most visible jazz band, has gathered an interesting group of musicians, all his former students. Despite a busy performing schedule in Los Angeles, Chicago and even Europe, Dr. Gordon keeps his hand in the academic scene teaching music at Brookhaven College. The most recent European jaunt in summer of '92 was to Monaco where the T-Byrd group represented Texas at "Texas in Monaco Day," playing for an 80,000 audience among the several events. T-Byrd is popular in Europe, with its "Give It Up" recording on Gordon's Le Me label in the top 20 in France and England. Locally, we've been lucky to hear T-Byrd at two Dallas Museum Beaux Arts Balls, the '92 Grand Heritage Ball at Old City Park, the author's' very own dance club and at several weddings. T-Byrd plays annually at the January 1 Cotton Bowl for a national television audience. The group has a wide musical range, although they excel at jazz. Size of the group can vary from five to 20, with prices from $2500. to $12,500.

◆ For Texas swing, the **Light Crust Doughboys** are a state treasure, dating back to their appearances in the 1930's Westerns with Gene Autry and at the opening of our very own Texas Centennial. The foot-stomping four-man group is led by original member and octogenarian legend Smokey Montgomery. Smokey also has a group called **Smokey and the Bearkats.** With fellow Bearkat Bud Dresser, they play a mix of music, though Dixieland is their forte. The latter trio, which can be stationary or mobile, charges $300. for two hours or $400. for four hours.

◆ **The Mal Fitch Orchestra.** As several newspaper portraits have said, "If you are invited to a charity ball or social gala, chances are the Mal Fitch Orchestra has been invited too." On the Texas scene for more than 25 years, Mal Fitch is perhaps the state's most popular society orchestra and has an impressive list of credits for anyone who might need a reference — the Dallas Symphony Ball, Yellow Rose Gala, Tyler Rose Festival, Idlewild deb cotillions and Texas inaugural balls galore. While distinctively Big Society Band in sound, Mal Fitch prides himself on versatility, to which we can attest. At a recent large wedding reception at Brook Hollow Golf Club, the Big Band sound was supplemented by numbers of strings, giving a huge symphonic sound for the capacity crowd. And, we loved him at an outdoor wedding under a big tent in early June. Unfortunately for those who have been his fans for so long, Mal has announced his retirement for June of '94. It would be wise to book him as soon as possible to get in under the wire. The expanded orchestra has a current fee of $4150.

▼ **Mariachis Los Reyes de Dallas.** The charm of the mariachi group will turn any Mexican-themed party into a fiesta. Mariachis Los Reyes, frequent performers at local Mexican celebrations, charge $300. per hour for the six-man ensemble of strings and brass. There is an option for a larger group.

● **One O'Clock Lab Band** is North Texas University's legendary showpiece band, an example of the school's prominent music department. The band, under the direction of Neil Slater, is a popular Dallas hire and is rated high by professional musicians. In fact, many of the area musicians are alums of the illustrious 20 man band. If your party does not warrant the full band, which goes for a $4150. fee, there is an opportunity to engage the **North Texas Quintet** or other group members, which we have done on occasion. The results have gone "dancingly."

■ **Panhandler's Steel Band.** The Caribbean sound in "in" and another North Texas group has been ahead of the wave. Recently, we enjoyed the Steel Band at a wedding where the tropical beat greeted the guests at the reception and then alternated with the Lab Band, making it a upbeat evening in every respect.

▲ **Phares Corder Orchestra** performs in the traditional Big Band style, playing selections from the 50's through the present. The orchestra is supplemented by several vocalists who can add the dimension of Frank Sinatra or even the Manhattan Transfer, depending on the occasion. Phares Corder's orchestra has been the choice for a number of high-profile events recently, including the 1992 Ambassadors' Ball and the Gala Opening of Catherine the Great. The group, which is in the $2000. range for an evening, definitely has the ability to get people on the dance floor. We've had the personal experience of hiring Phares for a late night post-opera supper, an occasion for which he assembled a five man ensemble.

◆ **The Project** is new on the scene, an offshoot of the popular Bill Tillman Band, mentioned above. Pianist Eddie Parker, with Tillman since 1986, has started his own group with other members from the Tillman Band. If you like the Tillman sound, chances are that you will like The Project, a combination of the alums involved and the fact that Eddie Parker had also been Tillman's arranger. The group has broadened its reportoire to include the Big Band sound and some Country and Western. Catch them while you can — while their prices are in the $2000. range.

▼ **Ran Wilde Orchestra** has long been popular on the local scene and commands a steadfast following. Director Ran Wilde also has a trio, quartet or quintet to meet the flexibility of his clients' needs. Rates begin at $600. for the trio to about $1000. for the five-man group.

● **Ron Lawrence Music.** Ron Lawrence is a serious musician of note, both as a trumpeter and as band leader of the Ron Lawrence Orchestra. His versatility is impressive, as a solo performer and as the backup to many nationally-known artists. As band leader, he is known for his role in the television series "Dallas" and appearances at the White House and frequently as the band of choice for touring artists, such as Ben Vareen, Lola Falana and Joel Grey, on their Dallas stops. He played at the Fairmount's Venetian Room for three years, once again providing dance music and back-up to the name stars who frequented the club "in the good old days." The 13 piece Ron Lawrence Orchestra with vocalist is $2750. and an abbreviated orchestra with vocalist is $1300. A trio and a quartet are also possible, as $600. and $800. respectively.

■ **Ronnie Renfrow Big Band** from Houston has made its mark on Dallas recently. The 19 piece band made the social columns when it was the band of choice for the wedding of Caroline Hunt's youngest offspring and the dancefloor was jammed. More recently, when selecting a "really swinging" band for the opening party for the opening of "Crazy for You," the benefit chairmen chose the popular Houston group. They will be performing at the '93 deb Assembly Ball in Fort Worth and at a few upcoming weddings. In fact their size is great for the new Dallas Museum atrium space and they are already booked for a major wedding there in May of '94. Prices are in the $8500. to $10,000 range depending on variables of size and hours.

▲ **Rotel and the Red Hots** are definitely hot! This high-energy female ensemble belts out 50's and 60's favorites and put on a great show for $4000. to $4500. Their agent, David Hinkley, also represents **Red and the Red Hots**, two Andrews Sisters-sounding vocalists whom we have not heard. David assures us that Red of the Red Hots is as popular now as Linda Ronstadt was at the time he played piano for her. This may be a vote of confidence in Red's ascendancy in the entertainment world.

◆ **Stone Savage Music** is a familiar name on the private party scene. Many of us know "Stoney" from frequent Dallas Museum of Art appearences. A graduate of London's Guild Hall of Music and Drama, he has a background in classical bass and uses his instrument as the nucleus for trios and quartets. A trio, such as the usual bass, piano and drums, starts at $500. (Or, it could be bass, guitar and sax.) A quartet starts at $850.

● **The Vicho Vincenzio Band** has been on the Dallas scene for more than ten years now. Recently, the classy orchestra's popularity seems to have soared with frequent appearances at weddings and big charity events, such as the '92 Dallas Opera Ball and the Dallas Symphony's "New Year's at the Meyerson." Vicho's sound is Big Band, but he has an added dimension in having assimilated musical styles from Europe, where he lived prior to coming to the United States, and from his native Chile. Vicho also has a four-piece combo, which starts at $500. for four hours and can vary sizes to fit your needs up to his 14 piece big band at $2500. His is "the perfect balance of traditional and contemporary music styles for listening and for dancing."

Out of town attractions

There is a certain *caché* involved with the nationally recognized big name music groups. You will find **Lester Lanin, Alex Donner, Michael Carney, Peter Duchin** and **Marshall Grant** playing at the most elegant of Dallas' charity functions, debutante balls and high-profile weddings. Their lively cafe society sound is not easily duplicated, although each has a distinctive sound and avid followings. Best known for their sophistication, they are all well-versed and deliver a full range of musical repertoire — waltz, jazz, rock n' roll, Latin and, of course, their signature Big Band sounds. Certainly, the Houston bands mentioned above are from "out-of-town," but we'd like to think that fellow Texans can be included in our "local" coverage.

▲ **Alex Donner**'s New York orchestra is synonymous with elegance and class. While some of us know Mr. Donner from private parties, he made many new friends at the 1992 Sweetheart Ball where he was quite a hit. His tempo and style are up-beat, and like all accomplished musicians, his range of musical talent is wide-ranging and his repertoire flexible to suit his audience.

◆ **Lester Lanin**, perhaps the best-known orchestra leader in the world after more than 65 years of performing, has earned the designation "Legend in his own time." Society columns the world over are peppered with his name, always having played for the major party of the moment. As a society staple, his band's name on the invitation can double the attendance at an event. For those who have not seen the orchestra in its non-stop action, Lanin has a well-known trade mark of throwing floppy crew hats to late-staying guests. Collectors of his hats are know to linger to add another hat to their prized collection. It's great fun to close an elegant evening with the sight of couture-attired ladies and men in black or white tie sweeping across the dance floor in their casual, colored chapeaux. We noted recently in THE NEW YORK TIMES that Mr. Lanin's non-stop  playing, which has set the standard now for other orchestras, is mastered by a well-tuned group of musicians who can switch into an arrangement merely by maestro Lanin's mentioning the first word of the song. Mr. Lanin is adept in synchronizing his musical tempo and selection to the mood and ages of his guests. His presence will assure a successful party, particularly a party marking one of life's great events.

Lester Lanin has entertained royalty, presidents and, fortunately, a good number of Dallas party goers. We've been so delighted that he has made numerous trips to Dallas over the last few months and anticipate many more local appearances. We count two weddings, a special birthday and the Idlewild Ball during the Fall of '92 alone. He was back in '93 for the elite Sweetheart Ball, and we will be certain that one of Dallas' charities or weddings will feature him before the end of '94. All of Mr. Lanin's musicians travel with him, unlike some of the other orchestras which supplement their nucleus with local talent.
Please see the advertisement for **Lester Lanin Orchestras** *on page .207.*

▼ **Michael Carney** leads his well-known orchestra with lively non-stop playing and singing. His name on an invitation is certain to draw crowds, as he will did for the December '92 Crystal Charity Ball and the September '93 Gala Opening of the Hamon Wing of the Dallas Museum of Art. We are also thrilled that he has made numerous Dallas appearances, including for small dinner dances marking special anniversaries and birthdays.

● **The Marshall Grant Orchestra** is no newcomer to the Dallas entertainment scene. We have enjoyed its music at balls and weddings, and many will remember its appearance at a Crystal Charity Ball. Marshall Grant plays around the country for numerous charity functions, and regularly for Bob Hope and Dinah Shore. Grant was a child prodigy who debuted in classical piano at age four and who has played professionally since age fourteen. Now in the business for more than 30 years, it is no surprise that he is the recipient of numerous honors, including being the only living musician to have been inducted into the Big Band Hall of Fame. His home town, Palm Beach, has proclaimed a Marshall Grant Day in his honor.

■ To round out this category, we still have other favorites, such as society pianist **Peter Duchin**, who makes occasional Dallas appearances, and **Drew-Corcoran**, who with his marvelous Rhode Island group, has entertained us at several private dances and weddings.

As a reminder, the phone numbers for the above-listed musicians and groups can be found in the "Directory of Sources," which starts on page 223. For added convenience, a "Telephone Directory" for each chapter begins on page 247.

Agents and other sources

Agents and agencies provide special services for the event giver, whether mother of the bride or corporate or charity party planner, in search of orchestra or specialty act. In fact, there are some music groups and entertainers who will work only through their agents on an agent-to-agent basis. The agencies function as entertainment consulting firms to satisfy the needs of their clients, from fact-finding about the groups that are available to services beyond, including assurances of reliability. With "big name" and out-of-town entertainment, the gamut runs from contract negotiations to production of the entertainment that can include staging and lighting.

So as not to frighten away the would-be hostess looking for the most appropriate entertainer even for small parties, the local agents know the scene and will be happy to help with the direction and selection of the most suitable musicians or alternate amusement. There are other representatives, such as the Dallas Symphony Orchestra and the Dallas Chamber Orchestra, which act as booking agents for their own musicians. The American Federation of Musicians is still another source for musicians, and they will be happy to recommend from among their membership.

▲ **Carol Marks Music** is one of the biggest names among Dallas agents. In addition to singing and having her own band, Spyce, Carol Marks has been an agent for a very diverse clientele for 20 years now. Her credentials are many. We know her as the agent for a number of charity groups, such as TACA (the fund-raising entity for the performing arts), the Richardson Symphony Ball and, occasionally, for the exclusive Sweetheart Ball. Carol also points out that much of her business comes through the local hotels, such as the Four Seasons, whose clients are looking for event entertainment. Weddings, private parties and local corporations make up the remainder of her clients. The objective, of course, is to pair the party or event giver with the most appropriate music, whether it is Big Band, Rock, or Country and Western, with the party's theme, size, budget and ages of the audience. Carol is not limited to music. Speciality acts include magicians, clowns, caricature artists and even Santa for the annual party.

◆ **Ed Bernet Entertainment** has been a familiar name on the Dallas music scene since the 50's, when Ed organized the Levee Singers. Ask almost anyone who was in Dallas at the time and they will attest to the popularity of his Dixieland group, which still makes appearances on special occasions. Ed has been in the booking business ever since and knows the scene as an insider. He can engage anyone, but specializes in local and regional talent on a non-exclusive basis, allowing him to explore new talent without the restriction of promoting in-house acts. Ed represents his clients' best interests by assuring that the entertainment component of their party runs smoothly and by overseeing the lighting, sound and other extras.

● **Encore Productions** is an agency with a 15 year record. Owner Luana Stoutmeyer, in addition to having her own band, will arrange the music you like for your party, wedding, corporate event, bar mitzvah and bat mitzvah with consideration for the type of function, and the age and budget of the group. The agency likes, among the variety of available talent, the Roof Raisers among bands, George Anderson among harpists, mariachi music and DJ's.

■ **The Entertainment Company** is a name always on the short list of recommended agencies to book for every occasion — private and corporate parties, weddings, bar mitzvahs, and the charity parties we love to stage. The agency is also high on the list for area hotels, such as the Westin, Galleria, where there is the assurance that the talent will be well-matched to the occasion. Congenial Debbie Meyers heads the office and knows the music and talent scene, with access to more than 350 local and national bands, acts and personalities. So, if the circumstances call for a variety group like the trendy Duck Soup from Austin, a nostalgia group with a 50's repertoire such as Dash Rip Rock and the Dragons, or a Country and Western group to go with the multiplying Cowboy-themed facilities, The Entertainment Company will locate the appropriate entertainment. In addition to suitability, they can focus on a budget as well — and we know their added effort that goes into each client and musi-cian match. The agents play a role in the arrangements for everything from contract negotiations to timing for breaks to directions on hotel loading docks. The agency has its favorites, particularly the outstanding "name" bands of the area — The Bill Tillman Band and Dallas Brass & Electric. For the Big Band sound, they like Cal Lewiston, Ron Lawrence and Dallas Jazz. Comedians and DJ's are also big on their lists, depending on the crowd. Their list of corporate clients reads like a Who's Who of the Dallas business community, who recognize the success ingredient The Entertainment Company brings to events. Repeat business is the norm, a reflection of a satisfied clientele. *Please see the advertisement for* **The Entertainment Company** *on page 215.*

▲ **Wynne Entertainment**. Bon-vivant-around-town Angus Wynne books more national talent than most other Dallas agents, but he is similarly at home with the local and regional scene. With almost 30 years in the concert business, Angus has a wealth of contacts and certainly leads the way with booking trendy new groups.

◆ A wealth of musical talent is available through the area's symphonies. Each symphony, starting with the esteemed **Dallas Symphony Orchestra**, maintains an office and a contact for their musicians who will perform for private events when not on schedule or on tour. And not all adhere to the classics when performing elsewhere. We know a few who are adept at jazz and who enjoy a change of pace from the more serious side of their profession. **The Dallas Opera Orchestra, Dallas Chamber Orchestra** and the community orchestras of **Richardson** and **Plano** all have professionally-trained musicians available for private parties. The representatives of these symphonies will be happy to match your needs with the expertise of their members. Rates are consistent, about $100. per musician per hour.

▲ Local educational institutions are sources for extraordinary student talent, in some cases experienced far beyond the fees they charge. **Southern Methodist University** has a wealth of resources and their Meadows School for the Arts can be called about available musicians. In addition, a number of the faculty members, all exceptional musicians, will play for certain events. **The Arts Magnet School** (officially the Booker T. Washington School for Performing Arts) also has a number of talented youngsters, not necessarily limited to field of music. The school's theatre department has a fine Mime Group, which has provided an added dimension to any number of local parties and benefits.

Other Acts

Not all entertainment means music. Alternate forms of entertainment, such as a dance group or a comedian, can supplement, or even supplant, music for an event. Finding the right "act" can be the cincher in providing your guests with an uncommon experience.

Another format is blending theme and entertainment, such as a casino party or carnival. There are outstanding local groups who can provide all the ingredients for an activity-oriented evening.

◆ **Anita M. Martinez Ballet Folklorico**. The Anita Martinez-sponsored Ballet Folklorico works hard to keep its dance form thriving. The colorfully-costumes young dancers add warmth and color to events and captivate audiences with their energy. Frequently seen at private events, such as a South-of-the-Border-themed debutante ball a few years ago, fees for the charming dancers are $150. per dancer per half hour.

▼ **The Arrangers** stage casino parties which are a wonderful amusement for all ages. The Arrangers did a high school graduation party for our children, a big hit for the evening. The Arrangers also work with the Crystal Charity Ball, Cattle Barons, the Junior League and other charities, as well as handle many corporate parties. Basically, The Arrangers have crap and blackjack tables and roulette wheels, plus all the dice, cards, chips and other equipment. Dealers and croupiers are part of the rental prices of $350. per crap table, $150. per blackjack table and $200. for roulette. Recently, The Arrangers have branched out to carnival and other parties. At the time, Shannon Molky is taking over the business from her father.

● **The Original Butt Sketch.** We have to admit that the name took us by surprise. Perhaps the real surprise is the attraction that artist Krandel Lee Newton provides at a party by sketching the upper torsos of mostly couples from the rear, usually with a backward glance of one of the parties. The sensitive pastel art work is a welcome addition to one's collection and a fabulous momento of a party.

■ **The Caroling Troubadours.** During the Christmas season, a group of strolling minstrels provide festive and lively Christmas entertainment. Dressed in Victorian costumes, the group, up to eight in number, sing seasonal selections and provide their own accompaniment with guitars, bells and tambourine to reinforce the feel of Christmas' past. Prices are on an event by event basis.

▲ **Cohen's Casino Parties.** Ken Cohen offers authentic casino parties at their Las Vegas-style parties. Croupiers are dressed in Nevada night club fashion, with wing-tipped tux shirts, as they operate crap, roulette and black-jack tables. Prices for the total evening's entertainment, and all the instruction needed for the novices, average about $17. per person. Ken is both knowledgeable and helpful in planning the number of tables and croupiers for maximum guest participation. Cohen's has now been in the business for more than ten years, and we particularly like the high level of professionalism among his personnel, who are as wholesome as they are proficient. Not surprisingly, Cohen's Casino Parties has been featured in Dallas and Fort Worth newspapers and on P.M. Magazine. After a recent party, we receiv0ed a photo album commemorating the evening, a very thoughtful and appreciated gift.

◆ **Magicland** might put some spark into a party. If you have a group that needs diversion or an "ice breaker," or if you are entertaining children as well, try Magicland for magicians who can put on a show or who can wander through a party doing a few tricks. Magicland also has recommendations for palm readers and other party entertainers. A purveyor of magic supplies, Magicland is one of Dallas' older business, having been established in 1915. If a costume shop is also a possibility, you might also check out the rental stock here. And, for the "Masked Ball," the shop has some wonderful feathered and sequined masks.

▼ And speaking of costumes, Dallas has several top-notch costume shops where living out one's fantasy is an easy reality. **The Dallas Costume Shoppe,** on Main Street near Fair Park has been around for some time. Its inventory is mostly authentic vintage, making it all the more fun. We also love **Incognito Costume World,** on Inwood Road north of Alpha, where the well-organized inventory can outfit Henry VIII, Southern Belles, Tin Men and just about any character worthy of masquerade. For those who prefer Halloween ghoul, there is a separate department to satisfy morbid tastes. Prices start about $25., but this is an easy place to be carried away. **Texas Costume,** on Ross Avenue and Routh Street, can meet all your masquerade and more serious theatrical needs. **Accardi Costume,** on Lovers Lane west of the Tollway, also appeals to the thespian world, with custom-made costumes and an inventory to suit every fantasy.

● **Sandy Trent's 1 Dance 2**. Sandy Trent is popular for teaching country and western dancing for the popular Western parties. She will come to the party and get the steps going with instruction and refresher courses for those who have not danced the "Cotton Eye Joe" since the seventh grade. Sandy will also teach ballroom and country dancing at her studio as well and rent the studio for groups who want to polish up their dancing in advance.

■ **Superior Productions** by Paul Williams does character/comedy entertainment for social and corporate occasions. For a fee of $150., Paul will liven up an event with any one of his hilarious characters to roast a guest of honor. Paul is perhaps best known for his portrayal of Saturday Night Live's "the Church Lady."

a few tips on hiring musicians

♪ Ask for a demo tape
(but keep in mind, these are often not good representations).

♪ Find out the musical qualifications of the artist or group. *Usually, you will find that the best musicians also work for the area's professional orchestras, such as the Dallas and Fort Worth Symphonies, or the Dallas Opera Symphony.*

♪ Ask for references.

♪ Observe the group if at all possible.

♪ Find out if the same musicians will be playing at your engagement. *Many complaints arise from the use of "pick-up" musicians, some of whom are not accustomed to playing with one another.*

♪ Discuss the terms to be included in your contract — *fees, length of time to play and breaks. Consider the opportunity for extended playing time, if you decide not to break up a good party with the end of the music.*

♪ Discuss the timing of breaks to work with the flow of the party, *so that the orchestra, for example, will not be taking a break at the conclusion of a meal when guests will want to dance.*

♪ Be specific about what you want them to play.

♪ Inquire about wearing apparel.

X

Finishing Touches
rentals, lighting, sound & such

The difference between a good and a great party can be a matter of place, guests, food, music and decor. Yet, there are many small touches that can enhance some of these ingredients and create a more polished and complete picture. The right china and silver, a tent to create a dramatic outside room, the right lighting and sound, parkers and party help, and photos for memories are all part of our final chapter.

The addresses and phone numbers of those listed in this chapter can be found in the "Directory of Sources," which begins on page 223.

rentals

Past a given number, the at-home party giver will likely exhaust his or her china pantry, and rentals will be needed. There is also the convenience of having everything coordinated in the numbers required — added to the fact that rental equipment is usually more durable than one's finest Spode, particularly for the large or outdoor party. Virtually all the equipment needed for a party can, in fact, be rented. Everything from tents and dance floors, props and plants, lighting and sound, tableware and dining furniture.

Party planners, designers and caterers know the sources, and if you are using professional help, they can obtain all these things for you. Often, it is more convenient for them to figure out your needs, to check the rental items in and pack them up when the party is over.

If your needs are simple for a party at home, Dallas has several good rental companies that can assist you. If you have not previously dealt with one of the rental companies, or if your needs go beyond the basics of extra tables and chairs, we recommend that you familiarize yourself with the quality and vast inventory offered. A visit to one of the companies, such as **CANNONBALL**, will leave an idea of what is available and the variety of entertaining looks that can be achieved.

There are also a few specialists in the rental market, such as those who rent very attractive table cloths, in addition to the larger companies who have inclusive inventories.

▲ **Abbey Party Rents** has been a Dallas fixture since 1924, so no wonder there are so many regular Abbey customers. Abbey has all the basics, including catering equipment and tents. The company's uniqueness comes with its lighting equipment and special effects' rentals. For that wonderfully dramatic table lighting, they can supply the pin spots, lighting trees and the like for staging. You might note that they even have a fog machine for Phantom of the Opera themes and a number of props to assist with nautical, Western and Mexican themes.

◆ **Blue Chipper** is a relative newcomer to the rental arena. The stock is narrower and smaller but the savings add up. A white garden chair here rents for $1.55, undercutting the larger companies' rate of $1.95., and this is only one of numerous examples. They are quickly making many new friends among the party-giving set.

▼ **CANNONBALL Party Rental Co.**, one of Dallas' major rental companies, can accommodate any size party, from a backyard children's party for 20 to the charity ball at the Meyerson for 1200. For one recent charity event in which we were involved, 30,000 rental items came from CANNONBALL — from knives and forks, china and stemware, to tablecloths, the dance floor and those elegant, gold chivari chairs that create instant elegance. CANNONBALL

has all the basics and then some! What we like beyond the basics are some of the new dinnerware rentals, especially the Masquerade pattern with black border and gold band for a fine china look, paired with cut crystal stemware at affordable prices, and silverplated flatware. For the contemporary look, the new, black, oversized buffet plate lends itself to interesting settings. What caterers, party planners and charity mavens also like are the dance floors, extensive inventory of off-site cooking equipment and tents for weddings and party overflow. Having used CANNONBALL for several major charity events, we can testify to the assistance in planning, and advice on everything from stage sizes for orchestras to the coordination of linens with decorations. Latest of the CANNONBALL involvements was the mammoth undertaking of recent years — the opening of the Hamon Building of the Dallas Museum of Art. To the participant, the planning went effortlessly. Behind the scenes was a veritable musical chairs, with CANNONBALL assisting in the smooth flow of more than a dozen events over a two week period. Not to be overlooked, owner Bick Jones can always be counted on for extra effort when last minute changes befall the hostess.

Please see advertisement for CANNONBALL Party Rental Co. on page 204.

● **Ducky-Bob's Party Rentals.** Ducky-Bob's vast Addison showroom reveals the breadth of inventory and the variety of looks that can be achieved with silver, copper and gardenware. There are endless combinations of china, linens, tables and chairs to individualize a party. The selection also is mind boggling. Cloths come in 26 solid colors (at last count) up to 118 inches in diameter to cover 60 inch tables to the floor. There are moires, laces, jacquards, plaids and prints — in all in prices $9. for 90 inch solid colors to $55. for the more special patterns. A new red, white and blue star pattern made its appearance in time for the Fall elections and will be equally patriotic and non-partisan for Fourth of July celebrations. Tents are also a major rental item for Ducky-Bob, with sizes available from 20 feet by 20 feet to 80 feet by 120 feet.

■ In addition to the area-wide major rental companies, there are a number of smaller companies with happy clienteles. Among those of note are **Rentals Unlimited** on Airport Freeway in Irving, **The Rent-All Place** in Plano and **United Rent-All** on Josey Lane in Carrollton. Both The Rent-All Place and United Rent-All have additional inventory of activity-oriented props, such as candy machines, hot dog carts, snow cone carts, balloon machines, space walks as well as a full range of china, glassware, tables, tablecloths and chairs.

As a reminder, the phone numbers for the rental companies can be found in the "Directory of Sources," which begins on page. 223. A "Telephone Directory" begins on page 247.

speciality rentals

Antique appointments

▲ **Perfect Party Rentals** is perhaps the city's most unique source in this category, offering rentals worthy of the popular Martha Stewart book on entertaining. In fact, owner Holly Huffines got the idea for her business while taking a course from Martha, the doyenne of entertaining style, at her Connecticut home. Since then, Holly has been collecting antique French and English china and linens, old quilts to use for tablecloths and party props as well. Holly keeps up with the looks of the moment, recently forgoing "depression glass" for cobalt blue Mexican glassware and pottery for the Southwestern look. Perfect Party Rentals will handle high-end special parties of a limited size, up to 50 to 100, depending on the selection. If you want a well-appointed tables, exquisitely set with china, crystal and linens, this is a special source!! Tables and white wooden chairs are also available.

Linens

◆ **Special Occasions.** Partners Joan Wing and Gail Lee work with party planners and caterers in providing table cloths and napkins with a unique look. Their cotton cloths in a variety of colors rent for $34.50 and taffetas and silks are $39.50. There are overlays in multitudinous patterns, with stripes and plaids starting at $7.50. They also drape and swag tables and hand-pin cloths for special receptions and weddings.

▼ **Tablecloths Unlimited.** Owner Dawn Cartwright has a superior collection of coordinating tablecloths and napkins for rent. Cloths that extend to the floor for 48 inch and 60 inch round tables are hand-pressed and are accompanied by overlays of similar or contrasting fabrics. The cloths, which are hand-pressed and delivered to your home, are priced at $40. per table and napkins at $.85 each. Dawn also has a limited selection of six foot and eight foot rectangular cloths for buffet tables. There is no minimum order required. We hope you will note the comments on Tablecloths Unlimited in Chapter III under "Linens." Many of you may be interested in the company's periodic sales of their stock. The owner suggests that you put your name on her list for notification of sales.

Drink Machines

Margarita machines are almost a prerequisite for the popular and casual Mexican-themed party. Judging from the number of companies in this business, the demand for serving frosty margaritas is enormous. Most of the companies charge about the same: $85. for the machine, including delivery, installation and pick-up. The margarita mix adds $18. and will make five gallons to serve 80 eight ounce drinks. The host supplies the liquor. Now, with the popularity of the bellini and near relatives, the machines are in demand for those drinks as well. Try **Margarita Man**, **Margaritas-R-Us**, and **Margarita Masters**, all of which have the machine and the mixes.

● Mike and Sharon Miller of **Margaritas-R-Us** were the originators, back in 1987, of Sfuzzi's favorite champagne drink, a variation on the bellini. Since the increasing trendiness of bellinis, margarita machines have certainly made many more party scenes, or so it seems. Along with the machine's rental, Margaritas-R-Us will mix the champagne, peach schnapps and rum with their ingredients to reproduce the popular drink which originated at Harry's Bar in Venice. Now, Margaritas-R-Us are recommending some new drinks, including a raspberry bellini, a strawberry relative named the Rossini, and a cactus juice margarita. Obviously, there will be no shortage to the uses for the machines.

■ **Margarita Man**, in business since 1984, has a large following, especially in Plano and Richardson, where margarita machines are popular accompaniments to swimming pool parties, according to owner Joe Wetmore. Margarita Man is a purist, sticking to margaritas and bellinis. His feature is the selection of colors for machines. Cowboy Blue is predicted to be the color for the near future.

▲ **Margarita Masters** is another frequently-mentioned company in the same line of business. Margarita Masters supplies the machines and mixes for several of the annual charity events, including the annual Cattle Baron's Ball, a recommendation in itself. Also in their inventory are ice cream and yogurt machines for another direction — and great fun for family and child-oriented gatherings.

◆ **H. I. Imports.** Something new has been added to the drink rental scene — that of the machines that have brought us the addictive coffee-based Cafesorbetto. Former La Crème Coffee and Tea owners Bonnie and Jerry Itzig have retained the importing of machinery for coffee and tea, including the dual-dispenser for Cafesorbetto and iced fruit drinks. Rental on a machine that can dispense two different drinks runs $180., including pick-up, delivery and the delicious mix to create the Cafesorbetto.

Jukebox rentals

● **Advance Music Company** is a recommended source for jukeboxes to enliven the party. For $125. they will stock the music of your choice, deliver and pick up. If you are sentimental about your own collection, Advance can include your own recordings on the machine. Advance is also a reliable source for video games, pool tables and other amusements for the entertainment scene.

■ **Jukebox Rentals/Brass Register** is a treasury of old brass cash registers (hence the name), slot machines, coke machines, barber poles and the like, all destined for collectors to purchase. A spin-off, for rental purposes, is their jukebox business, a popular item for class reunions and fortieth birthday parties, where favorite tunes of the past are momentous additions, and for teenage parties. Jukebox Rentals has an inventory of 20,000 records — just about everything on a "45," or so it would seem. The company keeps a list if you want to peruse your selection. Otherwise, they will stock the jukebox with the era or sound of your preference, deliver and pick up for $125. in the North Dallas area.

▲ **Eveready Vending** is another of the companies which rents jukeboxes — in addition to video games, of great amusement potential for the younger set.

Pianos

For the orchestra of the evening, or for background music in your living room, pianos are available for short-term rental. Dallas has several companies making rentals available and all charge much the same: about $350. for a baby grand, such as a Kawai or Young Chang, and $195. for an upright, including delivery, installation and pick up. A Steinway or other major instrument will be more expensive, usually $750. a day. There may be additional installation charges to a high stage or in a location without easy access, since additional manpower may be required.

▲ Piano companies offering rentals include the **Dallas Piano Warehouse** and **Keyboards Unlimited**, which we have used on several occasions and can recommend enthusiastically. There are also **Steinway Hall**, **Tyson Organ and Piano** and **Wadley Piano and Organ Company**. When it comes to visiting musicians and locating their needs, **Brooks Mays** is the place to go. Incidentally, if the need is for an electric keyboard, the source for rentals is **Keyboards Unlimited**.

Plants

As an extension of decor for a party, which is covered in Chapter VIII, green and flowering plant rental is a major component of large parties and for parties where the definition of space and the addition of warmth is important. There are numerous plant rental businesses in the area, many of which have a similar inventory. We have chosen a few, which are distinctive for their inventories and their service.

◆ **Bread "N" Butter Tropical Plants**, although not a green plant sounding name, seems to be rental company of choice among many prominent party planners and floral designers. Owners Kenneth Ofshe and his wife, Kacie, believe plants create magic and add warmth to unembellished spaces. Ofshe brings a sense of style from backgrounds in the clothing and floral businesses. Bread "N" Butter does all the usual — a seven foot ficus tree with lights, basket container and ferns around the base for a $35. rental. But, Bread "N" Butter adds more unusual trees such as cypress, Japanese maple and crepe myrtles to their list. We were so impressed with their softening of the Dallas Museum's new atrium space on the occasion of the dinner for the Hamon Building's major donors. It was an indoor garden when the installation was complete. In addition to their unusual stock, service is the key is their success. "Small and personalized" was the most frequent comment from their many clients who read like a who's who of party givers and planners.

▼ **Dallas Garden Interiors** has expanded the concept of plant rental to include landscaped pools, an idea they pioneered ten years ago. Ponds of almost any size and configuration can be constructed to add focus to a ballroom, or to dramatize an entrance or an outdoor setting. A recent client wanted a Monet garden scene which was created with a narrow pond, complete with bridge and gold fish. For an Austin client, a wonderful, rocky waterfall was created, lending both drama and sound effect. The company also has full lighting facilities to accent the ponds. As an example of the costs involved, a six foot by eight foot landscaped pond, fully installed rents for $550. and a 14 by 20 foot landscaped, rocky waterfall, complete with an eight foot fall of water, is $1500. Dallas Garden Interiors also has the usual rental green and flowering plants. Their minimum is $100. and, of course, they deliver and pick up.

● **Southern Greenhouse** gets high marks from a number of customers. For the previously-mentioned party with a Sherwood Forest theme (perhaps the ultimate use for large plantings), the host and hostess were delighted to work with Southern Greenhouse to produce their country club forest. The variety of plantings, the adherence to a tight timetable and the congenial service were duly noted by the party-givers. Certainly, the guests were in awe of the scene at hand. Southern Greenhouse has been involved in proms and parties for St. Marks School, where they have also made some real friends.

■ There are a number of other excellent plant rental companies who work with both individuals and party planners. Most have both green plants, such as ficus, areca palm and schefflera, and flowering plants, such as mums, kalanchoes, azaleas and bromeliads, at usually the same prices. Baskets may vary and most can offer trees either with or without the tiny lights. Our favorites include **Green Expectations, Green with Envy**, which has white washed baskets for larger trees and terra cotta for smaller plants as a distinction, **Plantscaping, The Plant Place** and **Touch of Green**. Be sure to ask about delivery prices.

Props

Please note that most of the party planners have large inventories of props that they will rent for the do-it-yourselfer, to non-profit organizations for their events and to the catering companies to augment their themes. **Gale Sliger, Bill Reed, Liland's Special Events** and **Kaleidoscope**, all have warehouses filled with treasures for fulfillment of ideas and fantasies.

▲ **Don Prince**. One of our good sources has reported the unusual work of Don prince, who has been in the slight-of-hand business for visuals for some time now. Recently, he has added party props to his repertoire, not by virtue of his inventory but by a unique talent of being able to fashion almost any desired prop out of formcore. So, if your next party has giant Italian urns or nymphs in the picture, call Don. We are sure that his sculpting in foamcore can produce the desired result or object.

◆ **Props of Texas.** Owner Derek Hill started out in the theatre, finding props for plays. Now, after stints in the film business and for Peter Wolf and Dallas Stage Scenery, Derek has opened a business to utilize his growing collection of movie props, mostly small items and excluding backdrops. If your party is Western, Hollywood or Halloween, we suggest you consider the resources at Props of Texas. Derek continues to work with films, most recently a Glenn Close film shot in the environs, and has some fabulous items with the history of their appearances. If you want to recreate the General Store for your next Western fete or stage a Broadway extravaganza, you might locate some interesting "finds" at his Deep Ellum warehouse. By appointment only.

Tents

The major rental companies, such as CANNONBALL Rental, have gotten into tent and canopy rental in a big way and can tent an area of any useable size. In many cases, if you are renting tables, chairs and china, it may be easier to include the dancefloor and tent rental from the same company. If the demands are unusual and you want to rely on a "specialist, " we have several tent and canopy experts in the area.

▼ **Alexander Tent Company.** A tent would be in your future should you want to expand the party potential of your home. Sizes and styles, center pole or frame, are seemingly endless from a 20 foot by 20 foot tent to cover an entrance (and perhaps house a bar and a coat check) at $200., to a 40 foot by 40 foot pole tent at $500. for accommodating 100 dinner guests, to a 60 foot by 150 foot at $2000. for 600 guests for dinner and dancing. Tenting, which can be heated or cooled depending on needs, has become a popular weatherproof concept. We have to admit that there is always a certain glamour to a party or a wedding under a tent and one that lends itself to wonderful garden-like decorating. In fact, our favorite weddings of the past few years have been at-home weddings receptions with garden dinner seating protected by tenting. The home settings were very personal and the tents made the outdoor rooms possible.

● CANNONBALL Party Rental Co. See listing above under "Rentals."
Please see the advertisement for CANNONBALL Party Rental Co. on page 204.

■ **Sandone Tents** is the name we've had heard most recently in connection with some big name "tented" parties. Newspaper accounts refer to Mike Sandone as the "tentmaker to the stars."

Ice Sculptures

▲ **Bifulco's Vanishing Sculptures.** We hear accolades about the national and internationally-acclaimed talents of Robert Bifulco. It could be that we have become more aware of ice sculptures because of the talents in our midst. There is something magical about ice and a sculpture adds another possible dimension to the decorative scheme. Frequently, the ice serves a practical purpose as well, paricularly for an elaborate seafood display. Bifulco carves subjects that fit traditional images for weddings and cocktail receptions and, more frequently now, personal messages reflecting a host's interests or company logo. All the sculptures are custom-made, of course, and very detailed in execution. Bifulco's subjects start vanishing in about three hours after installation and cost about $300. to $400. for a typical size.

◆ Brian Higgins of **Higgins Ice Carving** comes to sculpting by way of a 15 year professional food background and is in great demand for ice centerpieces for weddings, parties and hotel buffets. One of his favorite pieces was a wild life duo — a lion and a gazelle — for a safari-themed party at the Museum of Natural History. Another is an elegant and graceful pair of interlocking swans he recommends for wedding receptions. Prices depend on complexity, but a three and a half foot piece runs about $500. and a two by two foot piece about $150.

Lighting

One of the more important finishing touches, which is so subtle that it is frequently overlooked in planning a party, is lighting. For the small party at home, candelabra and votives provide the flattering glow to make a setting and our guests look their most flattering. For the out-of-doors, hurricane lamps and touches add drama and a hint of excitement, while at the same time solving the practical need for light.

For the large party, party planners frequently use lighting to enhance their setting and effect. Narrow beam spotlights are often used to pinpoint and highlight centerpieces. Other lights can be used to wash walls and ceilings with colors for drama in lieu of decorations or to add interest to decorations. Light patterns, such as stars, can be projected on walls and ceilings. Of course, one of the most theatrical techniques often used at parties is stage lighting for the entertainment and the dance floor.

▼ Several excellent lighting companies, which do lighting for theatres, exhibits and music shows, also work on large parties. These include **Samarco** and **Dallas Stage Lighting & Equipment**, both of which always seem to have a great inventory of special effects inventory, such as fog machines. It was at Dallas Stage where we found a revolving stage for a recent charity benefit, the same one that has been used annually by the Crystal Charity Ball to alternate their music groups. **Showco** is the area's largest lighting company, specializing primarily in concerts.

● **Gemini Stage Lighting and Sound**, annually provides the lighting for several large charity events, such as the Crystal Charity Ball and the Cattle Baron's Ball. Theirs is a talented group, considered one of Dallas' best, who can also handle other technical parts of an event.

■ There are also several talented theatre-trained specialists who will do large parties, such as charity events, balls and large corporate celebrations.

 We recommend John P. Hall, III of **Hall of Production Services**, an SMU theatre-trained alum whose recent credits include the Bob Hope Retrospective at SMU and the Gala Opening for the Catherine the Great exhibit at Fair Park. During 1993, he worked on the lighting for the Art Museum's 90th Birthday Bash and one particularly extraordinary wedding which was outdoors under a large tent. Lighting was an important feature in the overall ambiance. He also directed the lighting for the '93 Ambassador's Forum, both the casual, outdoor party featuring Clint Black at the Forest Lane EDS facility and the ball at the Anatole's Chantilly Ballroom featuring the Pointer Sisters. In each case, lighting was a subtle but key element in creating mood and highlighting the major focal points of the evening.

*Please see advertisement for **Hall of Production Services** on page 206.*

Sound

Most musicians and, certainly, all bands handle their own sound and have their own speaker equipment. In short, the sound for an event is not often a problem for the party giver, except for supplemental sound in unusual circumstances, such as playing out-of-doors or for a large audience. In these instances, a sound expert may have to be consulted and supplemental equipment may have to be rented. We have a few recommendations in the sound area, for those times when the room is immense or the area difficult, such as dealing with the hard acoustical surfaces at the Dallas Museum of Art and the Meyerson Symphony Center lobby.

As we have mentioned, the orchestras and groups usually have their own equipment as well as a sound mixer, who is important to their musical statement. Be certain that you know the electrical requirements of their equipment. We have known a major event or two to be plunged into darkness because of the total miscalculated amperage of music, plus theatrical lighting, plus catering needs. Secondly, ask what the sound equipment will look like and how much space it will require. We've had a few experiences where the equipment overwhelmed both the space and the well-thought-through and expensive decor.

▲ **Crossroads Audio, Inc.** is one of the premier sound "houses" in Dallas and provides both full service audio assistance and rental equipment. Crossroads has done the sound systems for the Crystal Charity Ball on several occasions and for numerous events at the Meyerson, including performances of the Dallas Wind Symphony. The company also has a lighting department, enabling it to handle both sound and lighting for events. Owner Chuck Conrad has put his experience touring with groups, such as Rare Earth and the Doobie Brothers, to good use and relies on a total of 20 years sound experience!

◆ **Sound Productions Inc.** "handles or rents anything that makes sound," so says President Charles Kitch. On the grand scale, Sound Productions oversees the audio for Starplex and major corporate productions. But, it also does a comprehensive rental business for local music groups in need of augmented sound. The "renting everything" in sound includes pianos (a seven foot Steinway for $750. a day) and a Hammond B3 organ. The organ might pair with the smoke machines to create a perfect "Phantom of the Opera" theme. Heavy duty smoke machines, popular at Halloween and for rock groups, cost $35. a day to rent with enough "fog juice" to last an evening. The list of miscellany is long — eerie sound machines (still another Halloween prospect), keyboard synthesizers and, in short, about "everything in sound."

▼ Freelancer **Stewart Bennett** is one of the young and very talented in this field. When not working on major road shows, he is available for consultations and installations. He's made impressions among those who have sought out his services.

Party Help

Beyond one table of six to eight guests for a formal seated dinner, or beyond a buffet of 12 to 16, it is helpful and almost indispensable to have a helping hand. Entertaining without some help, particularly for the novice, can be quite an effort.

Of course, if you use a caterer, the caterer will supply the party help. Rates are fairly standard — usually $15. to $18. an hour with varying minimums. Caterers usually estimate one helper to each eight to ten guests for a seated dinner and fewer for a buffet. For larger parties, bartenders are needed to supplement the wait staff.

Most hostesses, who do their own parties without the benefit of caterers, are possessive of the names of party helpers they have assembled through the years. We are no different. But, we have a few ideas on how you can develop your own sources to guard for future use.

🍴 Ask your friends or neighbors for names of bartenders or party servers who have worked for them. A recommendation is a must!

🍴 If you a are member of a club, inquire at the club who takes on outside jobs or has friends experienced in party service.

🍴 Likewise, ask at your favorite take-out shop. Most take-out shops now also cater so they already have the sources, which they might share, particularly if you are a recognizable customer.

🍴 Ask among the college crowd. Some of them have had experience and may even work at rates less than the norm — but be certain they know what will be expected of them.

When party help is located

🍴 Ask for references

🍴 Be specific about duties and how and what to serve.

🍴 Be prepared to have wait staff and bartenders come about an hour early to go over procedures and have the opportunity to familiarize them with your surroundings.

● **Liaison Party Service**. Until recently, finding party help was a hit and miss situation, unless you happened to have developed a few guarded names of part-time party helpers. Now, a new company has been formed by someone experienced in the area and who recognized the need to find help for not only the occasional private party, but for those large events when even caterers have to reach beyond their usual lists of trained individuals. After 20 years with the Fairmont Hotel and, more recently with the Dallas Museum of Art handling staffing for events, Ahmad Farahani recognized the need for a such a service. Liaison Party Service will supply you with waiters, bartenders and even chefs, whatever the occasion demands. Ahmad has a crew of regulars and has also begun a training school. For a service fee, which includes the insurance and bonding, the service provides servers at $16. an hour, bartenders at $18., butlers at $20. and chefs at $25. — all at minimums of four hours. What a relief to leave the calling up to someone else! Liaison Party Service may have found an indispensable niche to fill.

Parkers

Dallas and parking services seem synonymous. When time permits, we will research the reason — beyond weather and convenience — that has made the Dallas "the valet parking capital of the world," although Houston may be a contender. Out-of-town guests always marvel at the omnipresence of parkers. But, luckily for us, we and our cars are frequently pampered. We certainly do not have a minimum number of guests to suggest when car parkers become convenient, and even expected. At home parties, available space for cars, distance from parking to site, and weather conditions are all factors. For large parties and certainly for formal parties, valet parking is a necessity and provides a measure of security. Incidentally, all the parking companies will make arrangements for off-duty policeman where appropriate to direct traffic and to secure the parking areas insurance.

■ **Jack Boles Services** may have started it all here in Dallas, and is the obvious choice among private party and charity function services. Park Cities and North Dallas crowds like to be recognized, and usually be greeted by name, and have their cars treated with favoritism. Their private party customers are legion. The Boles parkers can also be found at The Mansion and at the Hotel Crescent Court, not to mention some of the area country clubs. Most charity organizers seek out Jack Boles Parking Services when they know their guests want the best as they arrive and leave their cars in the hands of the experienced Boles crew — and when they leave at the end of a function and want their cars returned pronto. There is no doubt that they know their business and can work out a parking plan, even when space and logistics seem unworkable. We know this from many first hand experiences. When parking spaces and numbers of expected cars do not equate, company president David Hamilton can charm any adjacent building owner out of spare space to make it all possible. Rates have increased slightly for 1994, thanks to the folks who decide insurance rates for protecting and handling your cars while you enter and exit an event with ease and grace. Valet attendants are from $18. to $20. an hour.

Few of our citizens realize that the Boles touch extends to Houston and Galveston as well. Jack Boles Services originally handled parking at Rosewood Hotels' Houston property, the Remington Hotel. Now, they park cars at the River Oaks Country Club and other spots around town, giving Houstonians a taste of how it is done in "Big D." The Galveston area gets favored treatment at San Luis Hotel. Suffice it to say, we should keep this in mind when entertaining for business or pleasure in Houston or Galveston — and don't forget to make recommendations to your friends who should know the full story. See the listing below for Boles Services under "Transportation," another aspect of the business.

*Please see advertisement for **Jack Boles Services** on page 218.*

▲ **MEDiPARK Valet Services** has a growing reputation among our citizens who like to have their cars parked. Only six years ago, Mark Glosser started by providing valet parking at area hospitals (hence the MEDiPARK name) and has branched out to private parties and regular accounts around town;

namely, the Sammons Center for the Arts, the Belo Mansion and Aldredge House. Recently, we saw them at numerous large charity events, such as the Zoo-To-Do, the Crazy for You benefit and the Dallas Junior League benefits. This year, they will be at the Jewel Charity Ball in Fort Worth. These are events where they can park 600 to 800 cars with the same efficiency as you will expect for a small party at your home. MEDiPARK has found a niche for their well-groomed, fast-moving, college-age-looking parkers. The walky-talky efficiency is noticeable, and the party planners are mentioning their name with greater frequency. Expect to pay $16.50 per hour per parker, fully insured, with a total of ten hours divided among the manpower for a minimum.

Owner Mark Glosser is branching out into other service-oriented areas, so don't be surprised if you hear the company name associated with other than parkers for parties and events.
Please see advertisement for MEDiPARK Valet Services on page 216.

◆ Several other parking services have sprouted up around Dallas over the years, many of them to serve restaurants, clubs and corporate events. All have branched into providing experienced parkers at parties as well. These include **Park Cities Valet**, whom we see regularly at the Dallas Country Club and private parties in the Park Cities, **Best Valet Services**, and **R.P. Valet** .

Photography

Past memories are important to many hostesses, particularly if the event is to commemorate a birthday or anniversary celebration, a graduation or any of the major highlights in life. Most portrait photographers, such as Gittings, John Haynsworth, John Derryberry and James Allen will do candids. Dallas is fortunate to have so many outstanding portrait photographers. There are times, however, when we want quick but well-done photos as a memory. Several area photographers specialize in events and work quickly to capture the spirit of the occasion.

● **BTV-Button TV.** A momento of a party can be a treasure for the future, particularly if it involves a visual image. Skip Waters is the largest vendor in town for creating instant photo buttons. His BTV Company gets around and makes appearances at every kind of party, from birthdays to graduations, from corporate holiday parties to charity events, such as the Crystal Charity Ball and the Cattle Baron's Ball. BTV images are black and white and are placed in a customized frame for wearing or displaying. About 100 buttons can be processed in an hour by one camera (and Skip now owns several), averaging about $2. per button cost.

■ **J. Allen Hansley** is a very familiar face on the charity event and big party scene. Allen specializes in putting your party in recorded memories and will come early to ensure that the setting is not forgotten. Allen charges $75. an hour and $35. a roll, presenting a photo album for you to keep. Reprints for your friends are $5. each. Allen is a good friend to the charities in town and has helped out on many an occasion in supplying and supplementing photos to be sent to the social press.

▲ **Kristina Bowman** specializes in both fashion and special events. Kristina charges $85. an hour and $40. a roll, averaging two rolls an hour. Within the week following an event, she will present a book of finished 4" x 6" photos for you to keep. Reprints are reasonable, at $3.50 for a 4" x 6". Kristina has a very full calendar and we suggest that you book early. Many who engage her know that they are working with one of Dallas' best.

◆ **"Party Pics" by Flash** has been in business for eight years (and during that time we have been personally responsible for large portions of their enterprise via momentos of school parties and proms!). Party Pics charges $30. an hour and typically will shoot five rolls in an hour to an hour and a half. Photos are then available at $2.25 for the first copy, enabling a hostess to share photos with her guests.

▲ **Photographique** has multi-purpose shop, studio, photo processing and exhibit space in Inwood Village for the photographers they represent. Among the "stable" of photographers are at least two, Cheryl Masterson and Jay Jennings, who excel at party photos in addition to portraits and weddings. Rates are $150. an hour plus expenses. Photographique also has three special events cameras that enable the host to provide instant photos for their guests at $4. each. Proprietor Carol Black can arrange for custom folders as a momento of the event. Perhaps the photos of your festivities will be so wonderful that you will want to use them for photo Christmas cards, also available through the shop.

● **Tom Jenkins and Scott Hagar,** both Dallas Museum of Art photographers, work singly or together and free lance for parties. Rates are $100. an hour, plus cost of film and developing.

Transportation

Getting to the party may be a major consideration if the site chosen is away from areas convenient for most of the guests. Certainly, if the destination is Billy Bob's in Fort Worth, or to one of the area ranches, this is the way to go. If using transportation for your guests' convenience, consider it as an extension of the party and provide refreshments and even a hostess for each bus of guests.

Another group of revelers may want to choose another mode of transport as a convenience, a luxury or as added security because of late hours. Dallas has a wealth of limousine services. We are listing several of the more reliable and unique of them.

■ **British Limousine Service** is something we think our readers would want to know about. Owner Gerald McGarvin owns a 1963 Rolls Royce, the last of the old body style with sloping fenders. It's quite popular for " Sweet 16" birthday parties, weddings, anniversaries and going to charity events in style. McGarvin charges $100. an hour with no real minimums. If the car is hired for only one hour, the charge is $150.

▲ **Dallas Surrey Services.** If riding in an open surrey or handsome cab takes your fancy, the folks at Dallas Surrey Services has a fleet of vintage, horse-drawn vehicles. Uses are primarily limited to short trips from the wedding to reception and Christmas parties to view the festive Highland Park decorations. We know one grandmother who annually treats her grandchildren to a nostalogic holiday ride. Dallas Surrey Services also owns a stagecoach which makes occasional appearances at area ranches.

◆ **DFW Towncars** offers airport and private transportation in luxury sedans or stretch limousines, and we can attest to their reliability. We would normally expect to use luxury sedan or limousine transportation for important events such as weddings, large charity events, or travel to Fort Worth to a party that may end late, but an important consideration is the arrangement of travel for older guests who find driving at night difficult but who still maintain an active social calendar by using professional drivers. Limousines holding up to 7 people are $55. an hour with a three hour minimum. DFW has 24 hour reservation and dispatch service. Coach and mini-bus transportation can also be arranged through DFW Towncars. Coaches holding up to 47 people are priced at $55. per hour with a five hour minimum. Mini-buses holding up to 30 people are also $55. with a four hour minimum and vans holding up to 15 are $40. with a three hour minimum.

▲ **Five Star Limo** has the biggest and the bestest of the limousines. With more on order, Five Star has 10 passenger extra-wide body Cadillac limousines, equipped with everything imaginable, to take an entire entourage along on an outing. Rates for the 10 passenger vehicles, with a four hour minimum, are $80. an hour. Six passenger are $55. an hour.

◆ **Jack Boles Services.** The parking specialists at Jack Boles will also provide car services, a convenience offered for those preferring chauffeur-driven transportation for the evening's outing, or for those unable to drive to evening events, or to the airport. This is a boon for older citizens who still maintain an active social life, or as a substitute for the "designated driver." Limousine rates are $65. an hour. See above for the write-up of Jack Boles Services above under "Parking Services."
*Please see the advertisement for **Jack Boles Services** on page 218.*

▼ **Mr. Limo** has been a reliable source for transportation since 1985 with a diversified fleet of vehicles to meet a variety of needs — chauffeur-driven business cars, limousines for eight passengers, three Rolls Royces for an ultimate in luxury, vans and a 27 passenger mini-bus. Rates start at $35. an hour for sedans with a three hour minimum, limousines at $65., Rolls at $75. and mini-buses at $55. With this variety, one can accommodate a need for an evening for a group to go to the Mesquite Rodeo in a van, or arrive in style at the annual Crystal Charity Ball in a Roll

● **Yellow Rose Touring and Special Events.** Touring out-of-town visitors is Yellow Rose's specialty. Yellow Rose is the perfect organization to provide a custom tour for your friends as a Christmas treat to view lights and decorations (an annual event for many families and groups, complete with catered beverages and snacks). Yellow Rose also does get-acquainted Dallas tours geared toward any number of subjects. One of the more popular is for weekend wedding guests. The tour can be personalized to include points of reference significant to the bridal couple, such as their schools, businesses and childhood abodes. Yellow Rose can help plan a Fort Worth museum trip or a jaunt to First Monday in Canton. Rates are $60. an hour with a three hour minimum. Tour guides are $30. an hour. Mini-vans hold seven and coaches up to 29. The company has the good fortune to own its own coaches and mini-vans as well as limousines. This may mean some flexibility in pricing during off peak days and seasons.

A reminder – *the names and addresses of the businesses listed above will be found in the "Directory of Sources," beginning on page 223.*

Advertisers

WINN MORTON DESIGNS

The theme, the design, the flowers. . . . the total ambiance
of your special event should be custom-designed for you.
Since returning to Texas from Broadway fifteen years ago,
Winn Morton has created Dallas' most glamorous charity balls,
weddings, debutante balls, private dinners and corporate events.

Deerwood Studio   1921 Nokomis Rd   Lancaster, TX 75146
2 1 4 / 2 2 7 - 0 1 7 7   F A X   2 1 4 / 2 2 7 - 1 3 5 5

Lester Lanin

ORCHESTRAS

a sophisticated sound

212-265-5208

157 West 57th Street
New York, NY 10019

Feel like a guest
at your own event.

Who wrote the rules that said you can't have fun at your own event? Well, whoever it was has never heard of Westin. Plan your next event at The Westin, and your catering manager will take care of details most people wouldn't even *think* of. Chris LaLonde, our award-winning executive chef, will create a custom menu so inventive your guests will be dazzled. And everyone from the doormen to the waiters will be talking about your event for weeks – even months – before it happens. Which means your guests will be talking about it for a long time *after*. For your next event, call Cindi Breen at **450-2916**. It's your party…have fun if you want to.

THE WESTIN HOTEL
Galleria Dallas

St. Michael's Woman's Exchange

#5 Highland Park Village
Dallas, Texas 75205
(214) 521-3862

Staffed by volunteers
supporting
Community service organizations

Invitations
* Traditional engraved wedding papers
* Party invitations featuring thermography, hot-stamped imprinting, laser printing and computerized calligraphy
* Unique selection of papers, napkins and coasters

Gift Wrapping Service
* Specialized attention to custom designs for individual and corporate gifts

Table Accoutrements   **Seasonal Decorations**

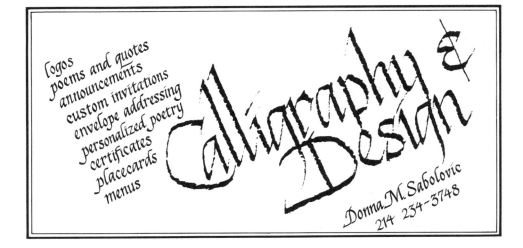

Quite Simply.

It just doesn't get any better.

Dallas' premier full service caterer.

Our services include Event Opportunitities
at the Dallas Museum of Art
and the Dallas Stars "Stars Club"

FOODS

CATERERS • PACKAGED FOODS
HOSPITALITY MANAGEMENT

2156 W. Northwest Hwy., Suit 311, Dallas 75220

(214) 444-9792

C R E A T I V E
U P S C A L E
C A T E R I N G

GOURMETDALLAS

Catering International Cuisine
10836 Grissom   Suite 108   Dallas 75229
2 1 4 / 4 8 4 - 4 9 5 4

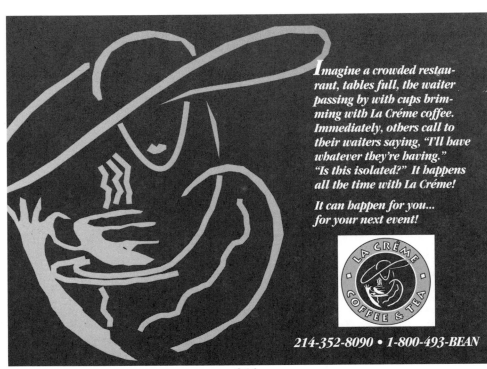

MEDiPARK
Valet Services Inc.

A Distinctive Name with Distinguished Serivce

Driven To Excellence
For more information call 214/828-0040
Mark A. Glosser, *Pres.*

Nestled in the shadows of Dallas' west end area is the city's only indoor,

three dimenisional frontier town party facility. A true western fantasy.

Specially designed buildings, unique bars and authentic decorations surround

*you to give you the best of the **old west atmosphere.***

Silverado City, 1322 North Industrial Blvd., Dallas, TX 75207 214/745-1870

THE
DALLAS
WORLD
AQUARIUM

A TWO-STORY WAREHOUSE, BUILT IN 1924 AND RECENTLY CONVERTED
TO A UNIQUE AQUARIUM, FEATURING LIVING REEF TANKS
REPRESENTING INTERNATIONAL DIVE DESTINATIONS,
ALONG WITH A WALK-THRU TUNNEL TANK.
SECOND FLOOR BANQUET CONFERENCE ROOM. ROOFTOP DECK.
CAPACITY 1000

1801 NORTH GRIFFIN DALLAS, TX 75202 214/720-2224
DARYL RICHARDSON, OWNER

Au Bon Goût

Catering for Elegance

Bettye Wellons, Incorporated
P.O. Box 7826 Dallas, TX 75209-0826 214/522-7345 522-0171 FAX 214/522-3285

wendy krispin caterer

KRISPIN - the restaurant
for lunch, for parties

DALLAS DESIGN CENTER • 1025 NORTH STEMMONS • SUITE 600 • DALLAS, TEXAS 75207 • (214) 748-5559

BOSTER'S
GOURMET CATERING

CUSTOMIZED CATERING
PLANNING FOR SPECIAL EVENTS
AND SOCIAL GATHERINGS

900 JACKSON STREET
DALLAS, TEXAS 75202

214/741-1158

DOUG BOSTER, OWNER

Directory

of Sources

8.0 Restaurant & Bar
2800 Routh Street
Dallas, Texas 75201
979-0880

A Catered Affair
387-5566

A Taste of Europe
4817 Brentwood Stair Rd
Ft. Worth, Texas 76103
817/654-9494(m)

A-Z Party House
2661 Midway, # 204
Carrollton, Texas 75006
732-8334

Abbey Party Rentals
2615 W. Mockingbird
Dallas, Texas 75235
350-5373

Abundio Ortiz
247-5317

Accardi Costume
5712 W. Lovers Lane
Dallas, Texas 75209
956-7280

Ace Mart Restaurant Supply
3050 W. Northwest Hwy
Dallas, Texas 75220
351-5444

Addison Cafe
5290 Belt Line Road
Dallas, Texas 75240
991-8824

Addison Farmers' Market
75659 Addison Road
Addison, Texas 75248
233-4619

Adelina's Catering
661-0644

Adelmo's
4357 McKinney
Dallas, Texas 75205
559-0323

Adolphus Hotel
1321 Main Street
Dallas, Texas 75202
742-8200

Advance Music Company
3100 Main Street
Dallas, Texas 75226
939-9014

Affaires Extraordinaire
11333 N. Central Exp, #219
Dallas, Texas 75243
373-9977

Affairs to Remember
14364 Marsh
Dallas, Texas 75244
247-8309

Aldredge House
5500 Swiss Avenue
Dallas, Texas 75214
823-8268

Alessio's
4117 Lomo Alto
Dallas, Texas 75205
521-3585

Alex Donner Orchestra
800/ITS-MUSIC

Alexander Tent Company
11324 Mathis Avenue
Dallas, Texas 75229
869-2405

Al's Import Foods
8209 Park Lane
Dallas, Texas 75231
363-3778

American Federation of
    Musicians
817/654-0063

American Food Service
4721 Simonton
Dallas, Texas 75244
233-5750

American Institute of Food & Wine
741-4072

Americas Ice Garden
600 North Pearl
Dallas, Texas 75201
922-9800

Amore (To Go)
6931 Snider Plaza
Dallas, Texas 75205
739-0502

Andrews Addison Grill
14930 Midway Road
Dallas, Texas 75240
702-0720

Angel in My Kitchen
373-6030

Anita M. Martinez Ballet Folklorico
The Majestic Theater
1925 Elm, Suite 400
Dallas, Texas 75201
720-7220

Ann Manning
522-4350

Apples to Zinnias
2800 Oak Lawn
Dallas, Texas 75219
559-2240

Arcodoro
2520 Cedar Springs
Dallas, Texas 75201
871-1924

Arnold's Gifts & Creations
14310 Preston Road
Dallas, Texas 75240
233-2957

Arnold's Texas B-B-Q
601 N. Haskell
Dallas, Texas 75246
826-1234 To-Go
289-0289 Catering

Arrangers, The
699-9076

Art Bar/Blind Lemon
    /Club Clearview
2805 Main Street
Dallas, Texas 75226
939-0202

ArtCakes by Oggetti
824-8601

Arts District Flower Market
2001 Ross Avenue
Dallas, Texas 75201
979-9002

Arts Magnet School
720-7300

Aston's English Bakery
6029 Luther Lane
Dallas, Texas 75225
368-6425

Atelier, A Work Shop
2800 Routh Street
Dallas, Texas 75201
350-4116

Au Bon Goût
522-7345

DIRECTORY OF SOURCES
alphabetical listing of sources

Austin Ranch
2009 Anderson-Gibson Road
Grapevine, Texas 76051
817/481-1536

Aziz Import Foods
9100 N. Central Exp
Dallas, Texas 75231
369-6982

Baby Routh
2708 Routh Street
Dallas, Texas 75201
871-2345

Bagel Chain, The
5555 W. Lovers Lane
Dallas, Texas 75209
350-2245

Bagel Emporium
7522 Campbell Road
Dallas, Texas 75248
980-1444

Bagelstein's Deli & Bakery
8104 Spring Valley
Dallas, Texas 75240
234-3787

Balloon Bonanza
4901 Keller Springs Road
Dallas, Texas 75248
250-1423

Balloon City USA
1922 N. Haskell
Dallas, Texas 75204
821-6482

Bagel Emporium, The
7522 Campbell Road
Dallas, Texas 75248
248-1569

Balloons Fantastique
4801 W. Park Blvd.
Plano, Texas 75093
964-2488

Balloon House, The
102 Tuesday Haus Lane
Highland Village, Tx 75067
317-1965

Balloons over Dallas - Innovators
2701 Fondren #A
Dallas, Texas 75206
373-9695

Balloons to You
2152 Chennault
Carrollton, Texas 75006
788-5022

Barbara Kirchhoff
931-1154

Barneys New York
333 North Park Center
Dallas, Texas 75225
692-5222

Belo Mansion
2101 Ross Avenue
Dallas, Texas 75201
220-0239

Bent Tree Country Club
5201 Westgrove
Dallas, Texas 75248
931-7326

Best Valet Service, Inc.
520-8830

Betty Barna Calligraphics
234-4075

Bifulco's Vanishing Sculptures
826-6980

Big Spur Corral
3094 N. Stemmons Freeway
Dallas, Texas 75247
905-0808

Big Town Farmers' Market
US 80 at Big Town Blvd.
Mesquite, Texas 75149
319-8093

Big-D-Dude Ranch
842-8440

Biggerstaff Flowers
900 Eighteenth Street
Plano, Texas 75074
423-2501

Bill Bates Cowboy Ranch
Rt. 4, Box 162, Ranch Rd 162
McKinney, Texas 75070
390-7790

Bill Reed Decorations
P.O. Box 153230
Dallas, Texas 75215
823-3154

Bill Tillman Band, The
424-8007

Billy Bob's Texas
2520 Rodeo Plaza,
Ft. Worth Stockyards
Ft. Worth, Texas 76106
817/589-1711(m)

Black Forest Bakery
5811 Blackwell
Dallas, Texas 75231
987-9090

Bloomingstock
4108 Lomo Alto
Dallas, Texas 75205
528-5801

Blue Chipper
350-2875

Blue Mesa Grill
5100 Belt Line Road
Dallas, Texas 75240
934-0165

Bodacious Baskets
285-1452

Bombay Cricket Club
2508 Maple
Dallas, Texas 75201
871-1333

Boster's Gourmet Catering
900 Jackson Street
Dallas, Texas 75202
741-1158

Botanicals
4258 Oak Lawn
Dallas, Texas 75219
521-5188

Bowed Creek Ranch
Route 1, Box 708
Prosper, Texas 75077
373-8940

Bread "N" Butter Tropical Plants
1512 Apple Street
Dallas, Texas 75204
824-7336

Brenda Schoenfeld
4346 Lovers Lane
Dallas, Texas 75225
368-4007

Bret Driver
948-1042

British Carriage Limousines
393-2088

British Emporium, The
130 North Main Street
Grapevine, Texas 76051
817/421-2311

British Trading Post
10892 Ferguson Road
Dallas, Texas 75228
686-8840

DIRECTORY OF SOURCES
alphabetical listing of sources

Brook Haven Country Club
3333 Golfing Green Drive
Dallas, Texas 75234
243-6151

Brook Hollow Golf Club
8301 Harry Hines
Dallas, Texas 75235
637-1900

Brook Mays Music Co.
5756 LBJ Freeway
Dallas, Texas 75240
233-9633

BTV - Button Television
942-8346

Bubba's Cooks Country
6617 Hillcrest
Dallas, Texas 75205
373-6527

Buddy Brock Orchestra
713/821-5202

Cafe Expresso
6135 Luther Lane
Dallas, Texas 75225
361-6984

Cafe Madrid Market
4501 Travis
Dallas, Texas 75205
234-5666

Cafe Margaux
4527 Travis
Dallas, Texas 75205
520-1985

Cafe Noir
821-6540

Cakery, The
396 Casa Linda Plaza
Dallas, Texas 75218
324-9292

Cake Carousel
510 Arapaho Central
Richardson, Texas 75081
690-4628

Caliente Ranch Grill & Cantina
6881 Greenville Avenue
Dallas, Texas 75231
369-8600

California Pizza Kitchens
5505 Belt Line Road
Dallas, Texas 75240
490-8550
8411 Preston Road
Dallas, Texas 75225
750-5691

Calligraphy & Design
234-3748

Calligraphic Arts, Inc.
4232 Herschel #201
Dallas, Texas 75219
522-4731

Calligraphy by Janet Travis
2531 B McKinney Avenue
Dallas, Texas 75201
871-6064

Calluaud's
5405 W. Lovers Lane
Dallas, Texas 75209
352-1997

Camellia Cafe
6617 Snider Plaza
Dallas, Texas 75205
691-8164

Campbell Stationers
8318 Preston Center East
Dallas, Texas 75225
692-8380

Campisi's Pizza To Go
7522 Campbell Rd., #106
Dallas, Texas 75248
931-2267

CANNONBALL Party Rental Co.
4514 McEwen Road
Dallas, Texas 75244
387-8900

Canyon Creek Country Club
625 Lookout Drive
Richardson, Texas 75080
231-1466

Capriccio Restaurant
2525 McKinney
Dallas, Texas 75201
871-2004

Card Art
341-8398

Carol Marks Music
615 Business Parkway
Richardson, Texas 75081
231-4091

Carol West
296-7247

Caroling Troubadours, The
713-0015

Carolyn Unsworth
521-9884

Carpenter House, The
1211 East 16th Street
Plano, Texas 75074
424-1889

Carté
4256 Oak Lawn
Dallas, Texas 75219
559-6168

Casa Dominguez
2408 Cedar Springs
Dallas, Texas 75201
871-9787

Casa Linda Bakery
10819 Garland Road
Dallas, Texas 75218
321-0355

Catering by Angela
520-3747

Catering by Arthur
3230 Towerwood, #A
Dallas, Texas 75234
620-7293

Catering by Don Strange
363-1155

Catering Company, The
696-1070

Cathy's Antiques
2200 Crescent Court, # 140
Dallas, Texas 75201
871-3737

Cato Company, The
352-3702

Carolcade of Stars
255-3967

Cedar Canyon Dude Ranch
4523 N. Houston School Rd
Lancaster, Texas 75134
214/224-8477

Celebrity Cafe & Bakery
65 Highland Park Village
Dallas, Texas 75205
528-6612
24118 Fairmount
Dallas, Texas 75201
922-9866
10720 Preston Road #1017
Dallas, Texas 75230
373-0783

Chamberlain's Prime Chop House
5330 Belt Line Road
Addison, Texas 75240
934-2467

Chantal Cookware Factory
6211 Denton Drive
Dallas, Texas 75235
351-2551

Chateau Magdalena Caterers
869-2167

Cheese House
11910 Preston Road
Dallas, Texas 75230
239-7051

Cheesecake Royale
9016 Garland Road
Dallas, Texas 75218
328-9102

Chef's Shadow
484-5533

Chenoweth Chamber Music
270-9366

Chez Gerard
4444 McKinney
Dallas, Texas 75205
522-6865

Chicken Chicken
Old Town Shopping Ctr #505
Dallas, Texas 75206
319-8550

China Cupboard, The
718 N. Paulus
Dallas, Texas 75214
528-6250

China Teacup, The
112 N. MacArthur Blvd.
Irving, Texas 75061
438-8074

Chris Whanger
319-8550

Christine Carbone
222-0517

Circle R Ranch
5901 Cross Timbers Road
Flower Mound, Texas 75028
817/430-1561

City Cafe
5757 W. Lovers Lane
Dallas, Texas 75225
351-2233

City Cafe to Go
5757 W. Lovers Lane
Dallas, Texas 75225
351-3366

City Club
901 Main Street
Dallas, Texas 75202
748-9525

City Market Catering
979-2696

Cityplace Club
2711 N. Haskell, Suite 2001
Dallas, Texas 75204
841-6830

Cityplace Conference Center
2711 N. Haskell, Suite 2001
Dallas, Texas 75204
841-6830

Civello's Raviolismo
1318 N. Peak
Dallas, Texas 75204
827-2989

CJ's Delight
3607 Greenville Avenue
Dallas, Texas 75206
827-7538

Clark's Outpost
Highway 379
Tioga, Texas 76271
817/437-2414

Classic China
1002 N. Central Expressway
Richardson, Texas 75080
238-7763

Coffee Company Inc.
6182 Berkshire
Dallas, Texas 75225
369-5704

Cohen's Casino Parties
276-2998

Colter's Bar-B-Q
5910 N. Central Expressway
Dallas, Texas 75206
265-8377

Columbian Country Club
2525 Country Club Drive
Carrollton, Texas
416-2131

Community Connection
526-7635

Constance Muller
522-5505

Container Store, The
3060 Mockingbird
Dallas, Texas 75205
373-7044
4939 Belt Line
Dallas, Texas 75240
458-9228
6060 Forest Lane
Dallas, Texas 75230
386-5054
additional locations

Cooking with Cammie
821-1506

Coosemans Dallas, Inc.
604 S. Central Avenue
Dallas, Texas 75226
741-7855

Copper Lamp, The
5500 Greenville Avenue
Dallas, Texas 75206
521-3711

Cowboy Chicken
3625 W. Northwest Hwy.
Dallas, Texas 75220
956-9288
6868 Shadybrook
Dallas, Texas 75231
361-7747
17437 Preston Road
Dallas, Texas
732-6281

Cowboys
7331 Gaston
Dallas, Texas 75214
321-0115

Crate & Barrel
220 North Park Center
Dallas, Texas 75225
696-8010
13350 Dallas Parkway
Dallas, Texas 75240
392-3411

Crate & Barrel Outlet Store
1317 Inwood Road
Dallas, Texas 75247
634-2277

Crescent Club
200 Crescent Court
Dallas, Texas 75201
871-8555

Crossroads Audio, Inc.
358-2623

Cuisine Concepts
1406 Thomas Place
Ft. Worth, Texas 76107
817/732-4758

Cuisine International
373-1161

D-ART Visual Art Center
2917 Swiss Avenue
Dallas, Texas 75204
821-2522

Dakota's
600 Akard
Dallas, Texas 75201
740-4001

Dallas Affaires
324-3082

Dallas Alley
2019 N. Lamar, Suite 200
Dallas, Texas 75202
702-0170

Dallas Aquarium
Fair Park
Dallas, Texas 75226
670-8441

Dallas Arboretum & Botanical
Garden
8617 Garland Road
Dallas, Texas 75218
327-8263

Dallas Brass & Electric
855-9754

Dallas Chamber Orchestra
520-3121

Dallas Civic Garden Center
Fair Park
Dallas, Texas 75226
428-7476

Dallas Communications Ctr.
6301 N. O'Connor Road
Irving, Texas 75039
869-0700

Dallas Country Club
4100 Beverly
Dallas, Texas 75205
521-2151

Dallas Costume Shoppe
3905 Main Street
Dallas, Texas 75226
428-4613

Dallas Eats! Newsletter
890-6666

Dallas Farmers Market
1010 S. Pearl Expressway
Dallas, Texas 75201
670-5880

Dallas Garden Interiors
327-6120

Dallas Grill
5708 Abrams Road
Dallas, Texas 75214
361-1387

Dallas Museum of Art
1717 N. Harwood
Dallas, Texas 75201
922-1200

Dallas Petroleum Club
2200 Ross Avenue
Dallas, Texas 75201
871-1500

Dallas Piano Warehouse
9292 LBJ Freeway
Dallas, Texas 75243
231-4607

Dallas Stage Lighting &
    Equipment
428-1818

Dallas Surrey Services
946-9911

Dallas Symphony Musicians
871-4067

Dallas Tortilla & Tamale Factory
2717 N. Harwood
Dallas, Texas 75201
742-3888
309 N. Marsalis
Dallas, Texas
943-7681

Dallas Women's Club
7000 Park Lane
Dallas, Texas 75225
363-7596

Dallas World Aquarium
1801 North Griffin Street
Dallas, Texas 75202
720-2224

Danals
10544 Harry Hines
Dallas, Texas 75220
357-0241
5011 Lemmon Avenue
Dallas, Texas 75209
528-8570
4438 Maple Avenue
Dallas, Texas 75219
526-4340

Dancemasters
10675 E. Northwest Hwy
Dallas, Texas 75238
553-5188

dani group, the
2156 W. Northwest Hwy #311
Dallas, Texas 75220
520-0890

Darrie Hinson Catering Co.
239-1213

Daryl's by Design
1801 N. Griffin Street
Dallas, Texas 75202
655-1444

Dave Tsnnen
635 Ranier Court
Highland Village, Texas
219-7315

Dave the Printer
2338 Irving Boulevard
Dallas, Texas 75207
630-4017

David J's
4885 Alpha, #125
Dallas, Texas 75240
991-1818

Deborah Orrill
343-1227

Deborah Youngblood
724-8410

Deep Ellum Cafe
2706 Elm Street
Dallas, Texas 75226
741-9012

Deep Ellum Party Warehouse
2808 Commerce
Dallas, Texas 75226
742-2091

Deli News
500 Crescent Court
Dallas, Texas 75201
922-deli
15575 Hillcrest
Dallas, Texas 75248
392-deli

Designs Behind the Scenes
11409 Broadmoor
Dallas, Texas 75218
691-7307

Designs in Bloom
118 Spring Creek Village
Dallas, Texas 75248
960-1114

Dessert Dreams
1451 East Northgate
Irving, Texas
438-7630

DFW Town Cars
956-1880

Diamond J Corral
Highway 380 and FM 1385
Frisco, Texas 75034
952-9809

Discount Party Warehouse
13619 Inwood Road
Dallas, Texas 75244
239-6717
additional locations

Dixie Chicks
P.O. Box 670444
Dallas, Texas 75367
369-9437

Dode Martin/Flowers
559-4701

Don Prince
214/775-1016

Donald Hill Flowers Etc.
522-6830

Donna Bonds Calligraphy
239-6423

**Donna Sabolovic
Calligraphy & Design
234-3748**

Doreen By Design
817/754-6111

Doubletree Hotel at Lincoln Center
5410 LBJ Freeway
Dallas, Texas 75240
934-8400

Dovie's Inc.
14671 Midway Road
Dallas, Texas 75244
233-4270

**Dr. Delphinium Designs
5806 Lovers Lane
Dallas, Texas 75225
522-9911**

Dragon Street Diner
Oak Lawn Design Plaza
1444 Oak Lawn
Dallas, Texas 75207
747-1566

Drew-Corcoran
401/885-3855

Drrew Ldt.
3313 Knox Street
Dallas, Texas 75205
521-0777

Ducky-Bob's Rentals
14500 Beltwood Pkwy East
Dallas, Texas 75244
702-8000

Earth Blooms
2101 Abrams
Dallas, Texas 75214
823-6222

East & Orient Co.
2901 N. Henderson
Dallas, Texas 75206
826-1191

eco-fluence
2936-D Elm Street
Dallas, Texas 75226
761-9979

Ed Bernet Entertainment
691-0001

**Edward Stalcup, Inc.
4017 Villanova
Dallas, Texas 75225
368-5530**

Eldorado Country Club
2604 Country Club Drive
McKinney, Texas 75070
548-8777

Ellum Beach Club
349-2002

Empire Baking Company
4264 Oak Lawn
Dallas, Texas 75219
526-3223

Empire Games
324-9858

Encore Productions
317-2336

Energy Club of Dallas
8080 N. Central Expressway
Dallas, Texas 75206
361-4468

**Entertainment Company, The
P.O. Box 860096
Plano, Texas 75086
423-1869**

Entrees on Trays
828-0452
980-7980

Ethel MacIntosh
421-3943

Eureka!
4011 Villanova
Dallas, Texas 75225
369-7767

European Market & Deli
11613 N. Central
Dallas, Texas 75243
696-5441

Events Unlimited
750-7226

Eveready Vending
1836 S. Central Expressway
Dallas, Texas 75215
428-5194

Fabian Seafood Co.
P. O. Box 2227
Galveston, Texas 77553

Fairmont Hotel
1717 N. Akard
Dallas, Texas 75201
720-2020

Ferrari's Italian Oven
703 McKinney
Dallas, Texas 75202
954-1112

Fiesta Mart
611 W. Jefferson
Dallas, Texas 75208
944-3300

**Fishburn's Cleaning & Laundry
3200 Ross Avenue
Dallas, Texas 75204
826-4101
21 area locations**

FishFinders, Inc.
4008 Commerce
Dallas, Texas 75226
823-3153

Fishmonger's Seafood Market
& Cafe
1915 N. Central, Suite 600
Plano, Texas 75074
423-3699

DIRECTORY OF SOURCES
alphabetical listing of sources

Fit-Kit Cuisine by dani
444-9792

Five Star Catering
520-9463

Five Star Limo
562-LIMO

Fleur Adel
625-6948

Flora Verde
Grand Kempinski Hotel
15201 Dallas Parkway
Dallas, Texas 75248
960-9893

Flower Studio, The
(Wesley Lujan)
4312 Elm Street
Dallas, Texas 75226
827-6950

Flowers (Carol Garner)
4106 Holland
Dallas, Texas 75219
526-4205

Flowers of Oak Lawn
2811 Oak Lawn
Dallas, Texas 75219
526-0912

Flowers on the Square
311 Main Street
Ft. Worth, Texas 76102
817/429-2888(m)

Folk Like Us
221-2416

Food Company
215 Henry Street
Dallas, Texas 75226
939-9270

Foster Child Advocate Services
827-8961

Four Seasons Resort & Club
4150 N. MacArthur Blvd.
Irving, Texas 75038
717-0700

Fred's Deli
243 Wynnewood Village
Dallas, Texas 75224
948-9090

French Direct Inc.
4008 Commerce St., #318
Dallas, Texas 75226
824-1659

French Room, The
Adolphus Hotel
1321 Main Street
Dallas, Texas 75202
742-8200

Fresh 'n Tender
747 Floyd Road
Richardson, Texas 75080
644-7224

Fresh Pasta Delights
901 W. Parker Road
Plano, Texas 75023
422-5907

Fresh Start Market
4108 Oak Lawn
Dallas, Texas 75219
528-5535

Frosted Art
3132 S. Skyway Circle So.
Irving, Texas 75038
258-0644

Fun-Ed's School of Cooking
13608 Midway, # 127
Dallas, Texas 75244
960-2666

Fun-Time Bakery
902-9369

Gale Sliger Productions
1261 Profit
Dallas, Texas 75247
637-5566

Garden Secret, The
2500 Routh Street
Dallas, Texas 75201
922-8860

Gardners Eden
800/822-9600

Gemini Stage Lighting & Sound
341-4822

Geppetto Designs
526-4857

Gil's Elegant Catering
254-1986

Gilbert's New York Deli
127 Preston Forest Village
Dallas, Texas 75229
373-3333

Ginette Albert
363-4543

Gittings Portraiture
5301 W. Lovers Lane
Dallas, Texas 75209
350-5581

Glazed Honey Hams
490-3023
multiple locations

Gleneagles Country Club
5401 Park Boulevard
Plano, Texas 75093
931-0984

Godiva Chocolatier Inc.
The Galleria
Dallas, Texas 75240
458-1821

Going Gourmet
4345 W. Northwest Hwy
Dallas, Texas 75220
351-6773

Golden Circle Herb Farm
Route 1, Box 4
Rice, Texas 75155
225-0500

Golden Pacific Supermarket
2108 East Arapaho
Richardson, Texas 75081
234-5666

Gone to Seed
943-2101

Goodies from Goodman
11661 Preston Forest Center
Dallas, Texas 75230
987-3591

Gorman's
423 N. Galloway
Mesquite, Texas 75...
288-7671
additional locations

Gourmet Cookery School
717-4189

Gourmet Foods Warehouse
    Outlet
6065 Forest Lane
Dallas, Texas 75230
788-5155
Hillside Village #362
Dallas, Texas 75214
824-0656

Gourmet Unlimited
14819 Inwood Road
Dallas, Texas 75244
233-9964

GOURMETDALLAS
10836 Grissom, #108
Dallas, Texas 75229
484-4954

Grailey's Fine Wines
6330 LaVista
Dallas, Texas 75214
823-8711

Granada Cinema & Grille
3524 Greenville Ave.
Dallas, Texas 75206
823-9619

Grand Kempinski Hotel
15201 N. Dallas Parkway
Dallas, Texas 75248
386-6000

Grassroots
220 E. Las Colinas Blvd.
Irving, Texas 75039
556-1244

Great American Food Co.
1818 Rodeo Drive
Mesquite, Texas 75149
285-8777

Green Produce
1430 Parker Street
Dallas, Texas 75215
421-4100

Green with Envy
1331 Dragon Street
Dallas, Texas 75207
748-2595

Guadalupe Pit Smoked Meats
800/880-0416

Guess Who's Coming to Dinner
340-0061

Gump's
800/284-8677

Gunter's Greenhouse
201 Campbell Road Village
Richardson, Texas 75080
234-3377

Haagen Dazs
73 Highland Park Village
Dallas, Texas 75205
559-3757

Hackberry Country Club
1901 Royal Lane
Irving, Texas 75063
869-2631

Hal Turner
348-5999

Hall of Production Services
P.O. Box 12614
Dallas, Texas 75225
931-3359

Hall of State
Fair Park
Dallas, Texas 75226
421-4500

Hans Mueller Sausage Co.
2459 Southwell Road
Dallas, Texas 75229
241-2793

Hao's
6920 Snider Plaza
Dallas, Texas 75205
361-2020

Heavenly Cheesecakes
13933 N. Central Exp, # 204
Dallas, Texas 75243
644-6314

Henk's European Deli & Black
Forest Bakery
5811 Blackwell
Dallas, Texas 75231
987-9090

Hiep Phong Supermarket & BBQ
10560 Walnut Street
Dallas, Texas 75243
272-4802

Hiep Thai Market
3530 Walnut Street
Garland, Texas 75042
272-1993

Higgins Ice Carving
748-5384

Highland Park Antique Shop
3117 Knox Street
Dallas, Texas 75205
528-0430

Highland Park Cafe
Highland Park Village
Dallas, Texas 75205
521-7300

Highland Park Cafeteria
4611 Cole

Dallas, Texas 75205
526-3801
Casa Linda Plaza
Dallas, Texas 75218
327-3663

Hines Nut & Produce Co.
2404 Canton
Dallas, Texas 75226
939-0253

Home Delivery Network
248-4006

Horchow Collection
556-6000

Horchow Finale
12300 Inwood Road
Dallas, Texas 75242
8074 Spring Valley
Richardson, Texas 75080

Hotel Crescent Court
400 Crescent Court
Dallas, Texas 75201
871-3200

Hotel St. Germain
2519 Maple Avenue
Dallas, Texas 75201
871-2516

Humble Pie & Cake Co.
5711 Bordeaux
Dallas, Texas 75209
358-3237

Huntington's Restaurant
The Westin Hotel
The Galleria
Dallas, Texas 75240
934-9494

I Can't Believe It's Yogurt
392-3011

I Love Flowers
4347 W. Northwest Hwy
Dallas, Texas 75220
357-9577

Ida Mae's Cakes
817/567-3439

Impofoods
1906 Promenade Shop. Ctr.
Richardson, Texas 75080
680-3232

In Bloom
1900 Coit
Plano, Texas 75075
596-4442

In Bloom　　　　　　　*Cont.*
6310 Gaston Avenue
Dallas, Texas 75214
827-6090
5420 LBJ Freeway
Dallas, Texas 75240
458-2958
2626 N. Josey Lane
Carrollton, Texas 75006
446-5666

In Good Company
2933 N. Henderson
Dallas, Texas 75206
826-0020

Inchon Oriental Food
839 N. Belt Line Road
Irving, Texas 75061
986-6939

Incognito Costume World
13621 Inwood Road
Dallas, Texas 75244
404-0584

India Imports
307 W. Airport Freeway
Irving, Texas 75062
255-5941

India Palace
12817 Preston Road #105
Dallas, Texas 75230
392-0190

**Inkcorporated Stationery
& Invitations
5949 Sherry Lane, # 835
Dallas, Texas 75225
361-5496**

International Bakery &
Sandwich Bar
359 Dal Rich Village
Richardson, Texas 75080
680-8513

International Wine Accessories
(IWA)
11020 Audelia Road, #B
Dallas, Texas 75243
800/527-4072

Invitations & Party Innovations
608-1805

Invite Your Guests
238-1754

It's A Wrap
25 Highland Park Village
Dallas, Texas 75205
520-9727

Ivy House, The
5500 Greenville Ave., #806
Dallas, Texas 75206
369-2411

J Pinnell's
2616 Maple Avenue
Dallas, Texas 75201
871-1181

J. Allen Hansley Photography
871-2949

J. Pepe's Mexican Restaurant
2800 Routh Street, #215
Dallas, Texas 75201
871-0366
3619 Greenville Avenue
Dallas, Texas 75206
821-6431

**Jack Boles Services, Inc.
357-4493**

Jack Cannon & Associates
647-8073

Javier's
4912 Cole
Dallas, Texas 75205
521-4211

Jed Mace
357-7686

Jennivine's Restaurant
3605 McKinney
Dallas, Texas 75204
528-6010

Jim Allen Photographic
Portraiture
5600 W. Lovers Lane
Dallas, Texas 75209
351-3200

Joan McIlyar
521-8658

John Haynesworth
Photography, Inc.
86 1/2 Highland Park Vlg.
Dallas, Texas 75205
559-3700

Jukebox Rentals/Brass Register
610 James Street
Richardson, Texas 75080
231-1386

Julia Sweeney & Associates
100 Highland Park Village
Dallas, Texas 75205
520-0206

Juniper
2917 Fairmount
Dallas, Texas 75201
855-0700

Just Delicious
521-2448

K & S Rental
245-6133

K2 Design
522-2344

Kaleidoscope Decor
1223 Security Drive
Dallas, Texas 75247
634-3778

Kaleidoscope, Inc.
3131 Turtle Creek Blvd. Dallas,
Texas 75219
522-5930

Kathleen's Art Bakery
4446 Lovers Lane
Dallas, Texas 75225
692-TOGO

Kazy's Food Market
8989 Forest Lane, Suite 106
Dallas, Texas 75243
235-4831

Kelly Durbin
817/382-4632

Ken Boome Musical Production
328-7995

Ken Knight
The Quadrangle
2800 Routh
Dallas, Texas 75201
754-0404

Keyboards Unlimited
630-2272

Kitchen Kakes
517-4827

Klown- Magician
226-1313

Kolache Station
3115 W. Parker
Plano, Texas 75023
519-8315

Kosher Link, The
7517 Campbell Road
Dallas, Texas 75248
248-3773

Kozy Kitchen
522-8504

Krispin — the restaurant
1025 N. Stemmons # 600
Dallas, Texas 75207
748-7151

Kristina Bowman
526-9683

Kuby's Sausage House, Inc
6601 Snider Plaza
Dallas, Texas 75205
363-2231

Kwik Kopy
6005 Berkshire Lane
Dallas, Texas 75225
691-8325

L'Ancestral
4514 Travis
Dallas, Texas 75205
528-1081

L'Epicurean
2025 Irving Blvd. #213
Dallas, Texas 75207
747-5885

La Botica Mexican Cafe
1902 N. Haskell
Dallas, Texas 75204
824-2005

La Cave Warehouse
1000 Munger #100
Dallas, Texas 75202
979-9463

La Cima Club
5215 N. O'Conner Road
Irving, Texas 75039
869-2266

La Créme Coffee & Tea
4448 Lovers Lane
Dallas, Texas 75225
369-4188

La Francaise French Bakery & Cafe
105 Lake Highlands Plaza
Dallas, Texas 75238
341-6365
6333 E. Mockingbird #130
Dallas, Texas 75214
823-8102

La Jardiniere
4310 Westside
Dallas, Texas 75209
522-3444

La Madeleine French Bakery
& Cafe
3072 Mockingbird
Dallas, Texas 75205
696-6960
3906 Lemmon Ave.
Dallas, Texas 75219
521-0182
11930 Preston Road
Dallas, Texas 75230
233-6448
4343 W. Northwest Hwy.
Dallas, Texas 75220
351-9542
additional locations

La Mariposa
2817 Routh Street
Dallas, Texas 75201
871-9100

La Musica String Quartet
363-6422

La Popular
4904 Columbia
Dallas, Texas 75214
824-7617

La Tosca
7713 Inwood
Dallas, Texas 75209
352-8373

Lady Primrose
The Crescent
2200 Cedar Springs
Dallas, Texas 75201
871-8334

Landlock Seafood Co.
1815 Trinity Valley Drive
Carrollton, Texas 75006
241-7500

LaRosa's Italian Bakery
907 W. Parker Road
Plano, Texas 75023
578-9497

Larry T-Byrd Gordon Show, The
286-6832

Las Americas
1146 Peavy Road
Dallas, Texas 75218
324-2604

Las Colinas Country Club
4900 N. O'Connor Road
Irving, Texas 75062
542-1141

LaserTations
618-3713

le gâteau cakery
3128 Harvard
Dallas, Texas 75205
528-6102

Les Antiques
3001 N. Henderson
Dallas, Texas 75206
824-7322

Les Dames d'Escoffier
821-0986

Lester Lanin Orchestras
212/265-5208

Liaison Party Service
247-5807
247-2998

Life's A Party
661-0330

Light Crust Dough Boys
247-4295

Liland's Flower Fashions
5606 E. Mockingbird
Dallas, Texas 75206
823-9505

Liland's Special Event Productions
1421 N. Industrial
Dallas, Texas 75207
748-1191

Linen Gallery, The
7001 Preston Road
Dallas, Texas 75205
522-6700

Linen Sisters, The
522-4289

Llewellyn & Lee
4020 Villanova
Dallas, Texas 75225
696-2114

Loews Anatole Hotel
2201 Stemmons Freeway
Dallas, Texas 75207
748-1200

Loma Luna
8201 Preston Road
Dallas, Texas 75225
691-1552

Lombardi's 311
311 Market Street
Dallas, Texas 75202
747-0322

Lovers Lane Antique Market
5001 W. Lovers Lane
Dallas, Texas 75209
351-5656

Loyd-Paxton
3636 Maple Road
Dallas, Texas 75219
521-1521

Luna's Tortilla Factory
1615 McKinney Avenue
Dallas, Texas 75202
747-2661

Luther P. Menke
824-0092

Lynn Townsend Dealey
P.O. Box 191406
Dallas, Texas 75219
890-8123

Macy's
The Galleria
Dallas, Texas 75240
851-5185

Magicland
340 Park Forest Shop. Ctr.
Dallas, Texas 75229
350-0966

Magnifico Fine Foods
5459 N. MacArthur Blvd.
Irving, Texas 75038
753-0093

Main Street News
2934 Main Street
Dallas, Texas 75226
746-2934

Making Statements
530-6191

Mal Fitch Orchestra, Inc.
279-3583

Mama's Daughter
2014 Irving Boulevard
Dallas, Texas 75207
742-8646

Mange-Tout Cooking School
5711 Bordeaux
Dallas, Texas 75209
350-9285

Mansion on Turtle Creek, The
2821 Turtle Creek
Dallas, Texas 75219
559-2100

Marc Jaco Productions
392-0469

Marco Polo
17194 Preston Road
Dallas, Texas 75252
931-2328

Margarita Man
298-6432

Margarita Masters
641-7926

Margaritas-R-Us
688-1880

Marguerite Green At Home
5655 W. Lovers Lane
Dallas, Texas 75209
352-8891

Mariachis Los Reyes
1925 Elm, Suite 400
Dallas, Texas 75201
720-7220

Marilee Mallinson Martinez
339-2954

Mario's Chiquita
4514 Travis Walk
Dallas, Texas 75205
521-0092

Marj's Stationery
5560 W. Lovers Lane
Dallas, Texas 75209
350-8246

Mark Carroll
824-8775

Market, The
Inwood Village
Dallas, Texas 75209
352-1220
434 NorthPark Ctr.
Dallas, Texas 75225
369-7161
Preston Park Village
Plano, Texas 75093
596-2699

Marshall Grant Orchestra
407/686-7000

Martha Tiller & Company
2811 McKinney

Dallas, Texas 75204
855-5140

Marty's
3316 Oak Lawn
Dallas, Texas 75219
526-4070 Gourmet
526-7796 Wine

Mary Cates & Co.
2701 State Street
Dallas, Texas 75204
855-5006

Massimo da Milano
5519 W. Lovers Lane
Dallas, Texas 75209
351-1426
Village on the Parkway
Dallas, Texas 75240
661-5255
6333 E. Mockingbird
Dallas, Texas 75214
826-9456
additional locations

Mattito's Cafe Mexicano
4311 Oak Lawn
Dallas, Texas 75219
526-8181

Matt's Rancho Martinez
6312 LaVista
Dallas, Texas 75214
823-5517

Maudee's Tearoom
4333 Lovers Lane
Dallas, Texas 75225
526-9750

McKinney Avenue Antiques
2710 McKinney Avenue
Dallas, Texas 75204
871-1904

McKinney Avenue Transit
3153 Oak Grove
Dallas, Texas 75204
855-0006

MEDiPARK Valet Parking
828-0040

Mediterraneo
18111 Preston at Frankfort
Dallas, Texas 75252
Opening Nov. '94

Melrose Hotel
3015 Oak Lawn
Dallas, Texas 75219
521-5151

Mercado Juarez
1901 W. Northwest Highway
Dallas, Texas 75220
556-0796
4050 Belt Line Road
Dallas, Texas 75244
458-2145

Mesquite Championship Rodeo
1818 Rodeo Drive
Mesquite, Texas 75149
285-8777

Messina's Culinary Center
3521 Oak Grove
Dallas, Texas 75204
559-0857

Mews, The
1708 Market Ctr Blvd.
Dallas, Texas 75207
748-9070

Michael Carney Music
212/986-4447

Michaels/MJ Designs
810 Preston Forest Shop. Ctr
Dallas, Texas 75230
696-5491
additional locations

Mille Fleurs, Inc.
5100 Beltline Road, # 860
Dallas, Texas 75240
960-1021

Mise en Place
7011 Lomo Alto
Dallas, Texas 75225
520-2424

Mitchell Lehr
392-1502

MoMo's Italian Restaurant
 & Grocery
9191 Forest Lane
Dallas, Texas 75243
234-6800

Momo's Pasta
3312 Knox Street
Dallas, Texas 75205
521-3009

Moreno Printing
1910 Greenville Avenue
Dallas, Texas 75206
827-7283

Morgen Chocolate, Inc.
703 McKinney Ave. #106
Dallas, Texas 75202
954-4424

Mori Music
644-8734

Morton. H. Meyerson Symphony
 Center
2301 Flora Street
Dallas, Texas 75201
670-3285

Mother Daughter Originals
613-1274
800'995-5499

Mozzarella Company
2944 Elm Street
Dallas, Texas 75226
741-4072

Mr. Fish Crabs 'n More
4008 Commerce St. #104
Dallas, Texas 75226
821-4833

Mr. G's Deli & Beverages
1453 Coit
Plano, Texas 75043
867-2821

Mr. Limo
437-3939

Nancy Beckham
821-8093

Nancy Himes
373-1789

Needle in a Haystack
6911 Preston Road
Dallas, Texas 75205
528-2850

Neiman Marcus
1618 Main Street
Dallas, Texas 75202
741-6911
NorthPark
Dallas, Texas 75225
363-8311
Prestonwood
Dallas, Texas 7524
233-1100

Nero's Italian
2104 Greenville Avenue
Dallas, Texas 75206
826-6376

Neuhaus Chocolate Cafe
10720 Preston Road
Dallas, Texas 75230
373-3590

Neuhaus Chocolates
427 North Park Center
Dallas, Texas 75225
691-9156
The Galleria
Dallas, Texas 75240
392-0281
Prestonwood Town Ctr.
Dallas, Texas 75240
980-9851

New Vintage Festival
Grapevine Heritage Foundation
817/481-0454

New York, TX Cheesecake
Box 222
LaRue, Texas 75770
800/225-6982

Newport's
703 McKinney
(In the Brewery)
Dallas, Texas 75202
954-0220

Nicholson Hardie
5725 W. Lovers Lane
Dallas, Texas 75209
357-4348

Nina Nichols Austin
871-3611

No Place
6310 LaVista
Dallas, Texas 75214
823-9077

Northwood Club
1524 Alpha Road
Dallas, Texas 75240
239-1366

Nuvo
3900 Cedar Springs
Dallas, Texas 75219
522-6886

O! Suzanna Design Studio
528-4289

O-K Paper Center
2601 McKinnon
Dallas, Texas 75201
871-0770
14540 Midway Road
Dallas, Texas 75244
239-6368
2618 Lingco Drive
Richardson, Texas 75081
644-2040
additional locations

DIRECTORY OF SOURCES
alphabetical listing of sources

Old City Park
1717 Gano
Dallas, Texas 75215
421-5141

Old Fort Dallas
315 Patrick Pike Road
Ferris, Texas 75125
225-5414

Omni Mandalay at Las Colinas
221 E. Las Colinas Blvd.
Irving, Texas 75039
556-0800

On the Border
3300 Knox Street
Dallas, Texas 75205
528-5900

One O'Clock Lab Band
P.O. Box 5038
Denton, Texas 76203
817/565-3743

Opus
Meyerson Symphony Ctr
Dallas, Texas 75201
670-3721

Opus Four String Quartet
390-7363

Orchid Gardens
9748 Brockbank
Dallas, Texas 75220
350-4985

Original Butt Sketch, The
943-2888

Out of a Flower
703 McKinney, Suite 202
Dallas, Texas 75202
754-0324

Palmer Sales Company
3510 E. Northwest Hwy
Dallas, Texas 75149
288-1026

Pam's Kitchen
278-6873

Panhandlers
11936 Preston Road
Dallas, Texas 75230
661-8021
130 Preston Park Village
Plano, Texas 75093
612-0155

Panhandlers Steel Band
817/565-4124

Paper Routes
3333 Elm Street
Dallas, Texas 75226
748-9322

Pappadeaux Seafood Kitchen
3520 Oak Lawn
Dallas, Texas 75219
521-4700

Pappas Catering
480-8585

Pappas Design
3518 Oak Lawn
Dallas, Texas 75219
522-9690

Papyrus
409 North Park Center
Dallas, Texas 75225
265-7187
The Galleria
Dallas, Texas 75240
386-8744

Park Cities Valet Parking
533-2319

Park City Club
5956 Sherry Lane
Dallas, Texas 75225
373-0756

Park Lane Ranch & Cattle
Highway 80 & Belt Line Rd.
Dallas, Texas 75217
349-2002

Parties-R-Us
100 Webb Royal Plaza
Dallas, Texas 75229
352-8386

Party & Event Designers
1914 Commerce
Dallas, Texas 75201
747-0025

Party Animals, Pony Party
  & Pet Zoo
613-9255

Party Art, Inc.
8311 Preston Road
Dallas, Texas 75225
987-0872

Party Bazaar
4435 Lovers Lane
Dallas, Texas 75225
528-4795

Party Cat
8306 Kate Street, # 3
Dallas, Texas 75225
739-2107
800/345-1213

Party in a Box
630-6673

"Party Pics" by Flash
6427 Hillcrest
Dallas, Texas 75205
443-9393

Party Place
8411 Preston Road, # 102
Dallas, Texas 75225
696-4550
Preston Park Village
Plano, Texas 75
867-6899

Party Plus
1017 North Central, # 150
Plano, Texas 75075
424-8770

Party Service
8333 Douglas
Dallas, Texas 75225
363-9366

Pasta Plus
225 Preston Royal East
Dallas, Texas 75230
373-3999
17194 Preston Road
Dallas, Texas 75248
713-7181

Peggy Sue BBQ
6600 Snider Plaza
Dallas, Texas 75205
987-9188

Pendery's
5450 W. Lovers Lane, # 227
Dallas, Texas 75209
357-1870
The Galleria
Dallas, Texas 75240
991-1870

Peregrinators Antiques
3109 Knox Street
Dallas, Texas 75205
521-1950

Perfect Party Rentals
P.O. Box 58625
Dallas, Texas 75258
750-7584

Perfect Setting, The
4270 Oak Lawn
Dallas, Texas 75219
559-3330

Petals & Stems
13319 Montfort
Dallas, Texas 75240
233-9037

Peter Duchin Orchestra
305 Madison Ave, # 1503
New York, N.Y. 10165
800/433-5064

Pettys Group, The
553-9707

Phares Corder
235-6319

Photographique
351-5144

Piccola Cucina
Barneys New York at NorthPark
Dallas, Texas 75225
691-0488

Pickens Design
5944 Luther Lane, # 122
Dallas, Texas 75225
363-9140

Pier One Imports
5427 W. Lovers Lane
Dallas, Texas 75209
3747 Forest Lane
Dallas, Texas 75244
247-4593
2048 Valley View Center
Dallas, Texas 75240
701-8081
additional locations

PIP Printing
7734 Forest Lane
Dallas, Texas 75230
987-3235
multiple locations

Plano Chamber Orchestra
1309 W. 15th Street
Plano, Texas 75074
423-6955

Plant Place, The
10704 Goodnight Lane
Dallas, Texas 75220
869-3808

Plantscaping
2320 N. Beckley Avenue
Dallas, Texas 75208
742-5222

Plate & Platter
4401 Lovers Lane
Dallas, Texas 75225
521-9980

Plaza of the Americas Hotel
650 N. Pearl Street
Dallas, Texas 75201
521-9980

Po-Go's Liquor
5360 W. Lovers Lane
Dallas, Texas 75209
350-8989
9669 N. Central Expressway
Dallas, Texas 75231
373-7646

Polish Delicatessen
10242 E. Northwest Hghwy
Dallas, Texas 75238
503-6510

Pollo Bueno
3438 Samuel Boulevard
Dallas, Texas 75223
826-0645

Polly Dupont
154 Spring Creek Village
Dallas, Texas 75248
991-3689

Polo Shop\Ralph Lauren
58 Highland Park Village
Dallas, Texas 75205
522-5270

Pomodoro
2520 Cedar Springs
Dallas, Texas 75201
871-1924

PoPolo's
707 Preston Royal Ctr.
Dallas, Texas 75229
692-5497

Potted Palm, The
5639 Merrimac
Dallas, Texas 75206
826-0075

Preferred Meats
318 Cadiz
Dallas, Texas 75207
565-0243

Preferred Parking
315-1140

Preizler's Deli & Bakery
116 Preston Valley Ctr
Dallas, Texas 75230
458-8896

Presto Print
131 Turtle Creek Village
Dallas, Texas 75219
528-9122

Print Shoppe, The
5019 Lovers Lane
Dallas, Texas 75209
350-1902

Private Collection Stamp Co.
6108 Luther Lane
Dallas, Texas 75225
360-0621

Project, The
250-3563

Props of Texas
2930 Canton
Dallas, Texas 75226
748-7767

Pullen Seafood
4008 Commerce
Dallas, Texas 75226
823-8222

Quadrangle Grille
2800 Routh Street
Dallas, Texas 75201
979-9022

Quarter J Ranch
Dublin Road
Plano, Texas 75094
235-6331

Quill Productions
620-1556

Quiltcraft Industries
1233 Levee Street
Dallas, Texas 75207
741-1662

R.P. Valet Dallas, Inc.
732-8800

R.S.V.P. Party Planning
5600 Lovers Lane
Dallas, Texas 75209
350-7787

Ralph Sanford
327-8325

Ralph's Fine Foods
6901 Snider Plaza
Dallas, Texas 75205
368-0931

Ran Wilde Orchestra
351-5040

Randall Morgan-Village Stationers
87 Highland Park Village
Dallas, Texas 75205
521-8240

Red Coleman Liquors
7560 Greenville Avenue
Dallas, Texas 75231
363-0201

Redwine Catering
4524 McKinney Ave., # 101
Dallas, Texas 75205
520-0502

Reichenstein House, The
4810 Cedar Springs
Dallas, Texas 75219
522-1075

Rent-All Place, The
2707 West 15th Street
Plano, Texas 75075
867-2121

Rentals Unlimited
1122 W. Airport Freeway
Irving, Texas 75062
259-7575

Resource 3, Inc.
6310 Lemmon Avenue
Dallas, Texas 75209
351-9806

Reunion Ranch
Route 2, Box 834
Terrell, Texas 75160
214/563-1170

Richardson Chamber Orchestra
7540 LBJ Freeway
Dallas, Texas 75251
385-7267

Richardson Woman's Club
2005 North Cliffe
Richardson, Texas 75082
238-0841

Rick Duren
505/984-2508

Ristorante Savino
2929 N. Henderson
Dallas, Texas 75206
826-7804

Riveria, The
7709 Inwood
Dallas, Texas 75209
351-0094

Romano's Cheesecake Co.
3131 Montecello, # C
Dallas, Texas 75205
521-1662

Ron Fink
817/565-3714

Ron Lawrence Orchestra
423-8467

Ronnie Renfrow Big Band
713/774-2263

Room Service
4354 Lovers Lane
Dallas, Texas 75225
369-7666

Rose Shop, The
5611 E. Grand
Dallas, Texas
827-1119

Rotel & the Red Hots
817/441-5488

Royal Oaks Country Club
7915 Greenville Avenue
Dallas, Texas 75231
691-6091

Royal Party +
11910 Preston Road
Dallas, Texas 75230
385-3885

Ruccus
3024 Mockingbird Lane
Dallas, Texas 75205
691-0828

Rudolph's Sausage Factory
2924 Elm Street
Dallas, Texas 75226
741-1874

Russell Glenn Floral Design
2114 Farrington
Dallas, Texas 75207
742-3001

Russian Room, The
(see Deli News)

Salli Goldstein
233-0976

Sally Jones
521-3119

Sam's Cafe
100 Crescent Court
Dallas, Texas 75201
855-2233
8411 Preston Road
Dallas, Texas 75225
739-3474

Samarco
1606 Gano
Dallas, Texas 75215
263-9969

Sammons Center for the Arts
3639 Harry Hines
Dallas, Texas 75219
520-7788

Sample House & Candle Shop
2811 Routh Street
Dallas, Texas 75201
871-1501
9835 N. Central Expressway
Dallas, Texas 75231
369-6521
122 Casa Linda Plaza
Dallas, Texas 75218
327-0486
1900 Preston Road
Plano, Texas
985-1616

Sandone Tents
8800 Chancellor Row
Dallas, Texas 75247
350-6334

Sandy Trent's 1 Dance 2
5706 East Mockingbird
Dallas, Texas 75206
827-3888

Sarah Jane Francis
373-7737

Savoire Faire
941-8939

Sazon International
783-7676

Schimelpfenig Showplace
920 18th Street
Plano, Texas 75074
424-2999

Schnitzer Productions
373-1245

Science Place
Fair Park
Dallas, Texas 75226
428-5555

Scott Hager Photography
922-1284

Seasonal Colour
4441 Lovers Lane
Dallas, Texas 75225
526-9800

Serge Stodolnik
324-9942

Sfuzzi
2504 McKinney
Dallas, Texas 75201
871-2606
15101 Addison Road
Dallas, Texas 75248
960-2606
2408 Preston Road
Plano, Texas 75093
964-0700

Shalibi Imported Foods
2121 E. Northwest Highway
Garland, Texas 75041
840-1375

Sharon Seaton
270-3791

Sheraton Park Central Hotel
12720 Merit Drive
Dallas, Texas 75251
385-3000

Shin Chon
4460 Walnut Street
Garland, Texas 75042
276-9792

Showco
201 Regal Row
Dallas, Texas 75247

Sigel's Liquor Stores
5757 Greenville
Dallas, Texas 75206
739-4012
15003 Inwood Road
Dallas, Texas 75244
387-9873
909 Abrams Road
Richardson, Texas 75081
480-8484

Silver Leopard
4100 Oak Lawn
Dallas, Texas 75219
559-3194

Silver Tray Catering
620 Haggard #608
Plano, Texas 75074
423-8322

Silver Vault, The
5655 Lovers Lane
Dallas, Texas 75209
357-7115
Preston Park Village #195
Plano, Texas 75093
867-8181

Silverado City
1322 N. Industrial Blvd.
Dallas, Texas 75207
745-1870

Simcha Kosher Catering
3230 Towerwood, #A
Dallas, Texas 75234
620-7295

Simon David
7177 Inwood
Dallas, Texas 75209
352-1781
6770 Abrams Road
Dallas, Texas
340-1119

Skylobby
Texas Commerce Tower
Dallas, Texas 75201
979-6100

Smiles Balloon Co.
361-8973

Smink, Inc.
3032 Mockingbird
Dallas, Texas 75205
691-1270

Smokey & the Bearcats
306-8200

Solly's
4801 Belt Line Road
Addison, Texas 75240
387-7120

Some Enchanted Evening
956-7302

Sonny Bryan's Barbecue
302 N. Market
Dallas, Texas 75202
744-1805, catering
2202 Inwood
Dallas, Texas 75235
357-7120

Soramy
4621 W. Park Blvd.
Plano, Texas 75093
612-0068
Preston Royal
Dallas, Texas 75230
Opening late '93

Sound Productions Inc.
10430 Shady Trail
Dallas, Texas 75220
351-5373

Southern Greenhouse
11357 Ferrell Drive
Dallas, Texas 75229
869-1679

Southern Methodist University
692-0000

Southfork Ranch
3700 Hogge Road
Parker, Texas 75002
442-7800

Special Affairs Catering
5541 Lovers Lane
Dallas, Texas 75209
351-1796

Special Occasions
233-3114

Spice of Life Catering
343-2598

Spirited Cakes
522-2806

Spirits Liquor Company,
2825 Canton Street
Dallas, Texas 75226
748-2459
8224 Park Lane
Dallas, Texas 75251
265-8085

St. Michael's Woman's Exchange
5 Highland Park Village
Dallas, Texas 75205
521-3862

Stanley Korshak
The Crescent
Dallas, Texas 75201
871-3600

Star Brand Ranch
P.O. Box 660
Kaufman, Texas 75242
214/932-2714

Star Canyon
Opening January '94

Stein's Bakery
417 Preston Valley Center
Dallas, Texas 75230
385-9911

Steinway Hall
5301 N. Central Exp.
Dallas, Texas 75205
526-1853

DIRECTORY OF SOURCES
alphabetical listing of sources

Steve Kemble Events
715 N. Oak Cliff Blvd.
Dallas, Texas 75208
943-5949

Stewart Bennett, Jr.
522-3991

Stone Savage Music
828-4555

Stonebriar Country Club
5050 Country Club Drive
Frisco, Texas 75034
625-5050

Stoneleigh Terrace Hotel
2927 Maple
Dallas, Texas 75201
871-7111

Stradivarius String Quartet
341-9142

Strictly Cheesecake
8139 Forest Lane
Dallas, Texas 75243
783-6545

Strictly Top Drawer
3214 Oak Lawn
Dallas, Texas 75219
521-1448

Studio on Hall, The
2816 Hall Street
Dallas, Texas 75219
871-9162

Sushi Sensei
520-1762

Sue Bohlin
686-4420

Superior Productions
824-8272

Suzanne Roberts Gifts
6718 Snider Plaza
Dallas, Texas 75205
369-8336

Swan Court
2435 N. Central
Richardson, Texas 75080
235-7926

Sweet Endings
2901 Elm Street
Dallas, Texas 75226
747-8001

Sweet Temptations Bakery
9090 Skillman #180

Dallas, Texas 75243
503-6007

Tablecloths Unlimited
363-8814

Taiwan Supermarket
221 W. Polk
Richardson, Texas 75081
783-2287

Taj Mahal
66 Richardson Heights
Richardson, Texas 75080
644-1329

Takeout Taxi
661-9991

Tapley Entertainment
255-3967

Taste Teasers
458-2873

Taxco Produce
1801 S. Good Latimer
Dallas, Texas 75226
421-7191

Teel Gray
351-6905

Texas Boys' Choir
817/924-1482

Texas Club
800 Main Street
Dallas, Texas 75202
761-6300

Texas Commerce Sky Lobby
2200 Ross Avenue, # 3700
Dallas, Texas 75201
979-6388

Texas Costume
2607 Ross Avenue
Dallas, Texas 75201
953-1255

Texas Hill Country Wine &
  Food Festival
512/345-3531

Texas Stadium Club
2401 E. Airport Freeway
Irving, Texas 75062
554-6368

Texas Wild Game Cooperative
P.O. Box 530
Ingram, Texas 78025
800/962-4263

Thai Oriental Food Store
2519 N. Fitzhugh
Dallas, Texas 75204
827-0978

Three Teardrops Tavern
1320 N. Industrial Blvd.
Dallas, Texas 75207
747-7464

Tienda Santa Rosa
521 W. Davis
Dallas, Texas 75208
943-3162

Tiffany & Co.
The Dallas Galleria
Dallas, Texas 75240
458-2800

Tillman's Corner
324 W. 7th Street
Dallas, Texas 75208
942-0988

Tim Louque Designs
526-5481

Tina Wasserman's Cooking School
7153 Lavendale
Dallas, Texas 75230
369-8741

TJ's Fresh Seafood Market
11661 Preston Road #149
Dallas, Texas 75230
691-2369

Today's Gourmet
373-0325

Todd Greer
522-0950

Tolbert's Chili Parlor
One Dallas Center,
350 N. St. Paul
Dallas, Texas 75201
953-1353

Tom Jenkins Photography
922-1284

Tommaso's Italian Fresh Pasta
5365 Spring Valley, #158
Dallas, Texas 75240
991-4040

Tony's Wine Warehouse & Bistro
2813 Oak Lawn
Dallas, Texas 75219
520-9463

DIRECTORY OF SOURCES
alphabetical listing of sources

Touch of Green
324-9432

Tower Club of Dallas
1601 Elm Street
Dallas, Texas 75202
220-0403

Trammell Crow Pavilions
2001 Ross Avenue
Dallas, Texas 75201
979-5100

Translations
4015 Villanova
Dallas, Texas 75225
373-8391

Très Bon Catering
946-1500

Truong Nguyen
3555 Walnut Street #221
Garland, Texas 75042
276-1185

Tulip Tree II, Inc., The
4410 Lovers Lane
Dallas, Texas 75225
691-9140

Tyson Organ & Piano Co.
3513 Oak Lawn
Dallas, Texas 75219
528-6123

Uncle Julio's
4125 Lemmon Avenue
Dallas, Texas 75219
520-6620

Union Station
400 S. Houston
Dallas, Texas 75202
651-0140

United Rent-All
3749 Josey Lane
Carrollton, Texas 75007
492-0550

University Club
13335 Dallas Pkwy, #4000
Dallas, Texas 75240
239-0050

Valet Limousines, Inc
690-1040

Valhalla
357-8383

Verandah Club
2201 Stemmons Freeway
Dallas, Texas 75207
761-7878

Vertu
4514 Travis
Dallas, Texas 75205
520-7817

Vicho Vincenzio Band
644-6846

Vick's Catering
368-3828

Villeroy & Boch
104 Interstate Highway 35NE
Hillsboro, Texas
817/582-0266

Vintage House, The
1101 Beltline Road
Carrollton, Texas 75006
242-5616

W.T. Greer, III
867-6307

Wadley Piano & Organ Co.
13536 Preston Road
Dallas, Texas 75240
239-2541

Wagon Wheel Ranch
816 Ruth Wall Road
Grapevine, Texas 76051
817/481-8284

Watel's
1923 McKinney Avenue
Dallas, Texas 75201
720-0323

Watson Food Service Industries
3712 Haggar
Dallas, Texas 75209
350-3561

Wendy Krispin Caterer
1025 N. Stemmons, #600
Dallas, Texas 75207
748-5559

Westin Hotel, The
13340 Dallas Parkway
Dallas, Texas 75240
934-9494

Westminster Lace
1022 North Park Center
Dallas, Texas 75225
373-1290

White House, The
6611 Forest Lane
Dallas, Texas 75230
991-9333

White Swan Cafe
2307 Abrams
Dallas, Texas 75214
824-8122

Whole Foods Market
2218 Greenville Avenue
Dallas, Texas 75206
824-1744
Coit & Beltline
Richardson, Texas 75080
699-8075

Wicker Basket, The
7817 Easton
Dallas, Texas 75209
353-0578

William Ernest Brown
524 NorthPark Center
Dallas, Texas 75225
691-5686

Williams Sonoma
51 Highland Park Village
Dallas, Texas 75205
696-0348
13350 Dallas Parkway
Dallas, Texas 75240
960-7575

Willow Bend Polo & Hunt Club
5845 W. Park Boulevard
Plano, Texas 75093
248-6298

Wine Emporium Etc.
5820 W. Lovers Lane
Dallas, Texas 75225
350-5686

Wine Letter
2152 Keller Court
Dallas, Texas 75208

Wine Press Bar & Bistro
4217 Oak Lawn
Dallas, Texas 75219
522-8720

Winn Morton Designs
Nakomia Drive
Lancaster, Texas 75146
227-0177

WMI Services
P.O. Box 509
Lewisville, Texas 75067
434-7977

Wolf & Company
4301 Bryan Street
Dallas, Texas 75204
381-8000

Wooden Spoon
1617 Avenue K
Plano, Texas 75074
424-6867

World Service U.K.
1923 Greenville Avenue
Dallas, Texas 7520
827-8886

Worldwide Food, Inc.
1907 Greenville Avenue
Dallas, Texas 75206
824-8860

Write Choice
361-7012

Write Selection
314 Preston Royal Shop Ctr
Dallas, Texas 75230
750-0531

Wynne Entertainment
4319 Oak Lawn
Dallas, Texas 75219
520-1111

Yellow Rose Special Events
1950 Stemmons Freeway
Dallas, Texas 75207
746-3780

York Street
6047 Lewis at Skillman
Dallas, Texas 75206
826-0968

Zen Floral Design Studio
Two Turtle Creek Village
Dallas, Texas 75219
526-9736

• **Advertisers** appear in **bold face**

Telephone Directory

Telephone Directory 248

TELEPHONE DIRECTORY
listing of sources by chapter

CHAPTER II

Cooking Classes

Anita Frank	520-1762
Brookhaven College	620-4715
Cake Carousel	690-4628
Christine Carbone	222-0517
Cooking with Cammie	821-1506
Cuisine Concepts	817/732-4758
Cuisine International	373-1161
Deborah Orrill	343-1227
eco-fluence	761-9979
Fun-Ed's School of Cooking	960-2666
Gourmet Cookery School	717-4189
Mange-Tout Cooking School	350-9285
Messina's Culinary Center	559-0857
Mountain View College	333-8612
North Lake College	659-5200
Out of a Flower	**754-0324**
Plano Parks & Recreation	578-7250
Tina Wasserman's School	369-6269

Organizations

American Heart Assoc.	748-7212
American Institute Wine & Food	741-4072
Dallas Opera, The	443-1043
Foster Child Advocate Services	827-8961
Les Dames D'Escoffier	821-0986
Texas Hill Country Wine & Food Festival	512/345-3531

CHAPTER III

Kitchenware & table accessories

Ace Mart Restaurant Supply	351-5444
Barneys New York	692-5222
Brenda Schoenfeld	368-4007
Cathy's Antiques	871-3737
Chantal Cookware Factory	351-2551
China Cupboard	528-6250
China Teacup	438-8074
Classic China	238-7763
Container Store	
Mockingbird	373-7044
Belt Line	458-9228
Forest Lane	386-5054
Plano	424-6060
Copper Lamp, The	521-3711
Crate & Barrel	
NorthPark	696-8010
Galleria	392-3411
Crate & Barrel Outlet	634-2277
Drrew Ldt.	521-0777
East & Orient Co.	826-1191
Edward Stalcup, Inc.	**368-5530**
Garden Secret, The	922-8860
Gardners Eden	800/822-9600
Gump's	800/284-8677

Highland Park Antique Shop	528-0430
Horchow Collection	556-6000
In Good Company	826-0020
International Wine Accessories	800/527-4072
Ivy House, The	369-2411
La Mariposa	871-9100
Lady Primrose	871-8334
Les Antiques	824-7322
Llewellyn & Lee	696-2114
Lovers Lane Antique Market	351-5656
Loyd-Paxton	521-1521
Macy's	851-5185
Marguerite Green At Home	352-8891
Market, The	
Inwood Village	352-1220
NorthPark	369-7161
Plano	596-2699
Mary Cates & Co.	855-5006
McKinney Avenue Antiques	871-1904
Mews, The	748-9070
Neiman Marcus	
Downtown	741-6911
NorthPark	363-8311
Prestonwood	233-1100
Nuvo	522-6886
Panhandlers	
Preston Royal	661-8021
Preston Park Village	612-0155
Pappas Design	522-9690
Perfect Setting, The	559-3330
Peregrinators Antiques	521-1950
Pier One Imports	
5427 W. Lovers Lane	351-5691
3747 Forest Lane	247-4593
Valley View Center	701-8081
Plate & Platter	521-9980
Polly Dupont	991-3689
Polo Shop, The	522-5270
Room Service	369-7666
Sample House	
Routh Street	871-1501
Walnut Creek	369-5148
Casa Linda	327-0486
Plano	985-1616
Mandalay Canal	556-1345
Silver Leopard	559-3194
Silver Vault, The	357-7115
Smink, Inc.	691-1270
St. Michael's Woman's Exchange	**521-3862**
Edward Stalcup, Inc.	**368-5530**
Stanley Korshak	871-3600
Tiffany & Co.	458-2800
Translations	373-8391
Tulip Tree II, Inc.	691-9140
Vertu	520-7817

TELEPHONE DIRECTORY
listing of sources by chapter

Villeroy & Boch	817/582-0266
Watson Food Service	350-3561
Westminster Lace	373-1290
Williams Sonoma	
Highland Park	696-0348
The Galleria	960-7575

Linens

Designs Behind the Scenes	691-7307
Fishburn's Cleaning & Laundry	**826-4101**
Ginette Albert	363-4543
Linen Gallery, The	522-6700
Linen Sisters, The	522-4289
Linens 'n Things	265-8651
Quiltcraft Industries	741-1662

CHAPTER IV
Invitations

Campbell Stationers	692-8380
Card Art	341-8398
Carté	559-6168
Geppetto Designs	526-4857
Inkcorporated Stationery & Invitations	**361-5496**
Invitations/Party Innovations	608-1805
Invite Your Guests	238-1754
It's A Wrap	520-9727
Ken Knight	754-0404
LaserTations	618-3713
Making Statements	530-6191
Marj's Stationery	350-8246
Needle in a Haystack	528-2850
O-K Paper Center	871-0770
Paper Routes	748-9322
Papyrus	
NorthPark	265-7187
The Galleria	386-8744
Party Art, Inc.	987-0872
Party Bazaar	528-4795
Party Cat	800/345-1213
Preston Center	3 739-2107
Party Place	
Preston Center	696-4550
Preston Park/Plano	867-6899
Print Shoppe, The	**350-1902**
Private Collection Stamp	360-0621
Randall Morgan	521-8240
Royal Party +	385-3885
Ruccus	691-0828
St. Michael's Woman's Exchange	**521-3862**
Suzanne Roberts Gifts	369-8336
William Ernest Brown	691-5686
Write Choice, The	361-7012
Write Selection	750-0531

Calligraphy

Betty Barna Calligraphics	234-4075
Calligraphic Arts, Inc.	522-4731
Calligraphy by Janet Travis	871-6064
Donna Bonds Calligraphy	239-6423
Donna Sabolovic Calligraphy & Design	**234-3748**
K2 Design	522-2344
Nancy Himes	373-1789
Quill Productions	620-1556
Sue Bohlin	686-4420
Teel Gray	351-6905

Invitation Design

Ann Manning	522-4350
Cato Company, The	352-3702
Donna Sabolovic Calligraphy & Design	**234-3748**
Inkcorporated Stationery & Invitations	**361-5496**
Lynn Townsend Dealey	890-8123
O! Suzanna Design Studio	**528-4289**
Pickens Design	363-9140

Printing

Dave the Printer	630-4017
Kwik Kopy	691-8325
Moreno Printing	827-7283
PIP Printing	987-3235
Presto Print	528-9122
Print Shoppe, The	**350-1902**

CHAPTER V
Food Markets

Addison Farmers' Market	233-4619
Al's Import Foods	363-3778
Big Town Farmers' Market	319-8093
Dallas Farmers Market	670-5880
Danals	
Harry Hines	357-0241
Lemmon Avenue	528-8570
Maple Avenue	526-4340
Fiesta Mart	944-3300
Golden Pacific Supermarket	234-5666
Hiep Phong Supermarket	272-4802
Hiep Thai Market	272-1993
Kazy's Food Market	235-4831
Ralph's Fine Foods	368-0931
Simon David	
Inwood	352-1781
Abrams Road	340-1119
Taiwan Supermarket	783-2287
Thai Oriental Food Store	827-0978
Truong Nguyen	276-1185

TELEPHONE DIRECTORY
listing of sources by chapter

Whole Foods Market	
Greenville Ave.	824-1744
Coit & Beltline	699-8075

Meat

Fresh n Tender	644-7224
Glazed Honey Hams	241-6799
Gorman's	288-7677
Guadalupe Meats	800/880-0416
Hans Mueller Sausage Co.	241-2793
Kosher Link, The	248-3773
Kuby's Sausage House	363-2231
Preferred Meats	565-0243
Rudolph's Market	741-1874
Tx Wild Game Co-op	800/962-4263

Seafood

FishFinders, Inc,	823-3153
Fishmonger's Seafood	423-3699
Landlock Seafood Co.	241-7500
Mr. Fish Crabs 'N More	821-4833
Pullen Seafood	823-8222
TJ's Fresh Seafood Market	691-2369

Gourmet

American Food Service	233-5750
Aziz Import Foods	369-6982
Bristish Emporium, The	817/421-3211
British Trading Post	686-8840
Cafe Madrid Market	234-5666
Civello's Raviolismo	827-2989
Coffee Company Inc.	369-5704
Coosemans Dallas, Inc.	741-7858
Dallas Tortilla & Tamale	
Downtown	742-3888
N. Marsalis	943-7681
European Market & Deli	696-5441
Fit-Fit Cuisine	**444-9792**
French Direct Inc.	824-1659
Fresh Pasta Delights	422-5907
Fresh Start Market	528-5535
Golden Circle Herb Farm	225-0500
Goodies from Goodman	987-3591
Gourmet Foods Warehouse	
Preston Forest	788-5155
Hillside Village	824-0656
Gourmet Unlimited	233-9964
Green Produce	421-4100
Hines Nut & Produce Co.	939-0253
Impofoods	680-3232
Inchon Oriental Food	986-6939
India Imports	255-5941
La Creme Coffee & Tea	**369-4188**
La Popular	824-7617
Las Americas	324-2604
Luna's Tortilla Factory	747-2661
Magnifico Fine Foods	596-2699

Marty's	**526-4070**
Momo's Italian Groceries	234-6800
Mozzarella Company	741-4072
Pasta Plus	
Preston Royal	373-3999
Plano	713-7181
Pendrey's	
Inwood Village	357-1870
The Galleria	991-1870
Polish Delicatessen	503-6510
Shalibi Imported Foods	840-1375
Shin Chon	276-9792
Taj Mahal	644-1329
Taste Teasers	
Taxco Produce	421-7191
Tommaso's Pasta	991-4040
Wooden Spoon	424-6867
World Service U.K.	827.8886
Worldwide Food, Inc.	824-8860

Gift Baskets

Bodacious Baskets	385-1452	800/645-1889
City Cafe to Go		351-3366
Eureka!		369-7767
Goodies from Goodman		987-3591
Gourmet Food Warehouse		788-5155
Kozy Kitchen		522-8504
La Creme Coffee & Tea		**369-4188**
L'Epicurean		747-5885
Marty's		**526-4070**
Mother-Daughter		613-1274
Mozzarella Factory		741-4072
Neiman Marcus		741-6911
Party in a Box		630-6673
Spirited Cakes		522-2806
Translations		375-8391

Desserts/Bakeries

A Taste of Europe	817/654-9494
Angel in My Kitchen	373-6030
ArtCakes by Oggetti	824-8601
Aston's English Bakery	368-6425
Bagel Chain, The	350-2245
Bagel Emporium	248-1569
Black Forest Bakery	987-9090
Cafe Partier	
Cakery, The	324-9292
Cakes of Elegance	343-2253
Casa Linda Bakery	321-0355
Celebrity Cafe & Bakery	
Highland Park	528-6612
Fairmount	922-9866
Preston & Royal	373-0783
Cheesecake Royale	328-9102
CJ's Delight	827-7538
Dallas Affaires	324-3082

David J's	991-1818	Richardson	480-8484
Dessert Dreams	438-7630	Spirits Liquor Company	
Empire Baking Co.	526-3223	Deep Ellum	748-2459
Frosted Art	258-0644	Park Lane	265-8085
Godiva Chocolatier Inc.	458-1821	Tony's Wine Warehouse	520-9463
Haagen Dazs	559-3757	Wine Emporium Etc.	350-5686
Heavenly Cheesecakes	644-6314		
Humble Pie & Cake Co.	358-3237	***Take-Out***	
Ida Mae's Cakes	817/567-3439	Amore (To Go)	739-0502
International Bakery	680-8513	**Arnold's Texas Bar-B-Q**	**826-1234**
Kathleen's Art Bakery	691-3968	Bagelstein's Deli and Bakery	234-3787
Kozy Kitchen	522-8504	Bubba's Cooks Country	373-6527
La Francaise French Bakery		California Pizza Kitchens	
Lake Highlands	341-6365	Belt Line	490-8550
Hillside Village	823-8102	Preston Center	750-5691
La Madeleine French Bakery		Camellia Cafe	691-8164
Mockingbird Ln	696-6962	Campisi's Pizza To Go	931-2267
Lemon Ave.	521-0182	Celebrity Cafe & Bakery	
Preston Forest	233-6448	Highland Park	528-6612
NW Hwy & Midway	357-5623	Fairmount	922-9866
LaRosa's Italian Bakery	578-9497	Preston & Royal	373-0783
le gâteau cakery	528-6102	Cheese House	239-7051
Massimo da Milano		Chicken Chicken	361-2222
Lovers Lane	351-1426	City Cafe to Go	351-3366
Village on the Parkway	661-5255	Colter's Bar-B-Q	265-8377
Hillside Village	826-9456	Cowboy Chicken	
Morgen Chocolate, Inc.	954-4424	Northwest Hghwy	956-9288
Neuhaus Chocolate Cafe	373-3590	Shadybrook	361-7747
NorthPark	691-9156	Preston Road	732-6281
The Galleria	392-0281	Dallas Grill	361-1387
Prestonwood	980-9851	Deli News	
New York, Tx Cheesecake	800/225-6982	Crescent Court	922-deli
Neuhaus Chocolate Cafe	373-3590	Richardson	392-deli
Out of a Flower	**754-0324**	Eureka!	369-7767
Romano's Cheesecake Co.	521-1662	Fred's Deli	948-9090
Sarah Jane Francis	373-7737	Gilbert's NY Deli	373-3333
Spirited Cakes	522-2806	Going Gourmet	351-6773
Stein's Bakery	385-9911	Hao's	361-2020
Strictly Cheesecake	783-6545	Henk's European Deli	987-9090
Sweet Endings	747-8001	Highland Park Cafeteria	
Sweet Temptations Bakery	503-6007	Knox Street	526-3801
Tim Louque Designs	526-5481	Casa Linda Plaza	327-3663
		Kathleen's Art Bakery	692-TOGO
Wine		**Marty's**	**526-4070**
Grailey's Fine Wines	823-8711	Maudee's Tearoom	526-9750
La Cave Warehouse	979-9463	Mise en Place	520-2424
Marty's	**526-7796**	Peggy Sue BBQ	987-9188
Mr. G's Deli & Beverages	867-2821	Pollo Bueno	826-0645
Po-Go's Liquor		Polish Delicatessen	503-6510
Inwood Village	350-8989	Preizler's Deli & Bakery	458-8896
9669 N. Central	373-7646	Solly's Barbecue	387-7120
Red Coleman Liquors		Sonny Bryan's Barbecue	744-1805
Greenville Ave.	363-0201	Soramy	
Sigel's Liquor Stores		Plano	612-0068
Greenville Ave.	739-4012	Preston Royal	N/A
Inwood Road	387-9873		

TELEPHONE DIRECTORY
listing of sources by chapter

Delivery Services

Entrees on Trays	828-0452
Home Delivery Network	248-4006
Takeout Taxi	661-9991

CHAPTER VI

Caterers

A Catered Affair	387-5566
Adelina's Catering	661-0644
Affairs to Remember	247-8309
Au Bon Goût	**522-7345**
Boster Gourmet Catering	**855-0700**
Carolyn Unsworth	521-9884
Catering by Angela	520-3747
Catering by Arthur	**741-1158**
Catering Company, The	696-1070
Catering by Don Strange	363-1155
Chateau Magdalena Caterers	869-2167
Chef's Shadow	484-5533
City Market Catering	979-2696
Constance Muller	522-5505
dani group, the	**520-0890**
Darrie Hinson Catering	239-1213
Daryl's by Design	**655-1444**
Ethel MacIntosh	421-3943
Five Star Catering	520-9463
Food Company	939-9270
Gil's Elegant Catering	254-1986
GOURMETDALLAS	**484-4954**
Great American Food Co.	285-8777
Guess Who's Coming	340-0061
Joan McIlyar	521-8658
Just Delicious	521-2448
L'Epicurean	747-5885
Nancy Beckham	821-8093
Pappas Catering	480-8585
Redwine Catering	520-0502
Savoire Faire	941-8939
Sazon International	783-7676
Silver Tray Catering	**423-8322**
Simcha Kosher Catering	**620-7295**
Some Enchanted Evening	942-8434
Special Affairs Catering	351-1796
Spice of Life	343-2598
Today's Gourmet	373-0325
Très Bon Catering	946-1500
Wendy Krispin Caterer	**748-5559**

Restaurants & Take-Outs That Cater

Arnold's Texas Bar-B-Q	**289-0289**
Blue Mesa Grill	**934-0165**
Caliente Ranch Grill	**369-8600**
Casa Domenguez	871-9787
City Cafe to Go	351-3366

Colter's Barbecue	265-8377
Deli News	
Crescent Court	922-deli
Richardson	392-deli
Goodies from Goodman	987-3591
Kathleen's Art Bakery	692-TOGO
Loma Luna	691-1552
Pasta Plus	373-3999
Marty's	**526-4070**
Newport's	**954-0220**
Sam's Cafe	**855-2233**
Uncle Julio's	905-3881

Party Planners & Designers

Affaires Extraordinaire	373-9977
Bill Reed Decorations	823-3154
Community Connection	526-7635
Creative Celebrations	350-1910
Events Unlimited	750-7226
Gale Sliger Productions	**637-5566**
Jed Mace	357-7686
Kaleidoscope, Inc.	522-5930
Kaleidoscope Decor	634-3778
Life's A Party	661-0330
Liland's Special Events	748-1191
Party & Event Designers	747-0025
Party Plus	424-8770
Party Service	363-9366
R.S.V.P. Party Planning	350-7787
Steve Kemble Events	**943-5949**
Winn Morton Designs	**227-0177**
Wolf & Company	381-8000
Yellow Rose Special Events	746-3780

Wedding Consultants

Nina Nichols Austin	871-3611
Salli Goldstein	233-0976
Sally Jones	521-3119

Public Relations

Julia Sweeney & Assoc.	520-0206
Martha Tiller & Co.	855-5140
Resource 3, Inc.	351-9806

CHAPTER VII

Hotels

Adolphus Hotel	**742-8200**
Doubletree Hotel at Lincoln Ctr	934-8400
Fairmont Hotel	720-2020
Four Seasons Resort & Club	717-0700
Grand Kempinski Hotel	386-6000
Hotel Crescent Court	871-3200
Hotel St. Germain	871-2516
Loews Anatole Hotel	748-1200

Mansion on Turtle Creek, The	559-2100
Melrose Hotel	521-5151
Omni Mandalay, Las Colinas	556-0800
Plaza of the Americas Hotel	521-9980
Sheraton Park Central Hotel	385-3000
Stoneleigh Terrace Hotel	871-7111
Westin Hotel, The	**934-9494**

Clubs

Bent Tree Country Club	931-7326
Brook Haven Country Club	243-6151
Brook Hollow Golf Club	637-1900
Canyon Creek Country Club	231-1466
City Club	748-9525
Cityplace Club	841-6830
Columbian Country Club	416-2131
Crescent Club	871-8555
Dallas Country Club	521-2151
Dallas Petroleum Club	871-1500
Dallas Women's Club	363-7596
Eldorado Country Club	548-8777
Energy Club of Dallas	869-2631
Gleneagles Country Club	867-6666
Hackberry Country Club	869-2631
La Cima Club	869-2266
Las Colinas Country Club	542-1141
Northwood Club	239-1366
Park City Club	373-0756
Royal Oaks Country Club	691-6091
Stonebriar Country Club	625-5050
Texas Club	761-6300
Tower Club of Dallas	220-0403
University Club	239-0050
Verandah Club	761-7878
Willow Bend Polo & Hunt Club	248-6298

Restaurants

8.0 Restaurant & Bar	979-0880
Addison Cafe	991-8824
Adelmo's	559-0323
Alessio's	521-3585
Andrews	702-0720
Arcodoro	871-1924
Art Bar/Blind Lemon /Club Clearview	939-0202
Baby Routh	871-2345
Big Spur Corral	905-0808
Blue Mesa Grill	**934-0165**
Bombay Cricket Club	871-1333
Cafe Expresso	361-6984
Cafe Margaux	520-1985
Caliente Ranch Grill	**369-8600**
Calluaud's	352-1997
Capriccio	871-2004
Chamberlain's Chop House	**934-2467**
Chez Gerard	522-6865

City Cafe	351-2233
Dakota's	740-4001
Deep Ellum Cafe	741-9012
Deli News	
The Crescent	922-deli
Hillcrest	392-deli
Dovie's Inc.	233-4270
Dragon Street Diner	747-1566
Ferrari's Italian Oven	954-1112
French Room, The	**742-8200**
Highland Park Cafe	521-7300
Huntington's	**934-9494**
India Palace	392-0190
J Pinnell's	871-1181
J. Pepe's	871-0366
Javier's	521-4211
Juniper	855-0700
Krispin – the restaurant	**748-7151**
L'Ancestral	528-1081
La Tosca	352-8373
Lady Primrose	871-8334
Lombardi's 311	747-0322
Main Street News	746-2934
Mama's Daughter	742-8646
Mario's Chiquita	521-0092
Matt's Rancho Martinez	823-5517
Mattito's Cafe Mexicano	526-8181
Mediterraneo	N/A
Mercado Juarez	
Northwest Hwy	556-0796
Belt Line Road	458-2145
Messina's Culinary Center	559-0857
Momo's Pasta	521-3009
Nero's Italian	826-6376
Newport's	**954-0220**
No Place	823-9077
On the Border	528-5900
Opus	670-3721
Pappadeaux Seafood	521-4700
Piccola Cucina	691-0488
Pomodoro	871-1924
PoPolo's	692-5497
Quadrangle Grille	979-9022
Ristorante Savino	826-7804
Riveria, The	351-0094
Russian Room, The	922-3333
Sam's Cafe	
Crescent Court	**855-2233**
Preston Center	**739-3474**
Sfuzzi	
McKinney Ave.	871-2606
Addison Road	960-2606
Plano	964-0700
Star Canyon	N/A
Swan Court	235-7926

White Swan Cafe	824-8122
Tillman's Corner	942-0988
Tolbert's Chili Parlor	953-1353
Watel's	720-0323
Wine Press	522-8720
York Street	826-0968

Special Places

Aldredge House	823-8268
Americas Ice Garden	922-9800
Belo Mansion	220-0239
Carpenter House	424-1889
Cityplace Conference Center	841-6830
D-Art	821-2522
Dallas Alley	702-0170
Dallas Aquarium	670-8441
Dallas Arboretum	327-8263
Dallas Civic Garden Center	428-7476
Dallas Communications Ctr	869-0700
Dallas Museum of Art	922-1200
Dallas World Aquarium	**720-2224**
Deep Ellum Party Warehouse	742-2091
Ellum Beach Club	349-2002
Granada Cinema & Grille	823-9619
Hall of State	421-4500
La Botica Mexican Cafe	824-2005
McKinney Avenue Transit	855-0006
Messina's Culinary Ctr	559-0857
Meyerson Symphony Ctr	670-3285
Old City Park	421-5141
Plano Civic Center	422-0296
Reichenstein Manor	522-1075
Richardson Woman's Club	238-0841
Sammons Center	520-7788
Science Place	428-5555
Schimelpfenig Showplace	424-2999
Silverado City	**745-1870**
Skylobby	979-6100
Southern Methodist University	692-0000
Studio on Hall, The	871-9162
Texas Commerce Sky Lobby	979-6388
Texas Stadium Club	554-6368
Three Teardrops Tavern	747-7476
Trammell Crow Pavilions	979-5100
Union Station	651-0140
Vintage House, The	242-5616
White House, The	991-9333

Country & Western

Austin Ranch	817/481-1536
Big-D-Dude Ranch	842-8440
Bill Bates Cowboy Ranch	390-7790
Billy Bob's Texas	817/589-1711
Bowed Creek Ranch	373-8940
Cedar Canyon Dude Ranch	214/224-8477
Circle R Ranch	817/430-1561
Clark's Outpost	817/437-2414

Cowboys	321-0115
Diamond J Corral	952-9809
Mesquite Championship Rodeo	**285-8777**
Old Fort Dallas	225-5414
Park Lane Ranch & Cattle	349-2002
Quarter J Ranch	235-6331
Reunion Ranch	214/563-1170
Silverado City	**745-1870**
Southfork Ranch	442-7800
Star Brand Ranch	214/932-2714
Wagon Wheel Ranch	817/481-8284

CHAPTER VIII

Flower Designers & Shops

Apples to Zinnias	559-2240
Arts District Flower Market	979-9002
Atelier, A Work Shop	350-4116
Biggerstaff Flowers	423-2501
Botanicals	521-5188
Bret Driver	948-1042
Charles Stephen Co., The	233-3838
Chris Whanger	319-8550
Designs in Bloom	960-1114
Dode Martin/Flowers	559-4701
Donald Hill...Flowers Etc.	522-6830
Doreen By Design	817/754-6111
Dr. Delphinium Designs	**522-9911**
Earth Blooms	823-6222
Fleur Adel	625-6948
Flora Verde	960-9893
Flower Studio, The	827-6950
Flowers by Carol Garner	526-4205
Flowers of Oak Lawn	526-0912
Flowers on the Square	817/429-2888
Gone to Seed	943-2101
Grassroots	556-1244
Gunter's Greenhouse	234-3377
I Love Flowers	522-3444
In Bloom	596-4442
La Jardinère	522-3444
Liland's Flower Fashions	823-9505
Luther P. Menke	960-1021
Marilee Mallinson Martinez	339-2954
Mille Fleurs	960-1020
Nicholson Hardie	357-4348
Orchid Gardens	350-4985
Petals & Stems	233-9037
Potted Palm, The	826-0075
Rick Duren	505/984-2508
Russell Glenn Floral Design	**742-3001**
Seasonal Colour	526-9800
Strictly Top Drawer	521-1448
The Rose Shop	827-1119
Todd Greer	522-0950
Marco Polo	931-2328

Valhalla	357-8383
Wesley Lujan	827-6950
Wicker Basket	353-0578
Zen Floral Design Studio	526-9736

Balloons

Balloon Bonanza	250-1423
Balloon City USA	821-6482
Balloon House, The	317-1965
Balloons Fantastique	964-2488
Balloons over Dallas	373-9695
Balloons to You	788-5022
Smiles Balloon Co.	361-8973

Party Supplies

A-Z Party Warehouse	732-8334
Arnold's Gifts	233-2957
Discount Party Warehouse	239-6717
Michaels/MJ Designs	696-5491
Palmer Sales	288-1026
Parties-R-Us	352-8386
Zaks Stores	404-8800

CHAPTER IX

Entertainment

Abundio Ortiz	247-5317
Alex Donner Orchestra	800/ITS-MUSIC
American Federation of Musicians	817/654-0063
Arts Magnet School	720-7300
Barbara Kirchhoff	931-1154
Bill Tillman Band	**424-8007**
Buddy Brock Orchestra	713/821-5202
Cafe Noir	821-6540
Calvalcade of Stars	255-3967
Carol West	296-7247
Caroling Troubadours, The	713-0015
Chenoweth Chamber Music	270-9366
Creative Alternatives	817/731-3219
Dallas Brass & Electric	855-9754
Dallas Chamber Orchestra	520-3121
Dallas Symphony Musicians	871-4067
Dave Tanner	219-7315
Deborah Youngblood	724-8410
Dixie Chicks	369-9437
Folk Like Us	221-2416
Hal Turner	348-5999
Jack Cannon & Assoc	647-8073
Kelly Durbin	817/382-4632
Ken Boone Musical Production	328-7995
La Musica String Quartet	363-6422
Larry T-Byrd Gordon Show	286-6832
Lester Lanin Orchestras	**212/265-5208**
Light Crust Dough Boys	247-4295
Mal Fitch Orchestra, Inc.	279-3583

Marc Jaco Productions	392-0469
Mariachis Los Reyes	720-7220
Mark Carroll	824-8775
Marshall Grant Orchestra	407/686-7000
Michael Carney	212/986-4447
Mitchell Lehr	392-1502
Mori Music	644-8734
One O'Clock Lab Band	817/565-3743
Opus Four String Quartet	390-7363
Panhandlers Steel Band	817/565-4124
Peter Duchin Orchestra	800/433-5064
Phares Corder	235-6319
Plano Chamber Orchestra	423-6955
Project, The	250-3563
Ralph Sanford	327-8325
Ran Wilde Orchestra	351-5040
Richardson Chamber Orchestra	385-7267
Ron Fink	817/565-3714
Ron Lawrence Orchestra	423-8467
Ronnie Renfrow Big Band	713/774-2263
Rotel & the Red Hots	817/441-5488
Schnitzer Productions	373-1245
Serge Stodolnik	324-9942
Sharon Seaton	270-3791
Smokey & the Bearcats	306-8200
Stone Savage Music	828-4555
Stradivarius String Quartet	341-9142
Tapley Entertainment	255-3967
Pettys Group, The	553-9707
Vicho Vincenzio Band	644-6846
W.T. Greer, III	867-6307

Other Acts

Accardi Costume	956-7280
Anita M. Martinez Ballet Folklorico	720-7220
Arrangers, The	699-9076
Cohen's Casino Parties	276-2998
Dallas Costume Shop	428-4613
Incognito Costume World	404-0584
Klown-Magician	226-1313
Magicland	350-0966
Party Animals	613-9255
Sandy Trent's 1 Dance 2	827-3888
Superior Productions	824-8272
Texas Costume	953-1255
The Original Butt Sketch	943-2888

Agents

Carol Marks Music	231-4091
Ed Bernet Entertainment	691-0001
Encore Productions	317-2336
Entertainment Company	**423-1869**
Wynne Entertainment	520-1111

CHAPTER X

Rentals

Abbey Party Rentals	350-5373
Blue Chipper	350-2875
CANNONBALL Party Rental Co.	**387-8900**
Ducky-Bob's Rentals	702-8000
K & S Rental	245-6133
Rent-All Place, The	867-2121
Rentals Unlimited	259-7575
United Rent-All	492-0550

Specialty

Alexander Tent Company	869-2405
Don Prince	214/775-1016
Perfect Party Rentals	750-7584
Props of Texas	748-7767
Sandone Tents	350-6334
Special Occasions	233-3114
Tablecloths Unlimited	363-8814
WMI Services	434-7977

Drink Machines

I. H. Imports	352-7190
Margarita Man	298-6432
Margarita Masters	641-7926
Margaritas-R-Us	688-1880

Plants

Bread "N" Butter Tropical	824-7336
Dallas Garden Interiors	327-6120
Green with Envy	748-2595
Plant Place, The	869-3808
Plantscaping	742-5222
Southern Greenhouse	869-1679
Touch of Green	324-9432

Piano and Juke Boxes

Advance Music Company	939-9014
Brook Mays Music Company	233-9633
Dallas Piano Warehouse	231-4607
Empire Games	324-9858
Eveready Vending	428-5194
Jukebox Rentals/ Brass Register	231-1386
Keyboards Unlimited	630-2272
Steinway Hall	526-1853
Tyson Organ & Piano Co.	528-6123
Wadley Piano & Organ Co.	239-2541

Lighting

Dallas Stage Lighting	428-1818
Gemini Stage Lighting & Equip.	341-4822
Hall of Production Services	**931-3359**
Samarco	263-9969

Ice Sculpture

Bifulco's Vanishing Sculptures	826-6980
Higgins Ice Carving	748-5384

Party Help

Liaison Party Service	247-5807

Parkers

Best Valet Service, Inc.	520-8830
Jack Boles Services	**357-4493**
MEDiPARK Valet Parking	**828-0040**
Park Cities Valet Parking	533-2319
Preferred Parking	315-1140
R. P. Valet Dallas, Inc.	732-8800

Photography

BTV - Button Television	942-8346
Gittings Portraiture	350-5581
J. Allen Hansley Photo	871-2949
Jim Allen Portraiture	351-3200
John Derryberry	357-5457
John Haynesworth	559-3700
Kristina Bowman	526-9683
"Party Pics" by Flash	443-9393
Tom Jenkins	922-1284
Scott Hagar	922-1284

Sound

Crossroads Audio, Inc.	358-2623
Sound Productions Inc.	351-5373
Stewart Bennett, Jr.	522-3991

Transportation

British Carriage Limousines	393-2088
Dallas Surrey Services	946-9911
DFW Town Cars	956-1880
Five Star Limo	562-LIMO
Jack Boles Services	**357-4493**
Mr. Limo	437-3939
Valet Limousines, Inc	690-1040
Yellow Rose Touring	746-3780

• **Advertisers** appear in **bold face**

Index

Index 260

INDEX

8.0 Restaurant & Bar   129, 225, 254
A Catered Affair   93, 225, 253
A Taste of Europe   225, 251
A-Z Party House   168, 225, 256
Abbey Party Rentals   186, 225, 257
Abundio Ortiz   170, 225, 256
Accardi Costume   183, 225, 256
Ace Mart Restaurant Supply   36, 225, 249
Addison Cafe   141, 225, 254
Addison Farmers' Market   225, 250
Adelina's Catering   93, 225, 253
Adelmo's   130, 225, 254
Adolphus Hotel   118, 210, 225, 253
Advance Music Company   189, 225, 257
Affaires Extraordinaire   110, 225, 253
Affairs to Remember   225, 253
Al's Import Foods   63, 72, 225, 250
Aldredge House   142, 225, 255
Alessio's   141, 225, 254
Alex Donner Orchestra   178, 225, 256
Alexander Tent Company   192, 225, 257
American Federation of Musicians   225, 256
American Food Service   63, 252, 251
American Heart Association   25, 249
American Institute
    of Food & Wine   22, 23, 225, 249
Americas Ice Garden   123, 225, 255
Amore (To Go)   82, 225, 252
Andrews   130, 225, 254
Angel in My Kitchen   72, 225, 251
Anita Frank   249,
    see also Sushi Sensei
Anita Martinez Ballet Folklorico 182,
    225, 256
Ann Manning   48, 225, 250
Apples to Zinnias   58, 225, 255
Arcodoro   89, 138, 225, 254
Arnold's Tx Bar-B-Q   82, 105, 225, 250, 253
Arnold's Gifts & Creations   225, 256
Arrangers, The   182, 225, 256
ArtCakes by Oggetti   73, 225, 251
Art Bar/Blind Lemon/
    ClubClearview   130, 225, 254
Arts District Flower Market   164, 225, 255
Arts Magnet School   182, 225, 256
Aston's English Bakery   73, 225, 251
Atelier, A Work Shop   158, 225, 255
Au Bon Goût   93-94, 219, 225, 253
Austin Ranch   150, 226, 255
Aziz Import Foods   226, 251
Baby Routh   20, 130, 226, 254
Bagel Chain, The   73, 226, 251
Bagel Emporium   226, 251
Bagelstein's Deli & Bakery   73, 89, 226, 252
Baked Honey Hams   61
Balloon Bonanza   226, 256

Balloon City USA   166-167, 226, 256
Balloons   166-167, 256
Balloons Fantastique   167, 226, 256
Balloons over Dallas   226, 256
Balloons to You   167, 226, 256
Barbara Kirchhoff   172, 226, 256
Barneys New York   27, 226, 249
Belo Mansion   142, 226, 255
Bent Tree Country Club   127, 226, 254
Best Valet Service, Inc.   199, 226, 257
Betty Barna Calligraphics   52, 226, 250
Bifulco's Vanishing Sculptures   193, 226, 257
Big Spur Corral   130, 226, 254
Big Town Farmers' Market   58, 226, 250
Big-D-Dude Ranch   153, 226, 255
Biggerstaff Flowers   164, 226, 255
Bill Bates Cowboy Ranch   150, 226, 255
Bill Reed Decorations   110, 226, 253
Bill Tillman Band   173, 226, 256
Billy Bob's Texas   151, 226, 255
Black Forest Bakery   73, 226, 251
Bloomingstock   226
Blue Chipper   186, 226, 257
Blue Mesa Grill   105, 131, 208, 226, 251, 254
Bodacious Baskets   69, 251
Bombay Cricket Club   141, 226, 254
Boster's Gourmet Catering   94-95, 222,
    226, 253
Botanicals   58, 226, 255
Bowed Creek Ranch   151, 226, 255
Bread "N" Butter Tropical Plants   190,
    226, 257
Brenda Schoenfeld   36, 226, 249
Bret Driver   162, 226, 255
British Carriage Limousines   201, 226, 257
British Emporium   63, 68, 226, 251
British Trading Post   63, 68, 226, 251
Brookhaven College   20, 249
Brook Haven Country Club   226, 254
Brook Hollow Golf Club   226, 254
Brook Mays Music Company   190, 226, 257
BTV - Button Television   199, 227, 257
Bubba's Cooks Country   82, 227, 252
Buddy Brock Orchestra   173, 227, 256
Cafe Expresso   83, 89, 227, 254
Cafe Madrid Market   227, 251
Cafe Margaux   141, 227, 254
Cafe Noir   227, 256
Cafe Partier   73, 251
Cake Carousel   17, 227, 249
Cakery, The   74, 227, 251
Cakes of Elegance   227, 251
Caliente Ranch Grill
    & Cantina   106, 227, 253, 254
California Pizza Kitchens   82, 89, 227, 252
Calligraphic Arts, Inc.   51, 227, 250

INDEX

Calligraphy   50-51, 250
Calligraphy by Janet Travis   51, 227, 250
Calluaud's   131, 227, 254
Camellia Cafe   83, 227, 252
Campbell Stationers   42, 227, 250
Campisi's Pizza To Go   89, 227, 252
CANNONBALL Party Rental Co.   186, 192, 204, 227, 257
Canyon Creek Country Club   227, 254
Capriccio Restaurant   131, 227, 254
Card Art   48, 227, 250
Carol Garner
   see also, Flowers
Carol Marks Music   180, 227, 256
Carol West   170, 227, 256
Caroling Troubadours   183, 227, 256
Carolyn Unsworth   95, 227, 253
Carpenter House, The   142, 227, 255
Carte   42, 227, 250
Casa Dominguez   108, 141, 227, 253
Casa Linda Bakery   74, 227, 251
Caterers   91-108, 253
Catering by Angela   95, 227, 253
Catering by Arthur   95-96, 204, 227, 253
Catering by Don Strange   96, 227, 253
Catering Company, The   96, 227, 253
Cathy's Antiques   28, 227, 249
Cato Company, The   53, 227, 250
Cedar Canyon Dude Ranch   151, 227, 255
Celebrity Cafe & Bakery   74, 227, 251
Chamberlain's Prime Chop
   House   132, 228, 254
Chantal Cookware Factory   28, 228, 249
Charles Stephens Co., The   158, 228, 255
Chateau Magdalena Caterers   96, 228, 253
Check list for caterers   109
Cheese House   88, 228, 252
Cheesecake Royale   80, 228, 251
Chef's Shadow   83, 228, 253
Chenoweth Chamber Music   170, 227, 256
Chez Gerard   132, 228, 254
Chicken Chicken   83, 228, 252
China Cupboard, The   28, 228, 249
China Teacup, The   28, 228, 249
Chris Whanger   162, 228, 255
Christian Gerber   20
Christine Carbone   17, 228, 249
Church Lady, The, see Superior
   Productions
Circle R Ranch   151, 228, 255
City Cafe   132, 228, 254
City Cafe to Go   69, 83, 228, 249, 252, 253
City Club   125, 228, 254
City Market Catering   97, 228, 253
Cityplace Club   125, 228, 254
Cityplace Conference Center   143, 228, 255

Civello's Raviolismo   63-64, 228, 251
CJ's Delight   227, 251
Clark's Outpost   151, 228, 255
Classic China   28, 228, 249
Clubs   124-128, 254
Coffee Company Inc.   64, 228, 251
Cohen's Casino Parties   183, 228, 256
Colter's Bar-B-Q   106, 228, 252, 253
Columbian Country Club   228, 254
Community Connection   116, 228, 253
Constance Muller   104, 228, 253
Container Store, The   228, 249
Cookbooks by Area Chefs   21
Cooking & Charity Events   22-23
Cooking Schools & Classes   16-21, 249
Cooking with Cammie   17, 228, 249
Coosemans Dallas, Inc.   69, 228, 251
Copper Lamp, The   28, 228, 249
Country & Western Places   150-154, 255
Cowboy Chicken   82, 228, 252
Cowboys   152, 228, 255
Crate & Barrel   28, 228, 249
Crate & Barrel Outlet Store   28, 228, 249
Creative Learning Center   25
Crescent Club   124, 228, 254
Crossroads Audio, Inc.   195, 228, 257
Cuisine Concepts   17, 228, 249
Cuisine International   21, 72, 228, 249
Custom Designed Invitations   52-55, 250
D-Art   143, 229, 255
Dakota's   132, 229, 254
Dallas Affaires   74, 229, 251
Dallas Alley   143, 229, 255
Dallas Aquarium   149, 229, 255
Dallas Arboretum & Botanical
   Garden   143-144, 229, 255
Dallas Brass & Electric   229, 256
Dallas Chamber Orchestra   181, 229, 256
Dallas Civic Garden Center   144, 229, 255
Dallas Communications Center   144, 229, 255
Dallas Costume Shop   183, 256
Dallas Country Club   229, 254
Dallas Eats! Newsletter   229, 254
Dallas Farmers Market   57, 229, 240
Dallas Garden Interiors   191, 229, 257
Dallas Grill   229, 252
DALLAS MORNING NEWS   16, 20, 25, 29
Dallas Museum of Art   144, 229, 255
Dallas Opera, The   25, 181, 249
Dallas Petroleum Club   124, 229, 254
Dallas Piano Warehouse   190, 229, 257
Dallas Stage Lighting & Equipment   194, 229, 257
Dallas Surrey Services   201, 229, 257, 257
Dallas Symphony Musicians   181, 229, 256
Dallas Tortilla & Tamale Factory   84, 229, 251

INDEX

Dallas Wind Symphony   174
Dallas Women's Club   229, 254
Dallas World Aquarium   144, 219, 229, 255
Danals   58, 229, 250
dani group, the   84, 97-98, 213, 229, 253
Darrie Hinson Catering & Co.   98, 229, 253
Daryl's by Design   98-99, 229, 253
Dave Tanner   174
Dave the Printer   50, 229, 250
David J's   74, 81. 229, 252
Dean Fearing   20
Deborah Orrill   18, 229, 249
Deborah Youngblood   170, 229, 256
Deep Ellum Cafe   108, 132, 229, 254
Deep Ellum Party Warehouse   229, 255
Deli News   88, 106, 229, 252, 253, 254
Delivery Services   90, 253
Designs Behind the Scenes   37, 229, 250
Dessert Dreams   23, 230, 252
Desserts   72-77, 251-252
DFW Town Cars   201, 230, 257
Diamond J Corral   230, 255
Directory of Sources   223- 243
Discount Party Warehouse   167, 230, 257
Dixie Chicks   174, 230, 256
Dode Martin/Flowers   162, 230, 255
Donald Hill Flowers Etc.   163, 230, 255
Donna Bonds Calligraphy   51, 230, 250
Donna Sabolovic Calligraphy &
   Design   51, 53-54, 212, 230, 250
Doreen By Design   163, 230, 255
Doubletree Hotel at Lincoln Center   119,
   230, 253
Dovie's Inc.   132, 230, 254
Dr. Delphinium Designs   158-159, 208,
   230, 255
Dragon Street Diner   101, 230, 254
Drew-Corcoran   179, 230, 256
Drrew Ldt.   29, 230, 249
Drink Machines   188-189, 257
Ducky-Bob's Rentals   187, 230, 257
Earth Blooms   230, 255
East & Orient Co.   29, 230, 249
eco-fluence   230, 249
Ed Bernet Entertainment   180, 230, 256
Eduardo's Aca Y Alla   141
Edward Stalcup, Inc.   35, 212, 230, 249
Eldorado Country Club   230, 254
Ellum Beach Club   146, 230, 255
Empire Baking Company   69, 74-75, 230, 252
Empire Games   230, 257
Encore Productions   181, 230, 256
Energy Club of Dallas   126, 230, 254
Entertainment   169-184, 256
Entertainment Agents   180-182, 256
Entertainment Company, The   181, 215,
   230, 256
Entrees on Trays   90, 230, 253
Ethel MacIntosh   99, 230, 253
Eureka!   69, 83, 230, 251, 252
European Market & Deli   64, 89, 230, 251
Events Unlimited   230, 253
Eveready Vending   189, 230, 257
Fabian Seafood Co.   62, 230
Fairmont Hotel   119, 230, 253
Ferrari's Italian Oven   133, 230, 254
Fiesta Mart   58, 230, 250
Fishburn's Cleaning & Laundry   38, 211
   230, 250
FishFinders, Inc,   62, 230, 251
Fishmonger's Seafood Market &
   Cafe   62, 230, 251
Fit-Kit Cuisine by dani   84, 231, 251
Five Star Catering   108, 231, 253
Five Star Limo   202, 231, 257
Fleur Adel   163, 231, 255
Flora Verde   159, 231, 255
Flower Studio, The   164, 231, 255
Flowers by Carol Garner   162, 231, 255
Flowers   157-166, 255
Flower Designers   162-164, 255
Flower Shops   255
Flowers of Oak Lawn   159, 231, 255
Flowers on the Square   159, 231, 255
FOCAS, see Foster Child Advocate Services
Folk Like Us   174, 231, 256
Food Company, The   99, 231, 253
Food Events   22-23
Foster Child Advocate Services   22, 231, 249
Four Seasons Resort & Club   120, 231, 253
Fred's Deli   231, 252
French Direct Inc.   69, 231, 251
French Room, The   133, 210, 231, 254
Fresh N Tender   60, 231, 251
Fresh Pasta Delights   64, 231, 251
Fresh Start Market   64, 231, 251
Frosted Art   75, 231, 252
Fun-Ed's School of Cooking   18, 231, 249
Gale Sliger Productions   111, 220, 231, 253
Garden Secret, The   30, 231, 249
Gardners Eden   29, 231, 249
Gemini Stage Lighting & Sound Co.   194,
   231, 257
Geppetto Designs   42, 231, 250
Gil's Elegant Catering   99, 231, 253
Gilbert's New York Delicatessen   88, 231,
   252
Ginette Albert   37, 231, 250
Gittings Portraiture   231, 257
Glazed Honey Hams   61, 231, 251
Gleneagles Country Club   127, 231, 254
Godiva Chocolatier Inc.   78, 231, 252

INDEX

Going Gourmet   84, 231, 252
Golden Circle Herb Farm   64, 231, 251
Golden Pacific Supermarket   59-60, 231, 250
Gone to Seed   231, 255
Goodies from Goodman   64, 69, 231, 249, 253
Gorman's   61, 231, 251
Gourmet Cookery School   17, 231, 249
Gourmet Foods Warehouse
    Outlet   65, 69, 231, 251
Gourmet Markets   60-69, 251
Gourmet Unlimited   65, 232, 251
GOURMETDALLAS   100, 214, 232, 253
Grailey's Fine Wines   70, 232, 252
Granada Cinema & Grille   146, 232, 255
Grand Kempinski Hotel   120, 231, 253
Grassroots   159, 232, 255
Great American Food Co.   163, 232, 253
Green Produce   68, 232, 251
Green Expectations   191, 257
Green with Envy   191, 232, 257
Guadalupe Pit Smoked Meats   61, 232, 251
Guess Who's Coming to Dinner   142, 232, 253
Gump's   29, 232, 249
Gunter's Greenhouse & Florist   164, 232, 255
Haagen Dazs   75, 232, 252
Hackberry Country Club   128, 232, 254
Hal Turner   174, 232, 256
Hall of Production Services   194, 206, 232, 257
Hall of State   146, 232, 255
Hans Mueller Sausage Co.   61, 232, 251
Hao's   232, 252
Heavenly Cheesecakes   80, 232, 252
Henk's European Deli   88, 232, 252
Hiep Phong Supermarket & BBQ   59, 232, 250
Hiep Thai Market   59, 232, 250
Higgins Ice Carving   193, 232, 257
Highland Park Antique Shop   29, 232, 249
Highland Park Cafe   141, 232, 254
Highland Park Cafeteria   84, 232, 252
Hines Nut & Produce Co.   68, 232, 251
Home Delivery Network   90, 232, 253
Horchow Collection   29, 232, 249
Horchow Finale   29, 232
Hotel Crescent Court   119, 232, 253
Hotel St. Germain   121, 232, 253
Hotels   118-124, 253
Humble Pie & Cake Co.   75, 232, 252
Huntington's Restaurant   134, 232, 254
I Can't Believe It's Yogurt   81, 232
I Love Flowers   159, 232, 255
Ice Sculptures   193, 257
Ida Mae's Cakes   75, 232, 252
Impofoods   65, 232, 251
In Bloom   165, 232, 255

In Good Company   29, 233, 249
Inchon Oriental Food   60, 233, 251
Incognito Costume World   183, 233, 257
India Imports   65, 233, 251
India Palace   141, 233, 254
Inkcorporated Stationery &
    Invitations   42-43, 54, 215, 233, 250
International Bakery & Sandwich
    Bar   76, 233, 252
International Wine Accessories   30, 233, 249
Invitations   41-55, 250
Invitation Design   52-55, 250
Invitations & Party Innovations   48, 233, 250
Invite Your Guests   48, 233, 250
It's A Wrap   43, 233, 250
Ivy House, The   30, 233, 249
J Pinnell's   134, 233, 254
J. Allen Hansley Photography   199, 233, 257
J. Pepe's Mexican Restaurant   141, 233, 254
Jack Boles Services   197-198, 201, 218, 233, 257
Jack Cannon & Associates   175, 233, 256
Javier's   134, 233, 254
Jed Mace   111, 233, 253
Jennivine's Restaurant   141, 233
Jim Allen Portraiture   233, 257
Joan McIlyar   104, 233, 253
John Haynesworth Photography   233, 257
Judy Terrell Ebrey   26, 233, see also
    Cuisine International
Jukebox Rentals   189, 257
Jukebox Rentals/Brass Register   189, 233, 257
Julia Sweeney & Associates   116, 233, 253
Juniper   20, 134-135, 233, 254
Just Delicious   104, 233, 253
K & S Rental   233, 257
K2 Design   52, 233, 250
Kaleidoscope, Inc.   112, 233, 253
Kaleidoscope Decor   112, 233, 253
Kathleen's Art Bakery   76, 233, 252, 253
Kazy's Food Market   60, 233, 250
Kelly Durbin   233, 256
Ken Knight   43, 233, 250
Kevin Garvin   21
Keyboards Unlimited   190, 233, 257
Kitchenware & Table Accessories   21-39, 249-250
Klown- Magician   233, 256
Kosher Link, The   234, 251
Kozy Kitchen   63, 76, 234, 251, 252
Krispin — the restaurant   135, 146, 221, 234, 254
Kristina Bowman   200, 234, 257
Kuby's Sausage House, Inc   61, 87, 234, 251
Kwik Kopy   234, 250
L'Ancestral   141, 234, 254

INDEX

L'Epicurean 63, 100-101, 234, 251, 253
La Botica Mexican Cafe 146, 234, 255
La Cave Warehouse 24, 65, 234, 252
La Cima Club 125, 234, 254
La Creme Coffee & Tea 63, 65-66, 69, 81, 214, 251
La Francaise French Bakery 76, 234, 252
La Jardiniere 160, 234, 255
La Madeleine French Bakery & Cafe 21, 77, 85, 234, 252
La Mariposa 30, 234, 249
La Musica String Quartet 171, 234, 256
La Popular 85, 234, 254
La Tosca 136, 234, 254
Lady Primrose 30, 135, 234, 249, 254
Landlock Seafood Co. 63, 234, 251
LaRosa's Italian Specialty Bakery 66, 234, 252
Larry T-Byrd Gordon Show, The 176, 234, 256
Las Americas 234, 251
Las Colinas Country Club 128, 234, 254
LaserTations 48, 234, 250
le gateau cakery 77, 234, 252
Les Antiques 29, 234, 249
Les Dames d'Escoffier 23, 234, 249
Lester Lanin Orchestras 178, 207, 234, 256
Liaison Party Service 197, 234, 257
Life's a Party 112, 234, 253
Light Crust Doughboys 175, 233, 256
Lighting 193-194, 257
Liland's Special Event Productions 112, 234, 253
Linen Gallery, The 37, 234, 250
Linen 'n Things 37, 250
Linen Sisters, The 38, 234, 250
Linens 37-38, 250
Llewellyn & Lee 30, 249
Loews Anatole Hotel 121, 234, 253
Loma Luna 107, 234, 253
Lombardi's 311 136, 235, 254
Lovers Lane Antique Market 30, 235, 249
Loyd-Paxton 235, 249
Luna's Tortilla Factory 235, 251
Luther P. Menke 163, 235, 255
Lynn Townsend Dealey 54, 235, 250
Macy's 31, 66, 235, 249
Magicland 183, 235, 256
Magnifico Fine Foods 66-67, 85, 235, 251
Main Street News 136, 235, 254
Making Statements 48, 235, 250
Mal Fitch Orchestra, Inc. 175, 235, 256
Mama's Daughter 77, 235, 254
Mange-Tout Cooking School 18, 235, 249
Mansion on Turtle Creek,The 21, 121, 235, 254
Marc Jaco Productions 235, 256

Marco Polo Shop 165, 255
Marco's Pizza 89, 235
Markets 57-69, 250-251
Margarita Man 189, 235, 257
Margarita Masters 189, 235, 257
Margaritas-R-Us 188, 235, 257
Marguerite Green At Home 31, 235, 249
Mariachis Los Reyes de Dallas 176, 235, 256
Marilee Mallinson Martinez 163, 235, 255
Mario's Chiquita Mexican Cuisine 136, 235, 254
Marj's Stationery 43, 235, 250
Mark Carroll 171, 235, 256
Market, The 31, 235, 249
Marshall Grant Orchestra 179, 235, 256
Martha Tiller & Company 116, 235, 253
Marty's 24, 67, 69, 70, 85, 107, 218, 235, 251, 252, 253
Mary Cates & Co. 31, 235, 249
Massimo da Milano 77, 86, 89, 235, 252
Matt's Rancho Martinez 235, 254
Mattito's Cafe Mexicano 141, 235, 254
Maudee's Tearoom 86, 235, 252
McKinney Avenue Antiques 31, 235, 249
McKinney Avenue Transit 146-147, 235, 255
Meat Markets 60-62, 251
MEDiPARK Valet Services 198, 216, 235, 257
Mediterraneo 136, 235, 254
Melrose Hotel 122, 135, 254
Mercado Juarez 136, 236, 254
Mesquite Championship Rodeo 152-153, 220, 236, 255
Messina's Restaurant & Culinary Ctr. 18, 236, 254, 255
Mews, The 32, 236, 249
Michael Carney Music 179, 236, 256
Michaels/MJ Designs 168, 236, 257
Mille Fleurs, Inc. 160, 236, 255
Mise en Place 86, 89, 236, 252
Mitchell Lehr 236, 256
Momo's Italian Groceries 67, 236, 251
Momo's Pasta 137, 236, 254
Moreno Printing 50, 236, 250
Morgen Chocolate, Inc. 63, 77, 236, 252
Mori Music 171, 236, 256
Morton H. Meyerson Symphony Center 147, 236, 255
Mother-Daughter Originals 69, 236, 251
Mountain View College 20, 249
Mozzarella Company 63, 67, 69, 236, 251
Mr. Fish Crabs 'n More 62, 236, 251
Mr. G's Deli & Beverages 71, 89, 236, 252
Mr. Limo 202, 236, 257
Music of the Harp, see Barbara Kirchhoff

INDEX

Nancy Beckham   101, 236, 253
Nancy Himes   52, 236, 250
Needle in a Haystack   43, 236, 250
Neiman Marcus   32, 47, 67, 69, 71, 78, 236, 249, 251
Nero's Italian   137, 236, 254
Neuhaus Chocolate Cafe   78, 236, 252
New Vintage Festival   25, 236
New York, Texas Cheesecake   80, 236, 252
Newport's   107, 137, 215, 236, 253, 254
Nicholson Hardie   164, 236, 255
Nina Nichols Austin   236, 253
No Place   141, 236, 254
North Lake College   20, 249
Northwood Club   236, 254
Nuvo   32, 236, 249
O! Suzanna Design Studio   54, 206, 236, 250
O-K Paper Center   50, 236, 2450
Old City Park   149, 237, 255
Old Fort Dallas   153, 237, 255
Omni Mandalay at Las Colinas   112, 237, 254
On the Border   137, 237, 254
One O'Clock Lab Band   176, 237, 256
Opus   137-138, 237, 254
Opus Four String Quartet   172, 237, 256
Organizations   249
Original Butt Sketch   183, 237, 256
Out of a Flower   19, 63, 78-79, 81, 212, 237, 249, 252
Palmer Sales Co.   237, 256
Panhandlers   32, 237, 249
Panhandlers Steel Band   176, 237, 256
Paper Routes   50, 237, 250
Pappadeaux Seafood Kitchen   138, 237, 254
Pappas Catering   138, 237, 253
Pappas Design   32, 237, 249
Papyrus   44, 237, 250
Parigi   21
Park Cities Valet Parking   199, 237, 257
Park City Club   126, 237, 254
Park Lane Ranch & Cattle Co.   153, 237, 255
Parkers   197-199, 257
Parties-R-Us   168, 237, 257
Party & Event Designers, The   112, 237, 253
Party & Event Planners   110-116, 253
Party Art, Inc.   44, 237, 250
Party Bazaar   44, 168, 237, 250
Party Cat   44, 237, 250
Party Help   196, 257
Party in a Box   69, 87, 237, 251
Party Pics" by Flash   199, 237, 257
Party Place   44-45, 168, 237, 250
Party Plus   237, 253
Party Service   45, 115, 237, 253

Party Supplies   167-168, 256
Pasta Plus   67, 87, 237, 249, 253
Peggy Sue BBQ   237, 252
Pendery's   68, 237, 251
Peregrinators Antiques   29, 237, 249
Perfect Party Rentals   187, 237, 257
Perfect Setting, The   33, 238, 249
Petals & Stems   160, 238, 255
Peter Duchin Orchestra   179, 238, 256
Pettys Group, The   238, 256
Phares Corder   176, 238, 256
Phil's Natural Foods   58
Photographique   200, 238, 257
Photography   199-200, 257
Piccola Cucina   89, 238, 254
Pickens Design   54-55, 238, 250
Pier One Imports   33, 238, 249
PIP Printing   50, 238, 250
Plano Chamber Orchestra   181, 256
Plano Civic Center   149, 255
Plano Parks & Recreation   20, 249
Plant Place, The   191, 238, 257
Plants   190-191, 257
Plantscaping   191, 238, 257
Plate & Platter   19, 33, 238, 249
Plaza of the Americas Hotel   112-113, 238, 254
Po-Go's Liquor   71, 238, 252
Polish Delicatessen   89, 238, 249, 252
Pollo Bueno   238, 252
Polly Dupont   33, 238, 249
Polo Shop\Ralph Lauren   33, 238, 249
Pomodoro   138, 238, 254
PoPolo's   89, 238, 254
Potted Palm, The   160, 238, 255
Preferred Meats   61, 238, 251
Preferred Parking   238, 257
Preizler's Deli & Bakery   238, 252
Presto Print   238, 252
Print Shoppe, The   46, 49, 221, 238, 250
Printing   49-50, 250
Private Collection Stamp Co.   50, 238, 250
Project, The   176, 238, 256
Props   191-192, 257
Props of Texas   192, 238, 257
Public Relations   116, 253
Pullen Seafood   62, 238, 251
Quadrangle Grille   24, 138, 238, 254
Quarter J Ranch   153, 238, 255
Quill Productions   52, 238, 250
Quiltcraft Industries   39, 238, 250
Ralph Sanford   238, 256
Ralph's Fine Foods   58, 238, 250
Ran Wilde Orchestra   176, 238, 256
Randall Morgan-Village Stationers   46, 239, 250
Red Coleman Liquors   71, 239, 252

INDEX

Redwine Catering   86, 101, 239, 253
Reichenstein Manor, The   142, 239, 255
Renie Steves   22
Rent-All Place   239, 257
Rentals   185-192, 257
Rentals Unlimited   239, 257
Resource 3, Inc.   116, 239, 253
Restaurants   129-141, 254
Reunion Ranch   154, 239, 255
Richardson Chamber Orchestra   181, 239, 256
Richardson Woman's Club   239, 255
Rick Duren   163-164, 239, 253
Ristorante Savino   141, 239, 254
Riveria, The   138, 239, 254
Romano's Cheesecake Company   79, 239, 252
Ron Fink   239, 256
Ron Lawrence Band & Orchestra 177, 239, 256
Ronnie Renfrow Big Band   177, 239, 256
Room Service   33, 239, 249
Rose Shop, The   239, 255
Rotel & the Red Hots   177, 256
Royal Oaks Country Club   128, 239, 254
Royal Party +   46, 239, 250
Ruccus   46, 239, 250
Rudolph's Market & Sausage Factory   61, 239, 251
Russell Glenn Floral Design   112-113, 161, 218, 239, 255
Russian Room , The   139, 239, 254
Salli Goldstein   239, 253
Sally Jones   239, 253
Sam's Cafe   107-108, 139-140, 215, 239, 253, 254
Samarco   194, 239, 257
Sammons Center for the Arts   147, 239, 255
Sample House & Candle Shop   33, 239, 249
Sandone Tents   192, 239, 256
Sandy Trent's 1 Dance 2   184, 239, 256
Sarah Jane Francis   79, 239, 252
Savoire Faire   239, 253
Sazon International   239, 253
Schimelpfenig Showplace   142, 239, 255
Schnitzer Productions   172, 239, 256
Science Place   149, 239, 255
Scott Hagar   200, 239, 257
Seafood Connection, The, see Pullen Seafood
Seafood Markets   62-63, 251
Seasonal Colour   165, 239, 255
Serge Stodolnik   172, 240, 256
Sfuzzi   21, 140, 240, 256
Shalibi Imported Foods   240, 251
Sharon Seaton   240, 256
Sheraton Park Central Hotel   123, 240, 254

Shin Chon   59, 240, 251
Showco   240
Sigel's Liquor Stores   71, 240, 252
Silver Leopard   34, 240, 249
Silver Tray Catering   102, 217, 240, 253
Silver Vault, The   34, 240, 249
Silverado City   148, 154, 216, 240, 255
Simcha Kosher Catering   96, 240, 253
Simon David   59, 71, 87, 240, 250
Skylobby   148, 240, 255
Smiles Balloon Co.   167, 240, 257
Smink, Inc.   34, 240, 249
Smith & Hawken   29
Smokey & the Bearkats   175, 240, 256
Solly's   240, 252
Some Enchanted Evening   102, 240, 253
Sonny Bryan's Barbecue   108, 240, 252
Soramy   89, 240, 252
SOS - Share Our Strength   22
Sound   194-195, 257
Sound Productions Inc.   194, 240, 257
Southern Greenhouse   191, 240, 257
Southern Methodist University   182, 240, 255
Southfork Ranch   154, 240, 255
Special Affairs Catering   79, 240, 253
Special Occasions   188, 240, 257
Special Places   141-150, 255
Spice of Life   103, 240, 253
Spirited Cakes   69, 79, 240, 251, 252
Spirits Liquor Company, Inc.   11, 252
St. Michael's Woman's Exchange   35, 46-47, 210, 240, 249, 250
Stalcup, Edward, Inc.   34-35, 212, 240, 249
Stanley Korshak   35, 47, 240, 249
Star Brand Ranch   154, 240, 255
Star Canyon   140, 254
Stein's Bakery   80, 240, 252
Steinway Hall   190, 240, 257
Stephan Pyles   22
Steve Kemble Events 113-114, 206, 241, 253
Stewart Bennett   195, 241, 257
Stone Savage Music   177, 241, 256
Stonebriar Country Club   128, 241, 254
Stoneleigh Terrace Hotel   123, 241, 254
Stradivarius String Quartet   241, 256
Strictly Cheesecake   80, 241, 252
Strictly Top Drawer   161, 241, 255
Studio on Hall, The   148, 241, 255
Sushi Sensei   20, 241
Superior Productions   184, 241, 256
Sue Bohlin   52, 241, 250
Suzanne Roberts Gifts   47, 241, 250
Swan Court   141, 241, 254
Sweet Endings   80, 241, 252
Sweet Temptations Bakery & Cafe   80, 241, 252

INDEX

Tablecloths Unlimited   38, 188, 241, 257
Taiwan Supermarket   60, 241, 250
Taj Mahal   65, 241, 251
Take-Out   82-90, 252
Takeout Taxi   90, 241, 253
Tapley Entertainment   173, 241, 256
Taste Teasers   63, 241, 251
Taxco Produce   68, 241, 251
Teel Gray   52, 241, 250
Tents   192, 257
Terry Van Willson, see Resource 3
Texas Club   241, 254
Texas Commerce Sky Lobby   148, 241, 255
Texas Costume   183, 241, 256
Texas Hill Country Wine & Food Festival
   23, 241, 249
Texas Stadium Club   149, 241, 255
Texas Wild Game Cooperative   61, 241, 251
Thai Oriental Food Store   60, 241, 250
Three Teardrops Tavern   149, 241, 255
Tienda Santa Rosa   241
Tiffany & Co.   35-36, 47, 241, 249
Tillman's Corner   141, 241, 255
Tim Louque Designs   80-81, 241, 252
Tina Wasserman's Cooking School   20,
   241, 249
TJ's Fresh Seafood Market   62, 241, 251
Today's Gourmet   103, 241, 253
Todd Greer   164, 241, 255
Tolbert's Chili Parlor   140, 241, 255
Tom Jenkins   200, 241, 257
Tommaso's Italian Fresh Pasta   68, 87, 241,
   252
Tony's Wine Warehouse & Bistro   24, 72,
   241, 252
Touch of Green   191, 242, 257
Tower Club of Dallas   126, 242, 254
Trammell Crow Center Pavilions   242, 255
Translations   36, 69, 242, 249, 251
Transportation   200-201, 257
Tres Bon Catering   104, 242, 253
Truong Nguyen   59, 242, 250
Tulip Tree II, Inc.   36, 242, 249
Tyson Organ & Piano Co.   190, 242, 257
Uncle Julio's   108, 242, 253
Union Station   149, 242, 255
United Rent-All   187, 242, 257
University Club   126, 242, 254
Valet Dallas, Inc.   242, 257
Valet Limousines, Inc   242, 257
Valet Parking Services   197-199, 257
Valhalla   164, 242, 256
Verandah Club   126, 242, 254
Vertu   29, 242, 249
Vicho Vincenzio Band   177- 178, 242, 256
Vick's Catering   104, 242

Victor Gielisse   22
Villeroy & Boch   242, 250
Vintage House, The   242, 255
Vintner Dinners   26
Visiting Nurses Assn., see AIWF
W.T. Greer, III   172, 242, 256
Wadley Piano & Organ Co.   190, 242, 257
Wagon Wheel Ranch   154, 242, 255
Waste Management Rental   257
Watel's   242, 255
Watson Food Service Industries,Inc.   36, 242,
   250
Wendy Krispin Caterer   **103, 221, 242, 253**
Wesley Lujan   164, 256,
   see also The Flower Studio
Westin Hotel, The   **123-124, 209, 242, 254**
Westminster Lace   39, 242, 250
White House, The   149, 242, 255
White Swan Cafe   140, 242, 255
Whole Foods Market   59, 72, 242, 251
Wicker Basket, The   36, 242, 256
William Ernest Brown   47, 242, 250
William Farrell   29
Williams Sonoma   36, 68, 69, 242, 250
Willow Bend Polo & Hunt Club   128, 242, 254
Wine   24, 70-72, 252
Wine Classes   24
Wine Emporium Etc.   24, 72, 242, 252
Wine Letter. The   90, 242
Wine Press Bar & Bistro   141, 242
Winn Morton Designs   **114, 205, 242, 253**
WMI Services   242, 257
Wolf & Company   115, 243, 253
Wooden Spoon   243, 251
World Service U.K.   68, 243, 251
Worldwide Food, Inc.   68, 243, 251
Write Choice, The   48, 243, 250
Write Selection   47, 243, 250
Wynne Entertainment   181, 243, 256
Yellow Rose Special Events   115, 202, 243,
   253, 257
York Street   141, 243, 255
Zaks Stores   168, 243
Zen Floral Design Studio   161, 243, 256

•**Advertisers** appear in **bold face** in
Directory of Sources & in the *Index*.

About The Author

*C*arol Fraser Hall brings considerable combined experience to ENTERTAINING IN DALLAS. In assessing that expertise, she decided to share her knowledge of community resources and talents.

Carol Hall, after early careers in politics and economics, plus stints in advertising and marketing, has devoted 25 years to community service. In so doing, she has chaired (and continues to chair) both organizations and events, including some of Dallas' most prestigious galas and civic endeavors. Her expertise with large-scale entertaining are a result of those many involvements. As related dimension, she has had a real interest in fine cuisine, ever since her first cooking lessons in Europe almost thirty years ago. She headed the local chapter of American Institute of Wine & Food and chaired its National Conference on Gastronomy in 1986. Carol is married to an attorney and is the mother of two grown children.

The author wants to thank Suzanna L. Brown of O! Suzanna Design for her substantial contribution to ENTERTAINING IN DALLAS! She has brought her usual flair and creativity to the book's production.

Acknowledgement is also is extended to Mary Tomás of Alma Graphics for the book's appropriate illustrations. Photo credits are numerous but, we especially thank Stewart Charles Cohen for Sam's Cafe, Tom Jenkins and Scott Hager of the Dallas Museum of Art, Kristina Bowman and the advertisers whose own photos have enhanced this edition.

Additional copies of **ENTERTAINING IN DALLAS!**
may be purchased from

PANACHE PRESS

P. O. Box 7044

Dallas, Texas 75209

Cost per book is $16.95
plus $1.40 sales tax and $2.00 postage and handling.